A SCHOOL OF PRAYER

POPE BENEDICT XVI

A SCHOOL OF PRAYER

The Saints Show Us How to Pray

General Audiences
4 May 2011–22 June 2011
3 August 2011–27 June 2012
1 August 2012–3 October 2012

IGNATIUS PRESS SAN FRANCISCO

English translation by *L'Osservatore Romano*

In Scripture references,
chapter and verse numbering varies
according to the Bible version used

Cover art:
The Agony in the Garden.
(Panel from the back of the *Maesta* altarpiece)
Duccio di Buoninsegna (c. 1260–1319)
Museo dell'Opera Metropolitana, Siena, Italy

Papal coat of arms image by www.AgnusImages.com

Cover design by Roxanne Mei Lum

Published 2013 by Ignatius Press, San Francisco
ISBN 978-1-62164-141-4
Library of Congress Control Number 2012953497
Printed in the United States of America ♾

CONTENTS

I

Man in Prayer (1)

WEDNESDAY, 4 MAY 2011
Saint Peter's Square

Dear Brothers and Sisters,

Today I would like to begin a new series of Catecheses. After the series on the Fathers of the Church, on the great theologians of the Middle Ages, and on great women, I would now like to choose a topic that is dear to all our hearts: it is the theme of prayer, and especially Christian prayer, the prayer, that is, which Jesus taught and which the Church continues to teach us. It is in fact in Jesus that man becomes able to approach God in the depth and intimacy of the relationship of a child to his father. Together with the first disciples, let us now turn with humble trust to the Teacher and ask him: "Lord, teach us to pray" (Lk 11:1).

In the upcoming Catecheses, in drawing near to Sacred Scripture, the great tradition of the Fathers of the Church, the Teachers of spirituality and the Liturgy, let us learn to live our relationship with the Lord even more intensely, as it were, at a "school of prayer". We know well, in fact, that prayer should not be taken for granted. It is necessary to learn how to pray, as it were, acquiring this art ever anew; even those who are very advanced in the spiritual life always feel the need to learn from Jesus, to learn how to pray authentically. We receive the first lesson from the Lord by his example. The Gospels describe Jesus to us in intimate and constant conversation with the Father: it is a profound communion of the One who came into the world to do, not his will, but that of the Father, who sent him for the salvation of man.

At this first Catechesis, as an introduction, I would like to propose several examples of prayer in the ancient cultures, to show that practically always and everywhere they were addressed to God.

I shall start with ancient Egypt, as an example. Here a blind man, asking the divinity to restore his sight, testifies to something universally human. This is a pure and simple prayer of petition by someone who is suffering. This man prays: "My heart longs to see you.... You who made me see the darkness, create light for me, so that I may see you! Bend your beloved face over me" (A. Barucq and F. Daumas, *Hymnes et prières de l'Egypte ancienne* [Paris, 1980]). That I may see you: this is the essence of the prayer!

In the religions of Mesopotamia, an arcane, paralyzing sense of guilt predominated, but it was not devoid of the hope of redemption and liberation on God's part. We may thus appreciate this entreaty by a believer of those ancient cultures, formulated in these words: "O God who are indulgent even in the greatest sin, absolve me from my sin.... Look, O Lord, at your tired servant, and blow your breeze upon him: forgive him without delay. Alleviate your severe punishment. Freed from bonds, grant that I may breathe anew, break my chains, loosen the fetters that bind me" (M.-J. Seux, *Hymnes et Prières aux Dieux de Babylone et d'Assyrie* [Paris, 1976]). These are words that demonstrate how the human being, in his search for God, had intuited, if vaguely, on the one hand, his own guilt and, on the other, aspects of divine mercy and goodness.

In the pagan religion of ancient Greece, a very significant development may be seen: prayers, while still invoking divine help to obtain heavenly favors in every circumstance of daily life and to receive material benefits, gradually became orientated to more disinterested requests, which enabled the believer to deepen his relationship with God and to become a better person. For example, the great philosopher Plato records a prayer of his teacher, Socrates, held to be one of the founders of Western thought. This was Socrates' prayer: "Grant to me that I be made beautiful in my soul within, and that all external possessions be in harmony with my inner man. May I consider the wise man rich; and may I have such wealth as only the self-restrained man can bear or endure" (Plato, *Phaedrus*, English trans.: Loeb, Harold North Fowler). Rather than to possess plenty of money, he wanted above all to be beautiful within and wise.

In the Greek tragedies, sublime masterpieces of the literature of all time which still, after twenty-five centuries, are read, thought about, and performed today, there is a content of prayer which expresses the desire to know God and to worship his majesty. One of these tragedies says: "O Earth's Upbearer, thou whose throne is Earth, Who'er thou be, O past our finding out, Zeus, be thou Nature's Law, or Mind of man, Thee I invoke; for, treading soundless paths, To Justice' goal thou bringest all mortal things" (Euripedes, *Trojan Women*, 884–86, English trans.: Loeb, Arthur S. Way). God remains somewhat nebulous; nevertheless, man knows this unknown god and prays to the one who guides the ways of the world.

Also among the Romans who made up that great Empire in which Christianity first came into being and spread, prayer, even if it is associated with a utilitarian conception and fundamentally associated with the request for divine protection of the life of the civil community, sometimes begins with invocations that are wonderful because of the fervor of personal devotion that is transformed into praise and thanksgiving. In the second century A.D., Apuleius, an author of Roman Africa, attested to this. In his writings he expresses his contemporaries' dissatisfaction with the traditional religion and the desire for a more authentic relationship with God. In his masterpiece, entitled *Metamorphoses*, a believer addresses these words to a goddess: "You are holy, you are in every epoch a savior of the human species, you, in your generosity, always help mortals, offer to the wretch in travail the tender affection of a mother. Neither a day nor a night nor even a second passes without you filling it with your benefits" (Apuleius of Madaura, *Metamorphoses* IX, 25).

In the same period, the Emperor Marcus Aurelius—who was also a philosopher who reflected on the human condition—affirmed the need to pray in order to establish a fruitful cooperation between divine action and human action. He wrote in his *Meditations*: "Who told you that the gods do not help us also in what depends on us? So begin to pray to them and you will see" (*Dictionnaire de Spiritualité* XII/2, col. 2213). This advice of the Emperor philosopher was effectively put into practice by innumerable generations prior to Christ, thereby demonstrating that human life without prayer, which opens our existence to the mystery of God, lacks sense and direction. Always expressed in every prayer, in fact, is the truth of the human creature who, on the one hand, experiences weakness and impoverishment, who therefore addresses his supplication to Heaven, and, on the other, is endowed with an extraordinary dignity, so that, in preparing to receive the divine revelation, finds himself able to enter into communion with God.

Dear friends, in these examples of prayer of different epochs and civilizations emerges the human being's awareness of his creatural condition and of his dependence on Another superior to himself and the source of every good. The human being of all times prays because he cannot fail to wonder about the meaning of his life, which remains obscure and discomforting if it is not put in relation to the mystery of God and of his plan for the world. Human life is a fabric woven of good and of evil, of undeserved suffering and of joy and beauty that spontaneously and irresistibly impel us to ask God for that light and that inner strength which support us on earth and reveal a hope beyond the boundaries of death. The pagan religions remain an invocation which from the earth awaits a word from Heaven. One of the last great pagan philosophers, who lived fully in the Christian era, Proclus of Constantinople, gives a voice to this expectation, saying: "Unknowable, no one contains you. All that we think belongs to you. Our evils and our good come from you, on you our every yearning depends, O Ineffable One, whom our souls feel present, raising to you a hymn of silence" (*Hymni*, ed. Vogt [Wiesbaden, 1957], in *Preghiere dell'umanità*, *op. cit.*, p. 61).

In the examples of prayer of the various cultures which we have considered, we can see a testimony of the religious dimension and of the desire for God engraved on the heart of every human being, which receives fulfillment and full expression in the Old and in the New Testament. The revelation is in fact purifying and brings to its fullness man's original yearning for God, offering to him, in prayer, the possibility of a deeper relationship with the heavenly Father.

At the beginning of our journey in the "school of prayer", let us now ask the Lord to illumine our minds and hearts so that the relationship with him in prayer may be ever more intense, affectionate, and constant. Once again, let us say to him: "Lord, teach us to pray" (Lk 11:1).

2

Man in Prayer (2)

WEDNESDAY, 11 MAY 2011

Saint Peter's Square

Dear Brothers and Sisters,

Today I wish to continue my reflection on how prayer and the sense of religion have been part of man throughout his history.

We live in an age in which the signs of secularism are glaringly obvious. God seems to have disappeared from the horizon of some people or to have become a reality that meets with indifference. Yet at the same time we see many signs of a reawakening of the religious sense, a rediscovery of the importance of God to the human being's life, a need for spirituality, for going beyond a purely horizontal and materialistic vision of human life. A look at recent history reveals the failure of the predictions of those who, in the age of the Enlightenment, foretold the disappearance of religions and who exalted absolute reason, detached from faith, a reason that was to dispel the shadows of religious dogmatism and was to dissolve the "world of the sacred", restoring to the human being freedom, dignity, and autonomy from God. The experience of the past century, with the tragedy of the two World Wars, disrupted the progress that autonomous reason, man without God, seemed to have been able to guarantee.

The *Catechism of the Catholic Church* says: "In the act of creation, God calls every being from nothingness into existence. . . . Even after losing through his sin his likeness to God, man remains an image of his Creator, and retains the desire for the one who calls him into existence. All religions bear witness to man's essential search for God" (no. 2566). We could say—as I explained in my last Catechesis—that there has been no great civilization, from the most distant epoch to our day, which has not been religious.

Man is religious by nature, he is *homo religiosus* just as he is *homo sapiens* and *homo faber*: "The desire for God", the *Catechism* says further, "is written in the human heart, because man is created by God and for God" (no. 27). The image of the Creator is impressed on his being, and he feels the need to find light to give a response to the questions that concern the deep meaning of reality; a response that he cannot find in himself, in progress, in empirical science. The *homo religiosus* does not only appear in the sphere of antiquity; he passes through the whole of human history. In this regard, the rich terrain of human experience has seen the religious sense develop in various forms, in the attempt to respond to the desire for fulfillment and happiness. The "digital" man, like the cave man, seeks in the religious experience ways to overcome his finiteness and to give security to his precarious adventure on earth. Moreover, life without a transcendent horizon would not have its full meaning, and happiness, for which we all seek, is spontaneously projected toward the future in a tomorrow that has yet to come. In the Declaration *Nostra Aetate*, the Second Vatican Council stressed in summary form:

> Men look to their different religions for an answer to the unsolved riddles of human existence. The problems that weigh heavily on the hearts of men are the same today as in the ages past. What is man?—[who am I?]—What is the meaning and purpose of life? What is upright behavior, and what is sinful? Where does suffering originate, and what end does it serve? How can genuine happiness be found? What happens at death? What is judgment? What reward follows death? And finally, what is the ultimate mystery, beyond human explanation, which embraces our entire existence, from which we take our origin and towards which we tend? (no. 1)

Man knows that, by himself, he cannot respond to his own fundamental need to understand. However much he is deluded and still deludes himself that he is self-sufficient, he experiences his own insufficiency. He needs to open himself to something more, to something or to someone who can give him what he lacks. He must come out of himself toward the One who is able to fill the breadth and depth of his desire.

Man bears within him a thirst for the infinite, a longing for eternity, a quest for beauty, a desire for love, a need for light and for truth which impel him toward the Absolute; man bears within him the desire for God. And man knows, in a certain way, that he can turn to God; he knows he can pray to him. Saint Thomas Aquinas, one of the greatest theologians of history, defines prayer as "an expression of man's desire for God". This attraction to God, which God himself has placed in man, is the soul of prayer, which then takes on a great many forms, in accordance with the history, the time, the moment, the grace, and even the sin of every person praying. Man's history has in fact known various forms of prayer, because he has developed different kinds of openness to the "Other" and to the Beyond, so that we may recognize prayer as an experience present in every religion and culture.

Indeed, dear brothers and sisters, as we saw last Wednesday, prayer is not linked to a specific context, but is written on the heart of every person and of every civilization. Of course, when we speak of prayer as an experience of the human being as such, of the *homo orans*, it is necessary to bear in mind that it is an inner attitude before being a series of practices and formulas, a manner of being in God's presence before performing acts of worship or speaking words. Prayer is centered and rooted in the inmost depths of the person; it is therefore not easily decipherable and, for the same reason, can be subject to misunderstanding and mystification. In this sense, too, we can understand the expression: prayer is difficult. In fact, prayer is the place par excellence of free giving, of striving for the Invisible, the Unexpected, and the Ineffable. Therefore, the experience of prayer is a challenge to everyone, a "grace" to invoke, a gift of the One to whom we turn.

In prayer, in every period of history, man considers himself and his situation before God, from God, and in relation to God and experiences being a creature in need of help, incapable of obtaining on his own the fulfillment of his life and his hope. The philosopher Ludwig Wittgenstein mentioned that "prayer means feeling that the world's meaning is outside the world." In the dynamic of this relationship with the one who gives meaning to existence, with God, prayer has one of its typical expressions in the gesture of kneeling. It is a gesture that has in itself a radical ambivalence. In fact, I can be forced to kneel—a condition of indigence and slavery—but I can also kneel spontaneously, declaring my limitations and therefore my being in need of

Another. To him I declare I am weak, needy, "a sinner". In the experience of prayer, the human creature expresses all his self-awareness, all that he succeeds in grasping of his own existence, and, at the same time, he turns with his whole being to the One before whom he stands, directs his soul to that mystery from which he expects the fulfillment of his deepest desires and help to overcome the neediness of his own life. In this turning to "Another", in directing himself "Beyond" lies the essence of prayer, as an experience of a reality that overcomes the tangible and the contingent.

Yet only in God who reveals himself does man's seeking find complete fulfillment. The prayer that is openness and elevation of the heart to God thus becomes a personal relationship with him. And even if man forgets his Creator, the living, true God does not cease to call man first to the mysterious encounter of prayer. As the *Catechism* says: "In prayer, the faithful God's initiative of love always comes first; our own first step is always a response. As God gradually reveals himself and reveals man to himself, prayer appears as a reciprocal call, a covenant drama. Through words and actions, this drama engages the heart. It unfolds throughout the whole history of salvation" (no. 2567).

Dear brothers and sisters, let us learn to pause longer before God, who revealed himself in Jesus Christ; let us learn to recognize in silence, in our own hearts, his voice that calls us and leads us back to the depths of our existence, to the source of life, to the source of salvation, to enable us to go beyond the limitations of our life and to open ourselves to God's dimension, to the relationship with him, which is Infinite Love.

3

Abraham's Intercession for Sodom (Gen 18:16–33)

WEDNESDAY, 18 MAY 2011
Saint Peter's Square

Dear Brothers and Sisters,

In the last two Catecheses we have reflected on prayer as a universal phenomenon which—although in different forms—is present in the cultures of all times. Today instead I would like to start out on a biblical path on this topic which will guide us to deepening the dialogue of the Covenant between God and man that enlivened the history of salvation to its culmination, to the definitive Word that is Jesus Christ. This path will lead us to reflect on certain important texts and paradigmatic figures of the Old and New Testaments. Abraham, the great Patriarch, the father of all believers (cf. Rom 4:11–12, 16–17), will offer us a first example of prayer in the episode of intercession for the cities of Sodom and Gomorrah. And I would also like to invite you to take advantage of the journey we shall be making in the forthcoming Catecheses to become more familiar with the Bible, which I hope you have in your homes, and, during the week, to pause to read it and to meditate upon it in prayer, in order to know the marvelous history of the relationship between God and man, between God who communicates with us and man who responds, who prays.

The first text on which we shall reflect is in chapter 18 of the Book of Genesis. It is recounted that the evil of the inhabitants of Sodom and Gomorrah had reached the height of depravity so as to require an intervention of God, an act of justice that would prevent the evil from destroying those cities. It is here that Abraham comes in, with his prayer of intercession. God decides to reveal to him what is about to happen and acquaints him with the gravity of the evil and its terrible consequences, because Abraham is his chosen one, chosen to become a great people and to bring the divine blessing to the whole world. His is a mission of salvation which must counter the sin that has invaded human reality; the Lord wishes to bring humanity back to faith, obedience, and justice through Abraham. And now this friend of God, seeing the reality and neediness of the world, prays for those who are about to be punished and begs that they be saved.

Abraham immediately grasps the problem in all its gravity and says to the Lord: "Will you indeed destroy the righteous with the wicked? Suppose there are fifty righteous within the city; will you then destroy the place and not spare it for the fifty righteous who are in it? Far be it from you to do such a thing, to slay the righteous with the wicked, so that the righteous fare as the wicked! Far be that from you! Shall not the Judge of all the earth do right?" (Gen 18:23–25). Speaking these words with great courage, Abraham confronts God with the need to avoid a perfunctory form of justice: if the city is guilty, it is right to condemn its crime and to inflict punishment, but—the great Patriarch affirms—it would be unjust to punish all the inhabitants indiscriminately. If there are innocent people in the city, they must not be treated as the guilty. God, who is a just judge, cannot act in this way, Abraham says rightly to God.

However, if we read the text more attentively, we realize that Abraham's request is even more pressing and more profound because he does not stop at asking for salvation for the innocent. Abraham asks forgiveness for the whole city and does so by appealing to God's justice; indeed, he says to the Lord: "Will you then destroy the place and not spare it for the fifty righteous who are in it?" (v. 24b). In this way he brings a new idea of justice into play: not the one that is limited to punishing the guilty, as men do, but a different, divine justice that seeks goodness and creates it through forgiveness that transforms the sinner, converts and saves him. With his prayer, therefore, Abraham invokes, not a merely compensatory form of justice, but rather an intervention of salvation which, taking into account the innocent, also frees the wicked from guilt by forgiving them. Abraham's thought, which seems almost paradoxical, could be summed up like this: obviously it is not possible to treat the innocent as guilty; this would be unjust; it would be necessary, instead, to treat the guilty as innocent, putting into practice a "superior" form of justice, offering them a possibility of salvation because, if evildoers accept God's pardon and confess their sin, letting themselves be saved, they will no longer continue to do wicked deeds; they, too, will become righteous and will no longer deserve punishment.

It is this request for justice that Abraham expresses in his intercession, a request based on the certainty that the Lord is merciful. Abraham does not ask God for something contrary to his essence; he knocks at the door of God's heart knowing what he truly desires. Sodom, of course, is a large city; fifty upright people seem few, but are not the justice and forgiveness of God perhaps proof of the power of goodness, even if it seems smaller and weaker than evil? The destruction of Sodom must halt the evil present in the city, but Abraham knows that God has other ways and means to stem the spread of evil. It is forgiveness that interrupts the spiral of sin, and Abraham, in his dialogue with God, appeals for exactly this. And when the Lord agrees to forgive the city if fifty upright people may be found in it, his prayer of intercession begins to reach the abysses of divine mercy. Abraham—as we remember—gradually decreases the number of innocent people necessary for salvation: if there are not fifty, perhaps forty-five might suffice, and so on down to ten, continuing his entreaty, which becomes almost bold in its insistence: "suppose forty . . . thirty . . . twenty . . . are found there" (cf. vv. 29, 30, 31, 32). The smaller the number becomes, the greater God's mercy is shown to be. He patiently listens to the prayer; he hears it and repeats at each supplication: "I will spare . . . I will not destroy . . . I will not do it" (cf. vv. 26, 28, 29, 30, 31, 32).

Thus, through Abraham's intercession, Sodom can be saved if there are even only ten innocent people in it. This is the power of prayer. For through intercession, the prayer to God for the salvation of others, the desire for salvation which God nourishes for sinful man is demonstrated and expressed. Evil, in fact, cannot be accepted; it must be identified and destroyed through punishment: the destruction of Sodom had exactly this function. Yet the Lord does not want the wicked to die but, rather, that they convert and live (cf. Ez 18:23; 33:11); his desire is always to forgive, to save, to give life, to transform evil into good. Well, it is this divine desire itself which becomes in prayer the desire of the human being and is expressed through the words of intercession. With his entreaty, Abraham is lending his voice, and also his heart, to the divine will. God's desire is mercy and love as well as the wish to save; and this desire of God found in Abraham and in his prayer the possibility of being revealed concretely in human history, in order to be present wherever there is a need for grace. By voicing this prayer, Abraham was giving a voice to what God wanted, which was not to destroy Sodom but to save it, to give life to the converted sinner.

This is what the Lord desires, and his dialogue with Abraham is a prolonged and unequivocal demonstration of his merciful love. The need to find enough righteous people in the city decreases, and in the end ten were to be enough to save the entire population. The reason why Abraham stops at ten is not given in the text. Perhaps it is a figure that indicates a minimum community nucleus (still today, ten people are the necessary *quorum* for public Jewish prayer). However, this is a small number, a tiny particle of goodness with which to start in order to save the rest from a great evil. However, not even ten just people were to be found in Sodom and Gomorrah, so the cities were destroyed; a destruction paradoxically deemed necessary by the prayer of Abraham's intercession itself. Because that very prayer revealed the saving will of God: the Lord was prepared to forgive, he wanted to forgive, but the cities were locked into a totalizing and paralyzing evil, without even a few innocents from whom to start in order to turn evil into good. This is the very path to salvation for which Abraham, too, was asking: being saved does not mean merely escaping punishment but being delivered from the evil that dwells within us. It is not punishment that must be eliminated but sin, the rejection of God and of love which already bears the punishment in itself. The Prophet Jeremiah was to say to the rebellious people: "Your wickedness will chasten you, and your apostasy will reprove you. Know and see that it is evil and bitter for you to forsake the Lord your God" (Jer 2:19). It is from this sorrow and bitterness that the Lord wishes to save man, liberating him from sin. Therefore, however, a transformation from within is necessary, some foothold of goodness, a beginning from which to start out in order to change evil into good, hatred into love, revenge into forgiveness. For this reason there must be righteous people in the city, and Abraham continuously repeats: "suppose there are . . .". "There": it is within the sick reality that there must be that seed of goodness which can heal and restore life. It is a word that is also addressed to us: so that in our cities the seed of goodness may be found; that we may do our utmost to ensure that there are not only ten upright people, to make our cities truly live and survive and to save ourselves from the inner bitterness which is the absence of God. And in the unhealthy situation of Sodom and Gomorrah that seed of goodness was not to be found.

Yet God's mercy in the history of his people extends further. If in order to save Sodom ten righteous people were necessary, the Prophet Jeremiah was to say, on behalf of the Almighty, that only one upright person was necessary to save Jerusalem: "Run to and fro through the streets of Jerusalem, look and take note! Search her squares to see if you can find a man, one who does justice and seeks truth; that I may pardon her" (5:1). The number dwindled further; God's goodness proved even greater. Nonetheless, this did not yet suffice; the superabundant mercy of God did not find the response of goodness that he sought, and under the siege of the enemy Jerusalem fell. It was to be necessary for God himself to become that one righteous person. And this is the mystery of the Incarnation: to guarantee a just person, he himself becomes man. There will always be one righteous person because it is he. God himself must become that just man. The infinite and surprising divine love was to be fully manifest when the Son of God became man, the definitive Righteous One, the perfect Innocent who would bring salvation to the whole world by dying on the Cross, forgiving and interceding for those who "know not what they do" (Lk 23:34). Therefore the prayer of each one will find its answer; therefore our every intercession will be fully heard.

Dear brothers and sisters, the prayer of intercession of Abraham, our father in the faith, teaches us to open our hearts ever wider to God's superabundant mercy so that in daily prayer we may know how to desire the salvation of mankind and ask for it with perseverance and with trust in the Lord who is great in love.

4

The Nocturnal Struggle and Encounter with God (Gen 32:23–33)

WEDNESDAY, 25 MAY 2011
Saint Peter's Square

Dear Brothers and Sisters,

Today I would like to reflect with you on a text from the Book of Genesis which recounts a rather curious incident in the narrative of the Patriarch Jacob. It is a passage that is not easy to interpret, but it is important for our life of faith and prayer; we are talking about the story of his struggle with God at the ford of the Jabbok, a portion of which we just heard.

As you will recall, Jacob had deprived his twin brother, Esau, of his birthright in exchange for a dish of lentils and then, by trickery, managed to receive the blessing from his father, Isaac, now very elderly, taking advantage of the latter's blindness. Having fled from Esau's wrath, he took refuge with one of his relatives, Laban; he married, acquired some wealth, and was returning to his homeland, ready to face his brother, having first put into place some prudent provisions. However, when everything was ready for this meeting, after having had those who were with him cross the ford of the stream that marked the boundary of Esau's territory, Jacob, who had remained behind alone, was suddenly set upon by an unknown man with whom he wrestled the whole night. This hand-to-hand combat, which we find described in chapter 32 of the Book of Genesis, became for him a singular experience of God.

Night is the favorable time for acting secretly, the best time, therefore, for Jacob to enter his brother's territory unseen, perhaps thinking to take Esau by surprise. It is he, however, who is surprised by an unforeseen attack, one for which he was unprepared. Having used his cleverness to try to escape a dangerous situation, he thought he had managed to have everything under control; instead, he now finds himself forced to enter a mysterious struggle that catches him alone and gives him no opportunity to organize a proper defense. Unarmed, in the night, the Patriarch Jacob wrestles with someone. The text does not specify the identity of the aggressor; it uses a Hebrew word that indicates "a man" in a generic sense, "one, someone"; it is, therefore, a vague, indeterminate definition that purposely keeps the assailant shrouded in mystery. It is dark; Jacob does not manage to see his opponent clearly, and even for the reader, for us, he remains anonymous; someone is opposing the Patriarch, and this is the only certain data supplied by the narrator. Only at the end, when the wrestling is over and that "someone" has disappeared, only then will Jacob name him and be able to say that he has wrestled with God.

The episode, therefore, takes place in darkness, and it is difficult to ascertain not only the identity of Jacob's assailant, but also how the struggle is going. On reading the passage, it is rather difficult to determine which of the two contenders is gaining the upper hand; the verbs used often lack a specific subject, and the actions take place almost in a contradictory manner, so that when it looks as though one of the two is winning, the next action immediately denies that and shows the other to be the victor. At the beginning, in fact, Jacob seems to be the stronger, and of his opponent, the text says, "he did not prevail over him" (v. 25); yet he strikes Jacob's hip at its socket, dislocating it. Thus one thinks that Jacob would have to give in, but instead it is his opponent who asks him to release him; and the Patriarch refuses, setting one condition: "I will not let you go, unless you bless me" (v. 27). The one who tricked his brother and robbed him of the blessing of the firstborn now claims it from the stranger, thus perhaps beginning to perceive some kind of divine meaning, but without yet being able to recognize it for certain.

His rival, who seems to be held back and therefore defeated by Jacob, rather than giving in to the Patriarch's request, asks him his name: "What is your name?" And the Patriarch replies: "Jacob" (v. 28). Here the struggle takes an important turn. In fact, knowing someone's name implies a kind of power over that person because in the biblical mentality the name contains the most profound reality of the individual; it reveals the person's secret and destiny. Knowing someone's name, therefore, means knowing the truth about the other person, and this allows one to dominate him. When, therefore, in answer to the unknown person's request, Jacob discloses his own name, he is placing himself in the hands of his opponent; it is a form of surrender, a total handing over of self to the other.

However, in this act of surrender, paradoxically Jacob, too, emerges victorious because he receives a new name with the recognition of his victory by his adversary, who says to him: "You shall no longer be spoken of as Jacob, but as Israel, because you have contended with divine and human beings and have prevailed" (v. 29). "Jacob" was a name that recalled the Patriarch's problematic beginnings; in Hebrew, in fact, it recalls the term "heel" and takes the reader back to the time of Jacob's birth, when, as he left his mother's womb, he held onto the heel of his twin brother (cf. Gen 25:26), almost prefiguring the unfair advantage he would take over his brother in adulthood; however, the name Jacob also recalls the verb "to deceive, to supplant". Well, now, in the struggle, the Patriarch, in this act of surrender and submission, reveals his true identity as a deceiver, the one who supplants; however, the other, who is God, transforms this negative reality into something positive: Jacob the deceiver becomes Israel; he is given a new name as a sign of a new identity. Here, too, the account maintains its deliberate duplicity because the more probable meaning of the name Israel is "God is strong, God is victorious."

Therefore Jacob has prevailed, he has won—his adversary himself says so—but his new identity, which he has received from the adversary himself, affirms and bears witness to God's victory. And when Jacob in turn asks his opponent his name, the latter refuses to say it, but he reveals himself in an unequivocal gesture, giving him the blessing. The blessing that the Patriarch had requested at the beginning of the struggle is now granted him. However, it is not a blessing obtained through deceit, but one given freely by God, which Jacob can receive because he is now alone, without protection, without cunning or tricks; he gives himself over unarmed, agrees to surrender, and confesses the truth about himself. Therefore, at the end of the struggle, having received the blessing, the Patriarch can finally recognize the other, the God of blessings: Truly, he says, "I have seen God face to face, and yet my life is preserved" (v. 30), and now he can cross the ford, the bearer of a new name but "conquered" by God and marked for ever, limping because of the injury he has received (v. 31).

Biblical exegetes give many interpretations to this passage; the scholars in particular recognize in it literary connotations and components of various genres as well as references to some popular accounts. But when these elements are taken up by the authors of the sacred texts and incorporated into the biblical narrative, they change their meaning and the text opens up to broader dimensions. For the believer, the episode of the struggle at the Jabbok thus becomes a paradigm in which the people of Israel speak of their own origins and outline the features of a particular relationship between God and humanity. Therefore, as is also affirmed in the *Catechism of the Catholic Church*, "from this account, the spiritual tradition of the Church has retained the symbol of prayer as a battle of faith and as the triumph of perseverance" (no. 2573). The Bible text speaks to us about a long night of seeking God, of the struggle to learn his name and see his face; it is the night of prayer that, with tenacity and perseverance, asks God for a blessing and a new name, a new reality that is the fruit of conversion and forgiveness.

For the believer, Jacob's night at the ford of the Jabbok thus becomes a reference point for understanding the relationship with God that finds in prayer its greatest expression. Prayer requires trust, nearness, almost a hand-to-hand contact that is symbolic, not of a God who is an enemy, an adversary, but of a Lord of blessing who always remains mysterious, who seems beyond reach. Therefore, the author of the sacred text uses the symbol of the struggle, which implies a strength of spirit, perseverance, tenacity in obtaining what is desired. And if the object of one's desire is a relationship with God, his blessing and love, then the struggle cannot fail but ends in that self-giving to God, in recognition of one's own weakness, which is overcome only by giving oneself over into God's merciful hands.

Dear brothers and sisters, our entire lives are like this long night of struggle and prayer, spent in desiring and asking for God's blessing, which cannot be grabbed or won through our own strength but must be received with humility from him as a gratuitous gift that ultimately allows us to recognize the Lord's face. And when this happens, our entire reality changes; we receive a new name and God's blessing. And, what is more: Jacob, who receives a new name and becomes Israel, also gives a new name to the place where he wrestled with God, where he prayed; he renames it Penuel, which means: "The Face of God". With this name he recognizes that this place is filled with the Lord's presence, making that land sacred and thus leaving a memorial of that mysterious encounter with God. Whoever allows himself to be blessed by God, who abandons himself to God, who permits himself to be transformed by God, renders a blessing to the world. May the Lord help us to fight the good fight of the faith (cf. 1 Tim 6:12; 2 Tim 4:7) and to ask, in prayer, for his blessing, that he may renew us in the expectation of beholding his Face.

5

The Intercession of Moses for the People (Ex 32:7–14)

WEDNESDAY, 1 JUNE 2011

Saint Peter's Square

Dear Brothers and Sisters,

As we read the Old Testament, we note one figure who stands out from among the others: Moses, precisely, as a man of prayer. Moses, the great Prophet and leader at the time of the Exodus, carried out his role as mediator between God and Israel by making himself a bearer of God's words and divine commands to the people, by leading it toward the freedom of the Promised Land, and by teaching the Israelites to live obeying God and trusting in him during their long sojourn in the desert. However, I would say also, and above all, by praying. Moses prayed for the Pharaoh when God, with the plagues, was endeavoring to convert the Egyptians' hearts (cf. Ex 8–10); Moses asked the Lord to heal his sister Miriam, afflicted with leprosy (cf. Num 12:9–13); he interceded for the people which had rebelled, fearful of what those who had spied out the land would report (cf. Num 14:1–19); he prayed when fire was about to burn down the camp (cf. Num 11:1–2) and when poisonous serpents decimated the people (cf. Num 21:4–9);

he addressed the Lord and reacted by protesting when the burden of his mission became too heavy (cf. Num 11:10–15); he saw God and spoke "to him face to face, as a man speaks to his friend" (cf. Ex 24:9–17; 33:7–23; 34:1–10, 28–35).

And on Sinai, even while the people were asking Aaron to make a golden calf, Moses prayed, explaining with symbols his own role as intercessor. The episode is recounted in chapter 32 of the Book of Exodus, and there is a parallel account in chapter 9 of Deuteronomy. It is this episode, and, in particular, on the prayer of Moses that we find in the Exodus narrative, on which I would like to reflect in today's Catechesis. The people of Israel were at the foot of Sinai, whereas Moses, on the mountain, was waiting for the gift of the Tables of the Law, fasting for forty days and forty nights (cf. Ex 24:18; Dt 9:9). The number forty has a symbolic value and suggests the totality of the experience, whereas fasting indicates that life comes from God, that it is he who sustains it. Indeed, the act of eating entails the assumption of the nourishment that keeps us going; hence fasting, giving up all food, in this case acquires a religious significance: it is a way of showing that man does not live by bread alone but by every word that comes from the mouth of the Lord (cf. Deut 8:3). By fasting, Moses showed that he was awaiting the gift of the divine Law as a source of life: this Law reveals God's will and nourishes the human heart, bringing men and women to enter into a covenant with the Most High, who is the source of life, who is life itself.

Yet, while the Lord, on the mountain, was giving the Law to Moses, at the bottom of the mountain the people were violating it. Unable to endure waiting and the absence of their mediator, the Israelites turned to Aaron: "Make us gods, who shall go before us; as for this Moses, the man who brought us up out of the land of Egypt, we do not know what has become of him" (Ex 32:1). Weary of the journey with an invisible God, now that Moses, their mediator, had disappeared, the people clamored for an actual, tangible presence of the Lord and in the calf of molten metal made by Aaron found a god made accessible, manageable, and within human reach. This is a constant temptation on the journey of faith: to avoid the divine mystery by constructing a comprehensible god who corresponds with one's own plans, one's own projects. What happened on Sinai shows the sheer folly and deceptive vanity of this claim because, as Psalm 106[105] ironically affirms: "They exchanged the glory of God for the image of an ox that eats grass" (v. 20). So it was that the Lord reacted and ordered Moses to come down from the mountain, revealing to him what the people were doing and ending with these words: "now therefore let me alone, that my wrath may burn hot against them and I may consume them; but of you I will make a great nation" (Ex 32:10). As he had to Abraham with regard to Sodom and Gomorrah, now too God revealed to Moses what his intentions were, almost as though he did not want to act without Moses' consent (Am 3:7). He said: "let ... my wrath burn hot." In fact, these words, "let ... my wrath burn hot", were spoken so that Moses might intervene and ask God not to do it, thereby revealing that what God always wants is salvation. Just as for the two cities in Abraham's day, the punishment and destruction—in which God's anger is expressed as the rejection of evil—demonstrate the gravity of the sin committed; at the same time, the request of the intercessor is intended to show the Lord's desire for forgiveness. This is God's salvation, which involves mercy but, at the same time, also the denunciation of the truth of the sin, of the evil that exists, so that the sinner, having recognized and rejected his sin, may let God forgive and transform him. In this way prayers of intercession make active in the corrupt reality of sinful man divine mercy, which finds a voice in the entreaty of the person praying and is made present through him wherever there is a need for salvation.

Moses' supplication was wholly based on the Lord's fidelity and grace. He referred first to the history of redemption, which God began by bringing Israel out of Egypt, and then recalled the ancient promise made to the Fathers. The Lord brought about salvation by freeing his people from slavery in Egypt; so "why", Moses asked, "should the Egyptians say, 'With evil intent did he bring them forth, to slay them in the mountains, and to consume them from the face of the earth?'" (Ex 32:12). Once the work of salvation has been begun, it must be brought to completion; were God to let his people perish, this might be interpreted as a sign of God's inability to bring the project of salvation to completion. God cannot allow this: he is the good Lord who saves, the guarantor of life; he is the God of mercy and forgiveness, of deliverance from sin that kills. Hence Moses appealed to God, to the interior life of God, against the exterior judgment. But, Moses then argued with the Lord, were his Chosen People to perish, even though they were guilty, God might appear incapable of overcoming sin. And this he could not accept. Moses had a concrete experience of the God of salvation; he was sent as a mediator of divine liberation, and then, with his prayers, he made himself the interpreter of a twofold anxiety; he was worried about his people's future, and at the same time he was also worried about the honor due to the Lord, about the truth of his name. In fact, the intercessor wanted the people of Israel to be saved because this people was the flock which had been entrusted to him, but also because it was in this salvation that the true reality of God was manifest. The prayer of intercession is permeated by love of the brethren and love of God; they are inseparable. Moses, the intercessor, is the man torn between two loves that overlap in prayer in a single desire for good.

Moses then appealed to God's faithfulness, reminding him of his promises: "Remember Abraham, Isaac, and Israel, your servants, to whom you swore by your own self, and said . . . 'I will multiply your descendants as the stars of heaven, and all this land [of which I have spoken] I will give to your descendants, and they shall inherit it for ever'"(Ex 32:13). Moses recalls the founding story of the origins, of the Fathers of the people and of their completely gratuitous election, a choice in which God alone took the initiative. Not for their own merits did they receive the promise, but because of God's free choice and his love (cf. Deut 10:15). And Moses then asked the Lord to continue in fidelity his record of election and salvation by forgiving his people. The intercessor did not ask for his people to be excused of their sin; he did not list any presumed merits, either the people's or his own, but appealed to God's bounty: a free God, total love, who does not cease to seek out those who have fallen away, who is always faithful to himself, who offers the sinner a chance to return to him and, through forgiveness, to become righteous and capable of fidelity. Moses asked God to show himself more powerful than sin and death and, with his prayer, elicited this divine revelation of himself. As a mediator of life, the intercessor showed solidarity with the people: anxious solely for the salvation that God himself desires, he gave up the prospect of it becoming a new people pleasing to the Lord. The sentence that God had addressed to him, "of you I will make a great nation", was not even taken into consideration by the "friend" of God, who, instead, was ready to take upon himself not only the guilt of his people, but also all its consequences. When, after the destruction of the golden calf, he returned to the mountain to ask salvation for Israel once again, he was to say to the Lord: "But now, if you will, forgive their sin—and if not, blot me, I pray you, out of your book which you have written" (Ex 32:32). With prayer, wanting what God wanted, the intercessor entered more and more deeply into knowledge of the Lord and of his mercy and became capable of a love that extended even to the total gift of himself. In Moses, on the summit of the mountain face to face with God, who made himself an intercessor for his people and offered himself—"blot me out"—the Fathers of the Church saw a prefiguration of Christ, who from the very top of the Cross was truly before God, not only as a friend, but as Son. And not only did he offer himself—"blot me out"—but with his pierced heart he had himself blotted out, he himself became sin; as Saint Paul himself says, he took *upon himself* our sins to ensure *our* salvation. His intercession was not only solidarity but identification with us: he bears all of us in his Body. And thus his whole life as a man and as Son is a cry to God's heart; it is forgiveness, but forgiveness that transforms and renews.

I think we should meditate upon this reality. Christ stands before God and is praying for me. His prayer on the Cross is contemporary with all human beings, contemporary with me. He prays for me; he suffered and suffers for me; he identified himself with me, taking our body and the human soul. And he asks us to enter this identity of his, making ourselves one body, one spirit with him because from the summit of the Cross he brought, not new laws, tablets of stone, but himself, his Body and his Blood, as the New

Covenant. Thus he brings us kinship with him; he makes us one body with him, identifies us with him. He invites us to enter into this identification, to be united with him in our wish to be one body, one spirit with him. Let us pray the Lord that this identification may transform and renew us, because forgiveness is renewal and transformation.

I would like to end this Catechesis with the Apostle Paul's words to the Christians of Rome: "Who shall bring any charge against God's elect? It is God who justifies; who is to condemn? It is Christ Jesus, who died, yes, who was raised from the dead, who is at the right hand of God, who indeed intercedes for us. Who shall separate us from the love of Christ? . . . neither death, nor life, nor angels, nor principalities . . . nor anything else in all creation, will be able to separate us from the love of God, [which is] in Christ Jesus our Lord" (Rom 8:33–35, 38, 39).

6

Prophets and Prayers in Confrontation (1 Kings 18:20–40)

WEDNESDAY, 15 JUNE 2011

Saint Peter's Square

Dear Brothers and Sisters,

The prophets, with their teaching and their preaching, had great importance in the religious history of ancient Israel. Among them the figure of Elijah stands out, impelled by God to bring the people to conversion. His name means "the Lord is my God", and his life develops in accordance with this name, entirely dedicated to kindling in the people gratitude to the Lord as the one God. The Book of Sirach [Ecclesiasticus] says of Elijah: "Then the prophet Elijah arose like a fire, and his word burned like a torch" (Sir 48:1). With this flame, Israel found its way back to God. In his ministry, Elijah prayed: he called upon the Lord to restore to life the son of a widow who had given him hospitality (cf. 1 Kings 17:17–24); he cried out to God in his weariness and anguish while fleeing to the desert, for Queen Jezabel sought to kill him (cf. 1 Kings 19:1–4); however, it was on Mount Carmel in particular that he showed his full power as an intercessor when, before all Israel, he prayed the Lord to show himself and to convert the people's hearts.

This is the episode, recounted in chapter 18 of the First Book of Kings, on which we are reflecting today.

It was in the kingdom of the north, in the ninth century before Christ at the time of King Ahab, at a moment when Israel had created for itself a situation of blatant syncretism. Beside the Lord, the people worshipped Baal, the reassuring idol from which it was believed that the gift of rain came and to which was therefore attributed the power of making fields fertile and giving life to people and animals. In spite of claiming to follow the Lord, an invisible and mysterious God, the people were also seeking security in a comprehensible and predictable god from whom they believed they could obtain fruitfulness and prosperity in exchange for sacrifices. Israel was capitulating to the seduction of idolatry, the continuous temptation of believers, deluding itself that it could "serve two masters" (cf. Mt 6:24; Lk 16:13) and facilitate the rugged paths of faith in the Almighty by also putting its faith in a powerless god, fashioned by men.

It was exactly in order to unmask the deceptive foolishness of this attitude that Elijah gathered the people of Israel on Mount Carmel and confronted it with the need to make a decision: "If the Lord is God, follow him; but if Baal, then follow him" (1 Kings 18:21). And the Prophet, a herald of God's love, did not abandon his people as they faced this decision; rather, he helped it by pointing out a sign that would reveal the truth. Both he and the prophets of Baal were to prepare a sacrifice and pray, and the true God would reveal himself, responding with fire that would burn the offering. Thus began the confrontation between the Prophet Elijah and the followers of Baal, which was in fact between the Lord of Israel, the God of salvation and of life, and the mute idol with no substance, which could do nothing, neither good nor evil (cf. Jer 10:5). And so the confrontation also began between two completely different approaches to God and to prayer.

The prophets of Baal, in fact, cried aloud, worked themselves up, danced and leaped about and fell into a state of ecstasy, even going so far as to cut themselves, "with swords and lances, until the blood gushed out upon them" (1 Kings 18:28). They had recourse to themselves in order to call on their god, trusting to their own devices to provoke his answer. In this way, the idol's deceptive reality was revealed: it was thought up by human beings as something that could be used, that could be managed with their own efforts, to which they could gain access through their own strength and their own vital force. Worship of an idol, instead of opening the human heart to Otherness, to a liberating relationship that permits the person to emerge from the narrow space of his own selfishness to enter the dimensions of love and of reciprocal giving, shuts the person into the exclusive and desperate circle of self-seeking. And the deception is such that in worshipping an idol, people find themselves forced to extreme actions, in the vain attempt to subject it to their own will. For this reason, the prophets of Baal went so far as to hurt themselves, to wound their bodies, in a dramatically ironic action: in order to get an answer, a sign of life out of their god, they covered themselves with blood, symbolically covering themselves with death.

Elijah's prayerful attitude was entirely different. He asked the people to draw close, thereby involving it in his action and his supplication. The purpose of the challenge he addressed to the prophets of Baal was to restore to God the people which had strayed, following idols; therefore, he wanted Israel to be united with him, to become a participator in and a protagonist of his prayer and of everything that was happening. Then the Prophet built an altar, using, as the text says, "twelve stones, according to the number of the tribes of the sons of Jacob, to whom the word of the Lord came, saying: 'Israel shall be your name'" (v. 31). Those stones represented the whole of Israel and are the tangible memorial of the story of the election, predilection, and salvation of which the people had been the object. The liturgical gesture of Elijah had crucial importance; the altar was a sacred place that indicated the Lord's presence, but those stones of which it was made represented the people which now, through the Prophet's mediation, was symbolically placed before God; it had become an "altar", a place of offering and sacrifice.

Yet it was necessary for the symbol to become reality, for Israel to recognize the true God and to rediscover its own identity as the Lord's people. Elijah therefore asked God to show himself, and those twelve stones that were to remind Israel of its truth also served to remind the Lord of his fidelity, for which the Prophet appealed in prayer. The words of his invocation are full of meaning and faith: "O Lord, God of Abraham, Isaac, and Israel, let it be known this day that you are God in Israel, and that I am your servant, and that I have done all these things at your word. Answer me, O Lord, answer me, that this people may know that you, O Lord, are God, and that you have turned their hearts back" (vv. 36–37). Elijah turned to the Lord, calling him the God of the Fathers, thus implicitly calling to mind the divine promises and the story of the election and Covenant that bound the Lord indissolubly to his people. The involvement of God in human history is such that his name was inseparably connected with that of the patriarchs, and the Prophet spoke that holy Name so that God might remember and show himself to be faithful, but also so that Israel might feel called by name and rediscover its faithfulness. In fact, the divine title spoken by Elijah seems somewhat surprising. Instead of using the customary formula, "God of Abraham, Isaac and Jacob", he used a less known title: "God of Abraham, Isaac and Israel". The replacement of the name "Jacob" by "Israel" calls to mind Jacob's struggle at the ford of the Jabbok, with the change of name to which the narrator explicitly refers (cf. Gen 32:31) and of which I spoke in one of the recent Catecheses. The substitution acquires a pregnant meaning in Elijah's invocation. The Prophet is praying for the people of the kingdom of the north, which was called, precisely, Israel, as distinct from Judah, which indicated the kingdom of the south. And now, this people, which seemed to have forgotten its own origins and privileged relationship with the Lord, heard itself called by name when the name of God, God of the Patriarch and God of the people, was spoken: "O Lord, God . . . of Israel, let it be known today that you are God in Israel."

The people for which Elijah prayed was faced with its own truth, and the Prophet asked that the truth of the Lord might also be shown and that he might intervene to convert Israel, detaching it from the deception of idolatry and thereby bringing it to salvation. His request was that the people might finally realize and know in fullness who truly is its God and make a decisive choice to follow him alone, the true God. For only in this way is God recognized for what he is, Absolute and Transcendent, ruling out the possibility of setting him beside other gods, which would deny that he was absolute and relativize him. This is the faith that makes Israel the People of God; it is the faith proclaimed by the well-known text of the *Shema' Israel*: "Hear, O Israel: The Lord our God is one Lord; and you shall love the Lord your God with all your heart, and with all your soul, and with all your might" (Dt 6:4–5). The believer must respond to the Absolute of God with an absolute, total love that binds his whole life, his strength, his heart. And it was for the very heart of his people that the Prophet, with his prayers, was imploring conversion: "that this people may know that you, O Lord, are God, and that you have turned their hearts back" (1 Kings 18:37). Elijah, with his intercession, asked of God what God himself wanted to do, to show himself in all his mercy, faithful to his reality as the Lord of life who forgives, converts, and transforms.

And this is what happened: "Then the fire of the Lord fell, and consumed the burnt offering, and the wood, and the stones, and the dust, and licked up the water that was in the trench. And when all the people saw it, they fell on their faces; and they said, 'The Lord he is God; the Lord, he is God'" (vv. 38–39). Fire, the element both necessary and terrible, associated with the divine manifestations of the burning bush and of Sinai, then served to mark the love of God that responds to prayer and was revealed to his people. Baal, the mute and powerless God, had not responded to the invocations of his prophets; the Lord, on other other hand, responded, and unequivocally, not only by burning the sacrifice but even by drying up all the water that had been poured round the altar. Israel could no longer have doubts; divine mercy came to meet its weakness, its doubts, its lack of faith. Now Baal, a vain idol, was vanquished, and the people which had seemed to be lost, rediscovered the path of truth and rediscovered itself.

Dear brothers and sisters, what does this history of the past tell us? What is the present of this history? First of all, it is a question of the priority of the first Commandment: worship God alone. Whenever God disappears, man falls into the slavery of idolatry, as the totalitarian regimes demonstrated in our time and as the various forms of nihilism that make man dependent on idols, on idolatry, also demonstrate; they enslave him. Secondly, the primary aim of prayer is conversion, the flame of God that transforms our heart and enables us to see God and so to live in accordance with God and live for others. And the third point. The Fathers tell us that this history of a prophet is itself prophetic, if, they say, it foreshadows the future, the future Christ; it is a step on the journey toward Christ. And they tell us that here we see God's true fire: the love that guided the Lord even to the Cross, to the total gift of himself. True worship of God, therefore, is giving oneself to God and to men and women; true worship is love. And true worship of God does not destroy but renews, transforms. Of course, the fire of God, the fire of love burns, transforms, purifies, but in this very way it does not destroy but rather creates the truth of our being, recreates our heart. And thus, truly alive through the grace of the fire of the Holy Spirit, of love of God, we are worshippers in spirit and in truth.

7

The People of God at Prayer: The Psalms

WEDNESDAY, 22 JUNE 2011
Saint Peter's Square

Dear Brothers and Sisters,

In recent Catecheses we have reflected on some of the Old Testament figures who are particularly significant for our reflection on prayer. I have talked about Abraham, who interceded for foreign cities, about Jacob, who in his nocturnal struggle received the blessing, about Moses, who invoked forgiveness for his people, and about Elijah, who prayed for the conversion of Israel. With today's Catechesis I would like to begin a new stretch of the journey: instead of commenting on specific episodes of people praying, we shall enter "the book of prayer" par excellence, the Book of Psalms. In the forthcoming Catecheses we shall read and meditate on several of the most beautiful Psalms that are dearest to the Church's tradition of prayer. Today I would like to introduce them by talking about the Book of Psalms as a whole.

The Psalter is presented as a "formulary" of prayers, a collection of 150 Psalms which the biblical tradition offers the people of believers so that they might become their and our prayer, our way of speaking and of relating to God. This Book expresses the entire human experience with its multiple facets and the whole range of emotions that accompany human existence. In the Psalms are expressed and interwoven joy and suffering, the longing for God and the perception of our own unworthiness, happiness and the feeling of abandonment, trust in God and sorrowful loneliness, fullness of life and fear of death. The whole reality of the believer converges in these prayers. The people of Israel first, and then the Church adopted them as a privileged mediation in relations with the one God and an appropriate response to God's self-revelation in history. Since the Psalms are prayers, they are expressions of the heart and of faith with which everyone can identify and in which that experience of special closeness to God—to which every human being is called—is communicated. Moreover, the whole complexity of human life is distilled in the complexity of the different literary forms of the various Psalms: hymns, laments, individual entreaties and collective supplications, hymns of thanksgiving, penitential Psalms, sapiential Psalms, and the other genres that are to be found in these poetic compositions.

Despite this multiplicity of expression, two great areas that sum up the prayer of the Psalter may be identified: supplication, connected to lamentation, and praise. These are two related dimensions that are almost inseparable, since supplication is motivated by the certainty that God will respond, thus opening a person to praise and thanksgiving; and praise and thanksgiving stem from the experience of salvation received; this implies the need for help which the supplication expresses.

In his supplication, the person praying bewails and describes his situation of anguish, danger, or despair, or, as in the penitential Psalms, he confesses his guilt, his sin, asking forgiveness. He discloses his needy state to the Lord, confident that he will be heard, and this involves the recognition of God as good, as desirous of goodness, and as one who "loves the living" (cf. Wis 11:26), ready to help, to save, and to forgive. In this way, for example, the Psalmist in Psalm 31[30] prays: "In you, O Lord, do I seek refuge; let me never be put to shame ... take me out of the net which is hidden for me, for you are my refuge" (vv. 2, 5). In the lamentation, therefore, something like praise, which is foretold in the hope of divine intervention, can already emerge, and it becomes explicit when divine salvation becomes a reality. Likewise, in the Psalms of thanksgiving and praise, recalling the gift received or contemplating the greatness of God's mercy, we also recognize our own smallness and the need to be saved, which is at the root of supplication. In this way we confess to God our condition as creatures, inevitably marked by death, yet bearing a radical desire for life. The Psalmist therefore exclaims in Psalm 86[85]: "I give thanks to you, O Lord my God, with my whole heart, and I will glorify your name for ever. For great is your steadfast love toward me; you have delivered my soul from the depths of Sheol" (vv. 12–13). In the prayer of the Psalms, supplication and praise are interwoven in this manner and fused in a single hymn that celebrates the eternal grace of the Lord who stoops down to our frailty.

It was precisely in order to permit the people of believers to join in this hymn that the Psalter was given to Israel and to the Church. Indeed, the Psalms teach how to pray. In them, the word of God becomes a word of prayer—and they are the words of the inspired Psalmist—which also becomes the word of the person who prays the Psalms. This is the beauty and the special characteristic of this Book of the Bible: the prayers it contains, unlike other prayers we find in Sacred Scripture, are not inserted in a narrative plot that specifies their meaning and role. The Psalms are given to the believer exactly as the text of prayers whose sole purpose is to become the prayer of the person who assimilates them and addresses them to God. Since they are a word of God, anyone who prays the Psalms speaks to God using the very words that God has given to us, addresses him with the words that he himself has given us. So it is that in praying the Psalms we learn to pray. They are a school of prayer.

Something similar happens when a child begins to speak, namely, he learns how to express his own feelings, emotions, and needs with words that do not belong to him innately but that he learns from his parents and from those who surround him. What the child wishes to express is his own experience, but his means of expression come from others; and little by little he makes them his own; the words received from his parents become his words, and through these words he also learns a way of thinking and feeling; he gains access to a whole world of concepts and in it develops and grows and relates to reality, to people, and to God. In the end, his parents' language has become his language; he speaks with words he has received from others but which have now become his own. This is what happens with the prayer of the Psalms. They are given to us so that we may learn to address God, to communicate with him, to speak to him of ourselves with his words, to find a language for the encounter with God. And through those words, it will also be possible to know and to accept the criteria of his action, to draw closer to the mystery of his thoughts and ways (cf. Is 55:8–9), so as to grow constantly in faith and in love. Just as our words are not only words but teach us a real and conceptual world, so too these prayers teach us the heart of God, for which reason not only can we speak to God but we can learn who God is, and, in learning how to speak to him, we learn to be a human being, to be ourselves.

In this regard, the title which the Jewish tradition has given to the Psalter is significant. It is called *tehillîm*, a Hebrew word which means "praise", from the etymological root that we find in the expression "Alleluia", that is, literally, "praised be the Lord". This book of prayers, therefore, although it is so multiform and complex with its different literary genres and its structure alternating between praise and supplication, is ultimately a book of praise which teaches us to give thanks, to celebrate the greatness of God's gift, to recognize the beauty of his works, and to glorify his holy Name. This is the most appropriate response to the Lord's self-manifestation and to the experience of his goodness. By teaching us to pray, the Psalms teach us that even in desolation, even in sorrow, God's presence endures; it is a source of wonder and of solace; we can weep, implore, intercede, and complain, but in the awareness that we are walking toward the light, where praise can be definitive. As Psalm 36[35] teaches us: "With you is the fountain of life; in your light do we see light" (Ps 36[35]:10).

However, in addition to this general title of the book, the Jewish tradition has given many Psalms specific names, attributing most of them to King David. A figure of outstanding human and theological depth, David was a complex figure who went through the most varied fundamental experiences of life. When he was young, he was a shepherd of his father's flock; then, passing through checkered and at times dramatic vicissitudes, he became King of Israel and pastor of the People of God. A man of peace, he fought many wars; unflagging and tenacious in his quest for God, he betrayed God's love, and this is characteristic: he always remained a seeker of God even though he sinned frequently and seriously. As a humble penitent, he received the divine pardon, accepted the divine punishment, and accepted a destiny marked by suffering. Thus David with all his weaknesses was a king "after the heart of God" (cf. 1 Sam 13:14), that is, a passionate man of prayer, a man who knew what it meant to implore and to praise. The connection of the Psalms with this outstanding King of Israel is therefore important because he is a messianic figure, an Anointed One of the Lord, in whom, in a certain way, the mystery of Christ is foreshadowed.

Equally important and meaningful are the manner and frequency with which the words of the Psalms are taken up in the New Testament, assuming and accentuating the prophetic value suggested by the connection of the Psalter with the messianic figure of David. In the Lord Jesus, who in his earthly life prayed with the Psalms, they were definitively fulfilled and revealed their fullest and most profound meaning. The prayers of the Psalter with which we speak to God speak to us of him, speak to us of the Son, an image of the invisible God (Col 1:15), which fully reveals to us the Father's Face. Christians, therefore, in praying the Psalms pray to the Father in Christ and with Christ, assuming those hymns in a new perspective which has in the Paschal Mystery the ultimate key to its interpretation. The horizon of the person praying thus opens to unexpected realities; every Psalm acquires a new light in Christ, and the Psalter can shine out in its full infinite richness.

Dear brothers and sisters, let us therefore take this holy book in our hands, let us allow God to teach us to turn to him, let us make the Psalter a guide which helps and accompanies us daily on the path of prayer. And let us, too, ask, as did Jesus' disciples, "Lord, teach us to pray" (Lk 11:1), opening our hearts to receive the Teacher's prayer, in which all prayers are brought to completion. Thus, made sons in the Son, we shall be able to speak to God, calling him "Our Father".

8

The Reading of Scripture: Food for the Spirit

WEDNESDAY, 3 AUGUST 2011
Castel Gandolfo

Dear Brothers and Sisters,

I am very glad to see you here in the square at Castel Gandolfo and to resume the audiences after the interval in July. I would like to continue with the subject on which we have embarked, that is, a "school of prayer", and today, in a slightly different way and without straying from this theme, I would also like to mention certain spiritual and concrete aspects which seem to me useful, not only for those who—in one part of the world—are spending their summer holidays like us, but also for all who are involved in daily work.

When we have a break from our activities, especially in the holidays, we often take up a book we want to read. It is on this very aspect that I would first like to reflect today. Each one of us needs time and space for recollection, meditation, and calmness.... Thanks be to God that this is so! In fact, this need tells us that we are not made for work alone, but also to think, to reflect, or even simply to follow with our minds and our hearts a tale, a story in which to immerse ourselves, in a certain sense "to lose ourselves" in order to find ourselves subsequently enriched.

Of course, many of these books to read, which we take in our hands during our vacation, are at best an escape, and this is normal. Yet various people, particularly if they have more time in which to take a break and to relax, devote themselves to something more demanding. I would therefore like to make a suggestion: why not discover some of the books of the Bible which are not commonly well known? Or those from which we hear certain passages in the Liturgy but which we never read in their entirety? Indeed, many Christians never read the Bible and have a very limited and superficial knowledge of it. The Bible, as the name says, is a collection of books, a small "library" that came into being in the course of a millennium. Some of these "small books" of which it is composed are almost unknown to the majority, even people who are good Christians. Some are very short, such as the Book of Tobit, a tale that contains a lofty sense of family and marriage; or the Book of Esther, in which the Jewish Queen saves her people from extermination with her faith and prayer; or the Book of Ruth, a stranger who meets God and experiences his providence, which is an even shorter book. These little books can be read in an hour. More demanding and true masterpieces are the Book of Job, which faces the great problem of innocent suffering; Ecclesiastes is striking because of the disconcerting modernity with which it calls into question the meaning of life and of the world; and the Song of Songs, a wonderful symbolic poem of human love. As you see, these are all books of the Old Testament. And what about the New? The New Testament is of course better known, and its literary genres are less diversified. Yet the beauty of reading a Gospel at one sitting must be discovered, just as I also recommend the Acts of the Apostles or one of the Letters.

To conclude, dear friends, today I would like to suggest that you keep the Holy Bible within reach, during the summer period or in your breaks, in order to enjoy it in a new way by reading some of its books straight through, those that are less known and also the most famous, such as the Gospels, but without putting them down. By so doing, moments of relaxation can become in addition to a cultural enrichment also an enrichment of the spirit which is capable of fostering the knowledge of God and dialogue with him, prayer. And this seems to be a splendid holiday occupation: to take a book of the Bible in order to have a little relaxation and at the same time to enter the great realm of the word of God and to deepen our contact with the Eternal One, as the very purpose of the free time that the Lord gives us.

9

"Oasis" of the Spirit

WEDNESDAY, 10 AUGUST 2011
Castel Gandolfo

Dear Brothers and Sisters,

In every age, men and women who have consecrated their lives to God in prayer—like monks and nuns—have founded their communities in particularly beautiful places: in the countryside, on hilltops, in mountain valleys, on the shores of lakes or of the sea, and even on small islands. These places combine two very important elements for contemplative life: the beauty of creation, which evokes the beauty of the Creator, and silence, which is guaranteed by living far from cities and the great thoroughfares of the media. Silence is the environmental condition most conducive to contemplation, to listening to God, and to meditation. The very fact of enjoying silence and letting ourselves be "filled", so to speak, with silence disposes us to prayer. The great Prophet Elijah on Mount Horeb—that is, Sinai—experienced a strong squall, then an earthquake, and finally flashes of fire, but he did not recognize God's voice in them; instead, he recognized it in a light breeze (cf. 1 Kings 19:11–13). God speaks in silence, but we must know how to listen. This is why monasteries are oases in which God speaks to humanity;

and in them we find the cloister, a symbolic place because it is an enclosed space yet open to Heaven.

Tomorrow, dear friends, we shall commemorate Saint Clare of Assisi. Therefore, I would like to recall one such "oasis" of the spirit that is particularly dear to the Franciscan family and to all Christians: the little convent of Saint Damian, situated just beneath the city of Assisi, among the olive groves that slope down toward Santa Maria degli Angeli [Saint Mary of the Angels]. It was beside this little church, which Francis restored after his conversion, that Clare and her first companions established their community, living on prayer and humble tasks. They were called the "Poor Sisters", and their "form of life" was the same as that of the Friars Minor: "To observe the Holy Gospel of our Lord Jesus Christ" (*Rule of Saint Clare* 1, 2), preserving the union of reciprocal charity (cf. ibid., X, 7) and observing in particular the poverty and humility of Jesus and of his Most Holy Mother (cf. ibid., XII, 13).

The silence and beauty of the place in which the monastic community dwells—a simple and austere beauty—are like a reflection of the spiritual harmony which the community itself seeks to create. The world, particularly Europe, is spangled with these oases of the spirit, some very ancient, others recent, yet others have been restored by new communities. Looking at things from a spiritual perspective, these places of the spirit are the backbone of the world! It is no accident that many people, especially in their breaks, visit these places and spend several days here: the soul, too, thanks be to God, has its needs!

Let us therefore remember Saint Clare. But let us also remember other saints who remind us of the importance of turning our gaze to the "things of Heaven", as did Saint Edith Stein, Teresa Benedicta of the Cross, Carmelite, co-Patroness of Europe, whom we celebrated yesterday. And today, 10 August, we cannot forget Saint Lawrence, deacon and martyr, with special congratulations to the Romans who have always venerated him as one of their Patrons. Lastly, let us turn our gaze to the Virgin Mary, that she may teach us to love silence and prayer.

10

Meditation

WEDNESDAY, 17 AUGUST 2011
Castel Gandolfo

Dear Brothers and Sisters,

We are still in the light of the Feast of the Assumption, which—as I said—is a Feast of hope. Mary has arrived in Heaven, and this is our destination: we can all reach Heaven. The question is: how? Mary has arrived there. It is she—the Gospel says—"who believed that there would be a fulfillment of what was spoken to her from the Lord" (Lk 1:45). Thus Mary believed, she entrusted herself to God, bent her will to the will of the Lord, and so was truly on the most direct road, the road to Heaven. Believing, entrusting oneself to the Lord, and complying with his will: this is the essential approach.

Today I do not want to talk about this whole journey of faith; I want to speak of only one small aspect of the life of prayer—which is life in contact with God—namely, meditation. And what is meditation? It means "remembering" all that God has done and not forgetting his many great benefits (cf. Ps 103[102]:2b). We often see only the negative things; we must also keep in mind all that is positive, the gifts that God has made us; we must be attentive to the positive signs that come from God and must remember them.

Let us therefore speak of a type of prayer which in the Christian tradition is known as "mental prayer". We are usually familiar with vocal prayer. The heart and the mind must of course take part in this prayer. However, we are speaking today of a meditation that does not consist of words but, rather, is a way of making contact with the heart of God in our mind. And here Mary is a very real model. Luke the Evangelist repeated several times that Mary, "kept all these things, pondering them in her heart" (2:19; cf. 2:51b). As a good custodian, she did not forget; she was attentive to all that the Lord told her and did for her, and she meditated, in other words, she considered various things, pondering them in her heart.

Therefore, she who "believed" in the announcement of the Angel and made herself the means of enabling the eternal Word of the Most High to become incarnate also welcomed in her heart the wonderful miracle of that human-divine birth; she meditated on it and paused to reflect on what God was working within her, in order to welcome the divine will in her life and respond to it. The mystery of the Incarnation of the Son of God and of Mary's motherhood is of such magnitude that it requires interiorization; it is not only something physical which God brought about within her, but it is something that demanded interiorization on the part of Mary, who endeavors to deepen her understanding of it, to interpret its meaning, to comprehend its consequences and implications. Thus, day after day, in the silence of ordinary life, Mary continued to treasure in her heart the sequence of marvelous events that she witnessed until the supreme test of the Cross and the glory of the Resurrection. Mary lived her life to the full, her daily duties, her role as a mother, but she knew how to reserve an inner space to reflect on the word and will of God, on what was occurring within her and on the mysteries of the life of her Son.

In our time we are taken up with so many activities and duties, worries, and problems: we often tend to fill all of the spaces of the day, without leaving a moment to pause and reflect and to nourish our spiritual life, our contact with God. Mary teaches us how necessary it is to find in our busy day moments for silent recollection, to meditate on what the Lord wants to teach us, on how he is present and active in the world and in our life: to be able to stop for a moment and meditate. Saint Augustine compares meditation on the mysteries of God to the assimilation of food and uses a verb that recurs throughout the Christian tradition, "to ruminate"; that is, the mysteries of God should continually resonate within us so that they become familiar to us, guide our lives, and nourish us, as does the food we need to sustain us. Saint Bonaventure, moreover, with reference to the words of Sacred Scripture, says that "they should always be ruminated upon so as to be able to gaze on them with ardent application of the soul" (*Coll. In Hex*, ed. Quaracchi 1934, p. 218). To meditate, therefore, means to create within us a situation of recollection, of inner silence, in order to reflect upon and assimilate the mysteries of our faith and what God is working within us; and not merely on the things that come and go. We may undertake this "rumination" in various ways: for example, by taking a brief passage of Sacred Scripture, especially the Gospels, the Acts of the Apostles, or the Letters of the Apostles, or a passage from a spiritual author that brings the reality of God closer to us and more present in our day; or we can even ask our confessor or spiritual director to recommend something to us; and then by reading and reflecting on what we have read, dwelling on it, trying to understand what it is saying to me, what it says today, to open our spirit to what the Lord wants to tell us and teach us. The Holy Rosary is also a prayer of meditation: in repeating the Hail Mary, we are asked to think about and reflect on the Mystery which we have just proclaimed. But we can also reflect on some intense spiritual experience or on words that stayed with us when we were taking part in the Sunday Eucharist. So, you see, there are many ways to meditate and thereby to make contact with God and to approach God; and, in this way, to be journeying on toward Heaven.

Dear friends, making time for God regularly is a fundamental element for spiritual growth; it will be the Lord himself who gives us the taste for his mysteries, his words, his presence and action, for feeling how beautiful it is when God speaks with us; he will enable us to understand more deeply what he expects of me. This, ultimately, is the very aim of meditation: to entrust ourselves increasingly to the hands of God, with trust and love, certain that in the end it is only by doing his will that we are truly happy.

11

Art and Prayer

WEDNESDAY, 31 AUGUST 2011
Castel Gandolfo

Dear Brothers and Sisters,

In this period I have recalled several times the need for every Christian, in the midst of the many occupations that fill our days, to find time for God and for prayer. The Lord himself gives us many opportunities to remember him. Today I would like to reflect briefly on one of these channels that can lead to God and can also be of help in the encounter with him. It is the way of artistic expression, part of that "*via pulchritudinis*"—the "way of beauty", of which I have spoken several times and whose deepest meaning must be recovered by men and women today.

It may have happened on some occasion that you paused before a sculpture, a picture, a few verses of a poem, or a piece of music that you found deeply moving, that gave you a sense of joy, a clear perception, that is, that what you beheld was not only matter, a piece of marble or bronze, a painted canvas, a collection of letters, or an accumulation of sounds, but something greater, something that "speaks", that can touch the heart, communicate a message, uplift the mind. A work of art is a product of the creative capacity of the human being who, in questioning visible reality, seeks to discover its deep meaning and to communicate it through the language of forms, color, and sound. Art is able to manifest and make visible the human need to surpass the visible; it expresses the thirst and the quest for the infinite. Indeed, it resembles a door open onto the infinite, onto a beauty and a truth that go beyond the daily routine. And a work of art can open the eyes of the mind and of the heart, impelling us upward.

However, some artistic expressions are real highways to God, the supreme Beauty; indeed, they help us to grow in our relationship with him, in prayer. These are works that were born from faith and express faith. We can see an example of this when we visit a Gothic cathedral: we are enraptured by the vertical lines that soar skyward and uplift our gaze and our spirit, while at the same time we feel small yet long for fullness. . . . Or when we enter a Romanesque church, we are spontaneously prompted to meditate and to pray. We perceive that these splendid buildings contain, as it were, the faith of generations. Or when we listen to a piece of sacred music that plucks at our heartstrings, our mind, as it were, expands and turns naturally to God. I remember a concert of music by Johann Sebastian Bach in Munich, conducted by Leonard Bernstein. At the end of the last passage, one of the *Cantatas*, I felt, not by reasoning but in the depths of my heart, that what I had heard had communicated truth to me, the truth of the supreme composer, and impelled me to thank God. The Lutheran bishop of Munich was next to me, and I said to him spontaneously: "In hearing this one understands: it is true; such strong faith is true, as well as the beauty that irresistibly expresses the presence of God's truth." Yet how many pictures or frescos, fruits of the artist's faith, in their form, in their color, in their light, urge us to think of God and foster within ourselves the desire to draw from the source of all beauty. What Marc Chagall, a great artist, wrote remains profoundly true: that for centuries painters have dipped their paintbrush in that colored alphabet which is the Bible. Thus how often artistic expression can bring us to remember God, to help us to pray, or even to convert our heart! Paul Claudel, a famous French poet, playwright, and diplomat, precisely while he was listening in the Cathedral of Notre Dame to the singing of the *Magnificat* during Christmas Mass in 1886, had a tangible experience of God's presence. He had not entered the church for reasons of faith but, rather, in order to seek arguments against Christians, and instead, God's grace worked actively in his heart.

Dear friends, I ask you to rediscover the importance of this path also for prayer, for our living relationship with God. Towns and villages throughout the world contain treasures of art that express faith and beckon to us to return to our relationship with God. May the visits to places filled with art, then, not only be opportunities for cultural enrichment—that, too—but may they become above all moments of grace, incentives to strengthen our bond and our dialogue with the Lord so that—in switching from simple external reality to the more profound reality it expresses—we may pause to contemplate the ray of beauty that strikes us to the quick, that almost "wounds" us, and that invites us to rise toward God. I end with a prayer from a Psalm, Psalm 27[26]: "One thing have I asked of the Lord, that will I seek after; that I may dwell in the house of the Lord all the days of my life, to behold the beauty of the Lord, and contemplate his temple" (v. 4). Let us hope that the Lord will help us to contemplate his beauty, both in nature and in works of art, so that we, moved by the light that shines from his Face, may be a light for our neighbor.

12

Psalm 3: "Arise, O Lord! Deliver me, O my God!"

WEDNESDAY, 7 SEPTEMBER 2011
Saint Peter's Square

Dear Brothers and Sisters,

Today we are resuming the Audiences in Saint Peter's Square and the "school of prayer" which we attend together during these Wednesday Catecheses. I would like to begin by meditating on several Psalms, which, as I said last June, constitute the "prayer book" par excellence. The first Psalm I shall consider is a Psalm of lamentation and supplication, imbued with deep trust, in which the certainty of God's presence forms the basis of the prayer that springs from the condition of extreme peril in which the person praying finds himself. It is Psalm 3, which Jewish tradition ascribes to David at the moment when he fled from his son Absalom (cf. v. 1): this was one of the most dramatic and anguishing episodes in the King's life, when his son usurped his royal throne and forced him to flee from Jerusalem for his life (cf. 2 Sam 15ff.). Thus David's plight and anxiety serve as a background to this prayer and help us to understand it by presenting a typical situation in which such a Psalm may be recited. Every man and woman can recognize in the Psalmist's cry those feelings of sorrow, bitter regret, and yet at the same time trust in God, who, as the Bible tells us, had accompanied David on the flight from his city.

The Psalm opens with an invocation to the Lord:

O Lord, how many are my foes! / Many are rising against me;
many are saying of me, "There is no help for him in God." (vv. 2–3)

The praying man's description of the situation is therefore marked by intensely dramatic tones. The idea of "multitude" is conveyed with the triple use of "many"—three words that in the original text are different terms with the same Hebrew root so as to give further emphasis to the enormity of the danger—in a repetitive manner, as it were, hammering it in. This insistence on the large number of his enemies serves to express the Psalmist's perception of the absolute disproportion between himself and his persecutors, which justifies and establishes the urgency of his plea for help; his oppressors are numerous, they get the upper hand, whereas the man praying is alone and defenseless, at the mercy of his assailants. Yet the first word the Psalmist says is "Lord"; his cry opens with a call to God. A multitude threatens him and rises against him, generating fear that magnifies the threat, making it appear greater and even more terrifying; but the praying person does not let this vision of death prevail; he keeps intact his relationship with the God of life and turns to him first in search of help. However, his enemies attempt to break this bond with God and to injure their victim's faith. They insinuate that the Lord cannot intervene; they say that not even God can save him. Hence the attack is not only physical but involves the spiritual dimension, too: "there is no help for him in God", they say, targeting the central principle of the Psalmist's mind. This is the extreme temptation to which the believer is subjected, the temptation to lose faith, to lose trust in God's closeness. The righteous pass the final test, remain steadfast in faith, in the certainty of the truth, and in full trust in God; in this way they find life and truth. It seems to me that here the Psalm touches us very personally: beset by many problems, we are tempted to think that perhaps God does not save me, that he does not know me, perhaps he is not able to; the temptation to lose faith is our enemy's ultimate attack, and if we are to find God, if we are to find life, we must resist it.

Thus in our Psalm the person praying is called to respond with faith to the attacks of the wicked: his foes—as I said—deny that God can help him; yet he invokes God; he calls him by name, "Lord", and then turns to him with an emphatic "thou/you" that expresses a solid, sturdy relationship and implies the certainty of the divine response:

But you, O Lord, are a shield about me, / my glory, and the lifter of my head.
I cry aloud to the Lord, / and he answers me from his holy hill. (vv. 4–5)

The vision of the enemies then disappears; they have not triumphed because the one who believes in God is sure that God is his friend. Only the "thou/you" of God is left. Now only One opposes the "many", but this One is far greater, far more powerful, than many adversaries. The Lord is help, defense, and salvation; as a shield he protects the person who entrusts himself to him and enables him to lift his head in the gesture of triumph and victory. Man is no longer alone; his foes are not invincible as they had seemed, for the Lord hears the cry of the oppressed and answers from the place of his presence, from his holy hill. The human being cries out in anguish, in danger, in pain; the human being calls for help, and God answers. In this interweaving of the human cry and the divine response we find the dialectic of prayer and the key to reading the entire history of salvation. The cry expresses the need for help and appeals to the other's faithfulness; crying out means making an act of faith in God's closeness and in his willingness to listen. Prayer expresses the certainty of a divine presence already experienced and believed in and fully expressed in God's salvific answers. This is important: that in our prayer the certainty of God's presence be given importance and be made present. Thus the Psalmist, who feels besieged by death, professes his faith in the God of life who, as a shield, surrounds him with an invulnerable protection; the one who believed he was as good as lost can raise his head because the Lord saves him; the praying person, threatened and mocked, is in glory, because God is his glory.

The divine response that hears his prayer totally reassures the Psalmist; even his fear is no more, and his cry is soothed in peace, in deep inner tranquility.

I lie down and sleep; I wake again, / for the Lord sustains me.
I am not afraid of ten thousands of people
who have set themselves against me round about. (vv. 6–7)

The praying person, even in peril, in the midst of battle, can sleep serenely in an unequivocal attitude of trusting abandonment. His foes have pitched camp around him; they are numerous, they besiege him, they rise up against him, taunting and trying to make him fall; instead, he lies down and sleeps, calm and serene, sure of God's presence. And, on reawakening he finds God still beside him, as a custodian who does not fall asleep (cf. Ps 121[120]:3–4), who sustains him, who holds his hand, who never abandons him. The fear of death is vanquished by the presence of One who never dies. And even the night that is peopled by atavistic fears, the sorrowful night of solitude and anguished waiting, is now transformed: what evoked death became the presence of the Eternal One.

The enemy's visible, massive, impressive attack is countered by the invisible presence of God with all his invincible power. And it is to him that the Psalmist, after his trusting words, once again addresses the prayer: "Arise, O Lord! Deliver me, O my God!" (v. 8a). His assailants "are rising" (cf. v. 2) against their victim; instead, the One who will "arise" is the Lord, and it will be to defeat them. God will deliver him, answering his cry. Thus the Psalm ends with the vision of liberation from the peril that kills and from the temptation that can cause us to perish. After addressing his plea to the Lord to arise and deliver him, the praying person describes the divine victory: the enemies—who with their unjust and cruel oppression are the symbol of all that opposes God and his plan of salvation—are defeated. Struck on the mouth, they will no longer attack with their destructive violence and will be unable to instill evil and doubt in God's presence and action. Their senseless and blasphemous talk is denied once and for all and is reduced to silence by the Lord's saving intervention (cf. v. 8bc). In this way the Psalmist can conclude his prayer with a sentence with liturgical connotations that celebrates the God of life in gratitude and praise: "Deliverance belongs to the Lord; your blessing be upon your people" (v. 9).

Dear brothers and sisters, Psalm 3 has presented us with a supplication full of trust and consolation. In praying this Psalm, we can make our own the sentiments of the

Psalmist, a figure of the righteous person persecuted, who finds his fulfillment in Jesus. In sorrow, in danger, in the bitterness of misunderstanding and offense, the words of the Psalm open our hearts to the comforting certainty of faith. God is always close—even in difficulties, in problems, in the darkness of life—he listens and saves in his own way. However, it is necessary to recognize his presence and accept his ways, as did David in his humiliating flight from his son, Absalom; as did the just man who is persecuted in the Book of Wisdom, and, ultimately and completely, as did the Lord Jesus on Golgotha. And when, in the eyes of the wicked, God does not seem to intervene and the Son dies, it is then that the true glory and the definitive realization of salvation is manifest to all believers. May the Lord give us faith, may he come to our aid in our weakness and make us capable of believing and praying in every anxiety, in the sorrowful nights of doubt and the long days of sorrow, abandoning ourselves with trust to him, who is our "shield" and our "glory".

13

Psalm 22 (21): "My God, my God, why have you forsaken me?"

WEDNESDAY, 14 SEPTEMBER 2011
Paul VI Audience Hall

Dear Brothers and Sisters,

In the Catechesis today I would like to apply myself to a Psalm with strong Christological implications which continually surface in accounts of Jesus' passion, with its twofold dimension of humiliation and glory, of death and life. It is Psalm 22 according to the Hebrew tradition and Psalm 21 according to the Greco-Latin tradition, a heartfelt, moving prayer with a human density and theological richness that make it one of the most frequently prayed and studied Psalms in the entire Psalter. It is a long poetic composition, and we shall reflect in particular on its first part, centered on the lament, in order to examine in depth certain important dimensions of the prayer of supplication to God.

This Psalm presents the figure of an innocent man, persecuted and surrounded by adversaries who clamor for his death; and he turns to God with a sorrowful lament, which, in the certainty of his faith, opens mysteriously to praise. The anguishing reality of the present and the consoling memory of the past alternate in his prayer in an agonized awareness of his own desperate situation in which, however, he does not want to give up hope. His initial cry is an appeal addressed to a God who appears remote, who does not answer and seems to have abandoned him:

My God, my God, why have you forsaken me?
Why are you so far from helping me, from the words of my groaning?
O my God, I cry by day, but you do not answer;
and by night, but find no rest. (vv. 3–4)

God is silent, and this silence pierces the soul of the person praying, who ceaselessly calls but receives no answer. Day and night succeed one another in an unflagging quest for a word, for help that does not come; God seems so distant, so forgetful, so absent. The prayer asks to be heard, to be answered; it begs for contact, seeks a relationship that can give comfort and salvation. But if God fails to respond, the cry of help is lost in the void and loneliness becomes unbearable. Yet, in his cry, the praying man of our Psalm calls the Lord "my" God at least three times, in an extreme act of trust and faith. In spite of all appearances, the Psalmist cannot believe that his link with the Lord is totally broken, and while he asks the reason for a presumed incomprehensible abandonment, he says that "his" God cannot forsake him.

As is well known, the initial cry of the Psalm, "My God, my God, why have you forsaken me?", is recorded by the Gospels of Matthew and Mark as the cry uttered by Jesus dying on the Cross (cf. Mt 27:46, Mk 15:34). It expresses all the desolation of the Messiah, Son of God, who is facing the drama of death, a reality totally opposed to the Lord of life. Forsaken by almost all his followers, betrayed and denied by the disciples, surrounded by people who insult him, Jesus is under the crushing weight of a mission that was to pass through humiliation and annihilation. This is why he cried out to the Father, and his suffering took up the sorrowful words of the Psalm. But his is not a desperate cry; nor was that of the Psalmist, who, in his supplication, takes a tormented path which nevertheless opens out at last into a perspective of praise, into trust in the divine victory. And since in the Jewish custom citing the beginning of a Psalm implied a reference to the whole poem, although Jesus' anguished prayer retains its burden of unspeakable suffering, it unfolds to the certainty of glory. "Was it not necessary that the Christ should suffer these things and enter into his glory?" the Risen Christ was to say to the disciples at Emmaus (Lk 24:26). In his passion, in obedience to the Father, the Lord Jesus passes through abandonment and death to reach life and to give it to all believers.

This initial cry of supplication in our Psalm 22[21] is followed in sorrowful contrast by the memory of the past,

In you our fathers trusted;
they trusted, and you did deliver them.
To you they cried, and were saved;
in you they trusted, and were not disappointed. (vv. 5–6)

The God who appears today to be so remote to the Psalmist is nonetheless the merciful Lord whom Israel experienced throughout its history. The People to whom the praying person belongs is the object of God's love and can witness to his fidelity to it. Starting with the patriarchs, then in Egypt and on the long pilgrimage through the wilderness, in the stay in the Promised Land in contact with aggressive and hostile peoples, to the night of the exile, the whole of biblical history is a history of a cry for help on the part of the people and of saving answers on the part of

God. And the Psalmist refers to the steadfast faith of his ancestors who "trusted"—this word is repeated three times—without ever being disappointed. Then, however, it seems that this chain of trusting invocations and divine answers has been broken; the Psalmist's situation seems to deny the entire history of salvation, making the present reality even more painful.

God, however, cannot deny himself, so here the prayer returns to describing the distressing plight of the praying person, to induce the Lord to have pity on him and to intervene, as he always has done in the past. The Psalmist describes himself as "a worm, and no man, scorned by men, and despised by the people" (v. 7). He was mocked, people made grimaces at him, (cf. v. 8), and he was wounded in his faith itself. "He committed his cause to the Lord; let him deliver him, let him rescue him, for he delights in him!" (v. 9), they said. Under the jeering blows of irony and contempt, it almost seems as though the persecuted man loses his own human features, like the suffering servant outlined in the Book of Isaiah (cf. 52:14; 53:2b–3). And like the oppressed righteous man in the Book of Wisdom (cf. 2:12–20), like Jesus on Calvary (cf. Mt 27:39–43), the Psalmist sees his own relationship with the Lord called into question in the cruel and sarcastic emphasis on what is causing him to suffer: God's silence, his apparent absence. And yet God was present with an indisputable tenderness in the life of the person praying. The Psalmist reminds the Lord of this: "Yet you are he who took me from the womb; you did keep me safe upon my mother's breasts. Upon you was I cast from my birth" (vv. 10–11a). The Lord is the God of life who brings the newborn child into the world and cares for him with a father's affection. And though the memory of God's fidelity in the history of the people has first been recalled, the praying person now re-evokes his own personal history of relations with the Lord, going back to the particularly significant moment of the beginning of his life. And here, despite the desolation of the present, the Psalmist recognizes a closeness and a divine love so radical that he can now exclaim, in a confession full of faith and generating hope: "and since my mother bore me you have been my God" (v. 11b).

The lament then becomes a heartfelt plea: "Be not far from me, for trouble is near and there is none to help" (v. 12). The only closeness that the Psalmist can perceive and that fills him with fear is that of his enemies. It is therefore necessary for God to make himself close and to help him, because enemies surround the praying man; they encircle him and are like strong bulls, like ravening and roaring lions (cf. vv. 13–14). Anguish alters his perception of the danger, magnifying it. The adversaries seem invincible; they become ferocious, dangerous animals, while the Psalmist is like a small worm, powerless and defenseless. Yet these images used in the Psalm also serve to say that when man becomes brutal and attacks his brother, something brutal within him takes the upper hand; he seems to lose any human likeness; violence always has something bestial about it, and only God's saving intervention can restore humanity to human beings. Now, it seems to the Psalmist, the object of so much ferocious aggression, that he no longer has any way out, and death begins to take possession of him: "I am poured out like water, and all my bones are out of joint ... my strength is dried up like a potsherd, and my tongue cleaves to my jaws ... they divide my garments among them, and for my raiment they cast lots" (vv. 15, 16, 19). The disintegration of the body of the condemned man is described with the dramatic images that we encounter in the accounts of Christ's passion, the unbearable parching thirst that torments the dying man that is echoed in Jesus' request "I thirst" (cf. Jn 19:28), until we reach the definitive act of his tormentors, who, like the soldiers at the foot of the Cross, divide the clothes of the victim whom they consider already dead (cf. Mt 27:35; Mk 15:24; Lk 23:34; Jn 19:23–24).

Here then, impelling, once again comes the request for help: "But you, O Lord, be not far off! O you my help, hasten to my aid! . . . Save me" (vv. 20; 22a). This is a cry that opens the Heavens, because it proclaims a faith, a certainty that goes beyond all doubt, all darkness, and all desolation. And the lament is transformed; it gives way to praise in the acceptance of salvation: He has heard. "I will tell of your name to my brethren; in the midst of the congregation I will praise you" (vv. 22c–23). In this way the Psalm opens to thanksgiving, to the great final hymn that sweeps up the whole people, the Lord's faithful, the liturgical assembly, the generations to come (cf. vv. 24–32). The Lord went to the rescue; he saved the poor man and showed his merciful Face. Death and life are interwoven in an inseparable mystery, and life triumphs; the God of salvation shows himself to be the undisputed Lord whom all the ends of the earth will praise and before whom all the families of the nations will bow down. It is the victory of faith which can transform death into the gift of life, the abyss of sorrow into a source of hope.

Dear brothers and sisters, this Psalm has taken us to Golgotha, to the foot of the Cross of Jesus, to relive his passion and to share the fruitful joy of the Resurrection. Let us therefore allow ourselves to be invaded by the light of the Paschal Mystery even in God's apparent absence, even in God's silence, and, like the disciples of Emmaus, let us learn to discern the true reality beyond appearances, recognizing humiliation itself as the way to exaltation and the Cross as the full manifestation of life in death. Thus, replacing in God the Father all our trust and hope, in every anxiety we will be able to pray to him with faith, and our cry of help will be transformed into a hymn of praise.

14

Psalm 23

WEDNESDAY, 5 OCTOBER 2011
Saint Peter's Square

Dear Brothers and Sisters,

Turning to the Lord in prayer implies a radical act of trust, in the awareness that one is entrusting oneself to God, who is good, "merciful and gracious, slow to anger, and abounding in steadfast love and faithfulness" (Ex 34:6–7; Ps 86[85]:15; cf. Joel 2:13; Jon 4:2; Ps 103 [102]:8; 145[144]:8; Neh 9:17). For this reason, I would like to reflect with you today on a Psalm that is totally imbued with trust, in which the Psalmist expresses his serene certainty that he is guided and protected, safe from every danger, because the Lord is his Shepherd. It is Psalm 23 [22, according to the Greco-Latin numbering], a text familiar to all and loved by all.

"The Lord is my shepherd, I shall not want": the beautiful prayer begins with these words, evoking the nomadic environment of sheep-farming and the experience of familiarity between the shepherd and the sheep that make up his little flock. The image calls to mind an atmosphere of trust, intimacy, and tenderness: the shepherd knows each one of his sheep and calls them by name; and they follow him because they recognize him and trust in him (cf. Jn 10:2–4). He tends them, looks after them as precious possessions, ready to defend them, to guarantee their well-being and enable them to live a peaceful life. They can lack nothing as long as the shepherd is with them. The Psalmist refers to this experience by calling God his shepherd and letting God lead him to safe pastures:

> He makes me lie down in green pastures.
> He leads me beside still waters;
> he restores my soul.
> He leads me in paths of righteousness
> for his name's sake. (Ps 23[22]:2–3)

The vision that unfolds before our eyes is that of green pastures and springs of clear water, oases of peace to which the shepherd leads his flock, symbols of the places of life toward which the Lord leads the Psalmist, who feels like the sheep lying on the grass beside a stream, resting rather than in a state of tension or alarm, peaceful and trusting, because it is a safe place, the water is fresh, and the shepherd is watching over them. And let us not forget here that the scene elicited by the Psalm is set in a land that is largely desert, on which the scorching sun beats down, where the Middle-Eastern semi-nomad shepherd lives with his flock in the parched steppes that surround the villages. Nevertheless, the shepherd knows where to find grass and fresh water, essential to life; he can lead the way to oases in which the soul is "restored" and where it is possible to recover strength and new energy to start out afresh on the journey.

As the Psalmist says, God guides him to "green pastures" and "still waters", where everything is superabundant, everything is given in plenty. If the Lord is the Shepherd, even in the desert, a desolate place of death, the certainty of a radical presence of life is not absent, so that he is able to say "I shall not want." Indeed, the shepherd has at heart the good of his flock; he adapts his own pace and needs to those of his sheep; he walks and lives with them, leading them on paths "of righteousness", that is, suitable for them, paying attention to their needs and not to his own. The safety of his sheep is a priority for him, and he complies with this in leading his flock.

Dear brothers and sisters, if we follow the "Good Shepherd"—no matter how difficult, tortuous, or long the pathways of our life may seem, even through spiritual deserts without water and under the scorching sun of rationalism—with the guidance of Christ the Good Shepherd, we, too, like the Psalmist, may be sure that we are walking on "paths of righteousness" and that the Lord is leading us, is ever close to us, and that we "shall lack nothing".

For this reason the Psalmist can declare his calm assurance without doubt or fear:

Even though I walk through the valley of the shadow of death,
I fear no evil; for you are with me;
your rod and your staff they comfort me. (v. 4)

Those who walk with the Lord, even in the dark valleys of suffering, doubt, and all the human problems, feel safe. You are with me: this is our certainty, this is what supports us. The darkness of the night frightens us with its shifting shadows, with the difficulty of distinguishing dangers, with its silence taut with strange sounds. If the flock moves after sunset when visibility fades, it is normal for the sheep to be restless; there is the risk of stumbling or even of straying and getting lost, and there is also the fear of possible assailants lurking in the darkness. To speak of the "dark" valley, the Psalmist uses a Hebrew phrase that calls to mind the shadows of death, which is why the valley to be passed through is a place of anguish, terrible threats, the danger of death. Yet the person praying walks on in safety undaunted since he knows that the Lord is with him. "You are with me" is a proclamation of steadfast faith and sums up the radical experience of faith; God's closeness transforms the reality; the dark valley loses all danger; it is emptied of every threat. Now the flock can walk in tranquility, accompanied by the familiar rhythmical beat of the staff on the ground, marking the shepherd's reassuring presence.

This comforting image ends the first part of the Psalm and gives way to a different scene. We are still in the desert, where the shepherd lives with his flock, but we are now set before his tent, which opens to offer us hospitality.

You prepare a table before me in the presence of my enemies;
you anoint my head with oil,
my cup overflows. (v. 5)

The Lord is now presented as the One who welcomes the person praying with signs of generous hospitality, full of attention. The divine host lays the food on the "table", a term which in Hebrew means, in its primitive sense, the animal skin that was spread out on the ground and on which the food for the common meal was set out. It is a gesture of sharing, not only of food, but also of life in an offering of communion and friendship that creates bonds and expresses solidarity. Then there is the munificent gift of scented oil poured on the head, which with its fragrance brings relief from the scorching of the desert sun, refreshes and calms the skin, and gladdens the spirit. Lastly, the cup overflowing with its exquisite wine, shared with superabundant generosity, adds a note of festivity. Food, oil, and wine are gifts that bring life and give joy, because they go beyond what is strictly necessary and express the free giving and abundance of love. Psalm 104[103] proclaims:

> You cause the grass to grow for the cattle,
> and plants for man to cultivate,
> that he may bring forth food from the earth,
> and wine to gladden the heart of man,
> oil to make his face shine,
> and bread to strengthen man's heart. (vv. 14–15)

The Psalmist becomes the object of much attention, for which reason he sees himself as a wayfarer who finds shelter in a hospitable tent, whereas his enemies have to stop and watch, unable to intervene, since the one whom they considered their prey has been led to safety and has become a sacred guest who cannot be touched. And the Psalmist is we ourselves, if we truly are believers in communion with Christ. When God opens his tent to us to receive us, nothing can harm us.

Then when the traveler sets out afresh, the divine protection is extended and accompanies him on his journey:

> Surely, goodness and mercy shall follow me all the days of my life;
> and I shall dwell in the house of the Lord for ever. (Ps 23[22]:6)

The goodness and faithfulness of God continue to escort the Psalmist who comes out of the tent and resumes his journey. But it is a journey that acquires new meaning and becomes a pilgrimage to the temple of the Lord, the holy place in which the praying person wants to "dwell" for ever and to which he also wants to "return". The Hebrew verb used here has the meaning of "to return" but with a small vowel change can be understood as "to dwell".

Moreover, this is how it is rendered by the ancient versions and by the majority of the modern translations. Both meanings may be retained: to return and dwell in the temple as every Israelite desires, and to dwell near God, close to him and to goodness. This is what every believer yearns and longs for: truly to be able to live where God is, close to him. Following the Shepherd leads to God's house; this is the destination of every journey, the longed for oasis in the desert, the tent of shelter in escaping from enemies, a place of peace where God's kindness and faithful love may be felt, day after day, in the serene joy of time without end.

With their richness and depth, the images of this Psalm have accompanied the whole of the history and religious experience of the people of Israel and accompany Christians. The figure of the shepherd, in particular, calls to mind the original time of the Exodus, the long journey through the desert, as a flock under the guidance of the divine Shepherd (cf. Is 63:11–14; Ps 77: 20–21; 78:52–54). And in the Promised Land, the king had the task of tending the Lord's flock, like David, the shepherd chosen by God and a figure of the Messiah (cf. 2 Sam 5:1–2; 7:8; Ps 78[77]:70–72). Then after the Babylonian Exile, as it were in a new Exodus (cf. Is 40:3–5, 9–11; 43:16–21), Israel was brought back to its homeland like a lost sheep found and led by God to luxuriant pastures and resting places (cf. Ezek 34:11–16, 23–31). However, it is in the Lord Jesus that all the evocative power of our Psalm reaches completeness, finds the fullness of its meaning: Jesus is the "Good Shepherd" who goes in search of lost sheep, who knows his sheep and lays down his life for them (cf. Mt 18:12–14; Lk 15:4–7; Jn 10:2–4, 11–18). He is the way, the right path that leads us to life (cf. Jn 14:6), the light that illuminates the dark valley and overcomes all our fears (cf. Jn 1:9; 8:12; 9:5; 12:46). He is the generous host who welcomes us and rescues us from our enemies, preparing for us the table of his body and his blood (cf. Mt 26:26–29; Mk 14:22–25; Lk 22:19–20) and the definitive table of the messianic banquet in Heaven (cf. Lk 14:15ff; Rev 3:20; 19:9). He is the Royal Shepherd, king in docility and in forgiveness, enthroned on the glorious wood of the Cross (cf. Jn 3:13–15; 12:32; 17:4–5).

Dear brothers and sisters, Psalm 23 invites us to renew our trust in God, abandoning ourselves totally in his hands. Let us therefore ask with faith that the Lord might also grant us on the difficult ways of our time that we might always walk on his paths as a docile and obedient flock and that he might welcome us to his house, to his table, and lead us to "still waters" so that, in accepting the gift of his Spirit, we may quench our thirst at his sources, springs of living water "welling up to eternal life" (Jn 4:14; cf. 7:37–39).

15

Psalm 126

WEDNESDAY, 12 OCTOBER 2011

Saint Peter's Square

Dear Brothers and Sisters,

In the preceding Catecheses, we have meditated on several Psalms of lamentation and trust. Today, I would like to meditate on a Psalm with a festive tone, a prayer that in joy sings the wonders of God. It is Psalm 126—125, according to the Greco-Latin numbering—which celebrates the great things the Lord has accomplished with his people and that he constantly accomplishes in every believer.

The Psalmist, in the name of all Israel, begins his prayer by recalling the exhilarating experience of salvation:

> When the Lord restored the fortunes of Zion,
>   we were like those who dream.
> Then our mouth was filled with laughter,
>   and our tongue with shouts of joy. (vv. 1–2a)

The Psalm speaks of "restored fortunes", that is, returned to its original state, in all its former positivity. It starts, then, from a situation of suffering and need, to which God responds by offering salvation and by leading the one praying back to his original condition, which is now even enriched and changed for the better. This is what happened to Job, when the Lord gave him back all that he had lost by doubling it and bestowing an even greater blessing (cf. Job 42:10–13), and it is what the people of Israel experienced when they returned to their homeland after the Babylonian Exile. It is precisely with reference to the end of the deportation in a foreign land that this Psalm is interpreted: the expression "restore the fortunes of Zion" is read and understood in tradition as "bring back the captives of Zion". In fact, the return from exile is a paradigm of all divine salvific intervention because the fall of Jerusalem and the deportation to Babylonia are a devastating experience for the Chosen People, not only on the political and social level, but also and especially on the religious and spiritual level. The loss of the land, the end of the Davidic monarchy, and the destruction of the temple appear to be a denial of the divine promises, and the people of the covenant, dispersed among pagans, ask themselves sadly about the God who seems to have abandoned them. That is why the end of the deportation and the return to their homeland are experienced as a miraculous return to faith, to trust, to communion with the Lord; it is a "restoration of fortunes" that also implies conversion of heart, pardon, refound friendship with God, awareness of his mercy, and the renewed possibility of praising him (cf. Jer 29:12–14; 30:18–20; 33:6–11; Ezek 39:25–29). It is an experience of extraordinary joy, of laughter and shouts of joy, so beautiful that it seems to be "like a dream". Divine interventions often take unexpected forms that go beyond what man can imagine; wonder and joy, then, are expressed through the praise: "The LORD has done great things for them!" This is what the nations say; it is what Israel proclaims:

Then they said among the nations,
"The LORD has done great things for them."
The LORD has done great things for us;
we are glad. (vv. 2b–3)

God works wonders in the history of men. By bringing salvation, he reveals himself to all as the powerful and merciful Lord, refuge against oppression, who does not forget the cry of the poor (cf. Ps 9:10, 13), who loves justice and right, and whose love fills the earth (cf. Ps 33:5). That is why, in the face of the liberation of the people of Israel, all the nations recognize the extraordinary great things God has accomplished for his people, and they celebrate the Lord in his reality as Savior. And Israel echoes the proclamation of the nations, and it resumes it by repeating it, but in the first person, as the direct recipients of the divine action: "The LORD has done great things for us"; "for us", or, more precisely still, "with us", in Hebrew "*immanû*", thereby affirming the privileged relationship that the Lord maintains with his elect and that will be found in the name Emmanuel, "God with us", which Jesus, his culmination and full manifestation, is called (cf. Mt 1:23).

Dear brothers and sisters, in our prayer we should look more often at how, in the events of our life, the Lord has protected, guided, and helped us and praise him for what he has done and continues to do for us. We must be more attentive to the good things that the Lord gives us. We are always attentive to problems, to difficulties, and it is as if we did not want to see that there are beautiful things that come to us from the Lord. This attentiveness, which becomes gratitude, is very important for us and creates in us a memory of the good that also helps us in dark hours. God accomplishes great things, and whoever experiences that—attentive to the goodness of the Lord with the attentiveness of the heart—is filled with joy. It is on this festive note that the first part of the Psalm concludes. To be saved and to return to one's homeland after exile is like being returned to life: liberation opens one to laughter but also to the expectation of a fulfillment for which one still must hope and ask. This is what the second part of the Psalm says:

> Restore our fortunes, O Lord,
> like the watercourses in the Negeb!
> May those who sow in tears
> reap with shouts of joy!
> He that goes forth weeping,
> bearing the seed for sowing,
> shall come home with shouts of joy,
> bringing his sheaves with him. (vv. 4–6)

If at the beginning of his prayer, the Psalmist celebrated the joy of fortunes by then restored by the Lord, he asks for it now, on the other hand, as something that still remains to be achieved. If we apply this Psalm to the return from exile, this apparent contradiction would be explained by Israel's historical experience of a difficult, only partial return to its homeland, which leads the intercessor to ask for a new divine intervention in order to accomplish fully the restoration of the people.

But the Psalm goes beyond the purely historical fact in order to open itself to fuller dimensions of a theological nature. The comforting experience of the liberation from Babylonia is still incomplete, "already" attained, but "not yet" marked by definitive fullness. So, while it celebrates with joy the salvation received, the prayer opens itself to the expectation of full realization. This is why the Psalm uses particular images that, with their complexity, refer to the mysterious reality of the redemption, in which are mixed the gift received and still to be expected, life and death, dreamlike joy and tears of sorrow. The first image refers to the dry streambeds of the Negeb desert, which during rain are filled with raging water that restores life to the arid terrain and makes it flourish again. The Psalmist's request, then, is that the restoration of the fortunes of the people and the return from exile might be like the water, overwhelming and unstoppable and capable of transforming the desert into an immense expanse of green grass and flowers.

The second image moves from the dry and rocky hills of the Negeb to the fields the farmers cultivate in order to gain food from them. To speak of salvation, we recall here the experience that is renewed every year in the agricultural world: the difficult and tedious time of sowing and then the immense joy of the harvest. Sowing that is accompanied by tears, for you throw what could still become bread, exposing yourself to a time of waiting filled with uncertainty: the farmer works, prepares the land, throws in the seed, but, as the parable of the sower illustrates, he does not know where this seed will fall, if birds will eat it, if it will rise, if it will take root, if it will become an ear of grain (cf. Mt 13:3–9; Mk 4:2–9; Lk 8:4–8). Throwing seed is a gesture of trust and hope; the work of man is necessary, but then he must enter into a time of impotent waiting, knowing well that numerous factors will be determinative for the good outcome of the harvest and that the risk of failure is always lurking. And yet, year after year, the farmer repeats his gesture and throws his seed. Then when the latter becomes grain and the fields are filled with wheat, the joy is manifest of one who finds himself before an extraordinary marvel. Jesus knew this experience well and spoke of it with his disciples: "And he said, 'The kingdom of God is as if a man should scatter seed upon the ground, and should sleep and rise night and day, and the seed should sprout and grow, he knows not how'" (Mk 4:26–27). It is the hidden mystery of life, those marvelous "great things" of salvation that the Lord works in the history of men and of which men do not know the secret. Divine intervention, when it is manifest in all its fullness, reveals a raging dimension, like the torrents of the Negeb and like the wheat in the fields, the latter also evoking a typical disproportion of the things of God: a disproportion between the fatigue of sowing and the immense joy of the harvest, between the uneasiness of waiting and the serene vision of full granaries, between the little seeds thrown into the earth and the piled-high stacks of wheat turned gold by the sun. At the time of harvesting, everything is transformed, tears stop; they give place to exultation, to shouts of joy.

The Psalmist refers to all that in order to speak of salvation, of liberation, of the restoration of fortune, of the return from exile. The deportation to Babylonia, like any other situation of suffering and crisis, with its painful darkness of doubt and apparent estrangement from God, is in reality, our Psalm says, like sowing. In the Mystery of Christ, in the light of the New Testament, the message becomes even more explicit and clear: the believer who goes through this darkness is like the grain of wheat that has fallen into the earth and dies, but in order to bear much fruit (cf. Jn 12:24); or rather, in taking up another image dear to Jesus, it is like the woman who suffers the pains of childbearing in order to be able to arrive at the joy of having given birth to a new life (cf. Jn 16:21).

Dear brothers and sisters, this Psalm teaches us that, in our prayers, we must always remain open to hope and solid in our faith in God. Our history, even if it is often marked by sorrow, by uncertainty, by moments of crisis, is a history of salvation and of a "restoration of fortunes". In Jesus, each exile ends and every tear is dried, in the mystery of his Cross, of death transformed into life, like the grain of wheat that opens up in the earth and becomes an ear of grain. For us, too, this discovery of Jesus Christ is the great joy of God's "yes", of the restoration of our fortunes. But like those who—having come back from Babylonia filled with joy—found an impoverished, devastated land, just like the difficulty of sowing and those who suffer in tears, not knowing if the restoration of their fortunes will really take place in the end, we, too, after the great discovery of Jesus Christ—our life, truth, way—in entering into the soil of faith, into the "land of faith", we too often find a somber, hard, difficult life, sowing in tears, but in the assurance that the light of Christ will give us, in the end, in reality, the great harvest. And we must learn that also in times of dark nights; we must not forget that the light exists, that God is already in the midst of our life and that we can sow with great confidence that God's "yes" is stronger than all of us. It is important not to lose this memory of the presence of God in our life, this profound joy that God has entered into our life by freeing us: it is gratitude for the discovery of Jesus Christ, who has come to us. And this gratitude is transformed into hope; it is the star of hope that gives us confidence; it is the light, for precisely the sufferings of sowing are the beginning of a new life, of God's great and definitive joy.

16

The Great Hallel:

Psalm 136 (135)

WEDNESDAY, 19 OCTOBER 2011
Saint Peter's Square

Dear Brothers and Sisters,

Today I would like to meditate with you on a Psalm that sums up the entire history of salvation recorded in the Old Testament. It is a great hymn of praise that celebrates the Lord in the multiple, repeated expressions of his goodness throughout human history: it is Psalm 136, or 135 according to the Greco-Latin tradition.

A solemn prayer of thanksgiving, known as the "Great Hallel", this Psalm is traditionally sung at the end of the Jewish Passover meal and was probably also prayed by Jesus at the Last Supper celebrated with his disciples. In fact, the annotation of the Evangelists, "and when they had sung a hymn, they went out to the Mount of Olives" (cf. Mt 26:30; Mk 14:26), would seem to allude to it. The horizon of praise thus appears to illumine the difficult path to Golgotha. The whole of Psalm 136 unfolds in the form of a litany, marked by the antiphonal refrain: "for his steadfast love endures for ever". The many wonders God has worked in human history and his continuous intervention on behalf of his people are listed in the composition. Furthermore, to every proclamation of the Lord's saving action the antiphon responds with the basic impetus of praise. The eternal love of God is a love which, in accordance with the Hebrew term used, suggestive of fidelity, mercy, kindness, grace, and tenderness, is the unifying motif of the entire Psalm. The refrain always takes the same form, whereas the regular paradigmatic manifestations of God's love change: Creation, liberation through the Exodus, the gift of land, the Lord's provident and constant help for his people and for every created being.

After a triple invitation to give thanks to God as sovereign (vv. 1–3), the Lord is celebrated as the One who works "great wonders" (v. 4), the first of which is the Creation: the heavens, the earth, the heavenly bodies (vv. 5–9). The created world is not merely a scenario into which God's saving action is inserted; rather, it is the very beginning of that marvelous action. With the Creation, the Lord shows himself in all his goodness and beauty; he commits himself to life, revealing a desire for goodness which gives rise to every other action of salvation. And in our Psalm, re-echoing the first chapter of Genesis, the principal elements of the created world are summed up, with special insistence on the heavenly bodies, the sun, the moon, and the stars, magnificent created things that govern the day and the night. Nothing is said here of the creation of human beings, but they are ever present; the sun and the moon are for them—for men and women—so as to structure human time, setting it in relation to the Creator, especially by denoting the liturgical seasons.

And it is precisely the Feast of Easter that is immediately evoked, when, passing to God's manifestation of himself in history, the great event of the Exodus, freedom from slavery in Egypt, begins, whose most significant elements are outlined: the liberation from Egypt with the plague of killing the Egyptian firstborn, the Exodus from Egypt, the crossing of the Red Sea, the journey through the desert to the entry into the Promised Land (vv. 10–20). This is the very first moment of Israel's history; God intervened powerfully to lead his people to freedom; through Moses, his envoy, he asserted himself before Pharaoh, revealing himself in his full grandeur, and at last broke down the resistance of the Egyptians with the terrible plague of the death of the firstborn. Israel could thus leave the country of slavery, taking with it the gold of its oppressors (cf. Ex 12:35–36), and "defiantly" (Ex 14:8), in the exultant sign of victory. At the Red Sea, too, the Lord acted with merciful power. Before an Israel so terrified by the sight of the Egyptians in pursuit as to regret its departure from Egypt (cf. Ex 14:10–12), God, as our Psalm says, "divided the Red Sea in sunder ... and made the people of Israel pass through the midst of it ... but overthrew Pharaoh and his host" (136:13–15). The image of the Red Sea "divided" into two seems to call to mind the idea of the sea as a great monster hacked into two and thereby rendered harmless. The might of the Lord overcomes the danger of the forces of nature and of these soldiers deployed in battle array by men: the sea, which seemed to bar the way of the People of God, let Israel cross on dry ground and then swept over the Egyptians, submerging them. Thus the full salvific force of the Lord's "mighty hand, and an outstretched arm" (cf. Deut 5:15; 7:19; 26:8) was demonstrated: the unjust oppressor was vanquished, engulfed by the waters, while the People of God "walked on dry ground through the sea", continuing its journey to freedom.

Our Psalm now refers to this journey, recalling in one short phrase Israel's long pilgrimage toward the Promised Land: he "led his people through the wilderness, for his steadfast love endures for ever" (v. 16). These few words refer to a forty-year experience, a crucial period for Israel, which in letting itself be guided by the Lord learned to live in faith, obedience, and docility to God's law. These were difficult years, marked by hardship in the desert, but also happy years, trusting in the Lord with filial trust. It was the time of "youth", as the Prophet Jeremiah describes it in speaking to Israel in the Lord's name with words full of tenderness and nostalgia: "I remember the devotion of your youth, your love as a bride, how you followed me in the wilderness, in a land not sown" (Jer 2:2). The Lord, like the shepherd of Psalm 23[22] whom we contemplated in a Catechesis, for forty years guided, taught, and cherished his people, leading it right to the Promised Land, also overcoming the resistance and hostility of enemy peoples that wished to block its way to salvation (cf. 136:17–20).

So as the "great wonders" that our Psalm lists unfold, we reach the moment of the conclusive gift, the fulfillment of the divine promise made to the Fathers: "gave their land as a heritage, for his steadfast love endures for ever; a heritage to Israel his servant, for his steadfast love endures for ever" (136:21–22). Then, in celebrating the Lord's eternal love, the gift of land was commemorated, a gift that the people were to receive but without ever taking possession of it, continuing to live in an attitude of thankful acknowledgment and gratitude. Israel received the land it was to live in as "a heritage", a generic term which designates the possession of a good received from another person, a right of ownership which specifically refers to the paternal patrimony. One of God's prerogatives is "giving"; and now, at the end of the journey of the Exodus, Israel, the recipient of the gift, enters as a son the land of the promise now fulfilled. The time of wandering, of living in tents, of living a precarious life, is over. It was then that the happy period of permanence began, of joy in building houses, of planting vineyards, of living in security (cf. Deut 8:7–13). Yet it was also the time of the temptation to idolatry, contamination with pagans, self-sufficiency that led to the Origin of the gift being forgotten. Accordingly, the Psalmist mentions Israel's low estate and foes, a reality of death in which the Lord once again reveals himself as Savior: "He . . . remembered us in our low estate, for his steadfast love endures for ever; and rescued us from our foes, for his steadfast love endures for ever" (136:23–24).

At this point a question arises: how can we make this Psalm our own prayer; how can we ourselves claim this Psalm as our own prayer? What is important is the Psalm's setting, for at the beginning and at the end is the Creation. Let us return to this point: the Creation as God's great gift by which we live and in which he reveals himself in his great goodness. Therefore, to think of the Creation as a gift of God is a common point for all of us. The history of salvation then follows. We can of course say: this liberation from Egypt, the time in the desert, the entry into the Holy Land, and all the other subsequent problems are very remote from us; they are not part of our own history. Yet we must be attentive to the fundamental structure of this prayer. The basic structure is that Israel remembers the Lord's goodness. In this history, dark valleys, arduous journeys, and death succeed one another, but Israel recalls that God was good and can survive in this dark valley, in this valley of death, because it remembers. It remembers the Lord's goodness and his power; his mercy is effective for ever. And this is also important for us: to remember the Lord's goodness. Memory strongly sustains hope. Memory tells us: God exists, God is good, his mercy endures for ever. So it is that memory unfolds, even in the darkest day or time, showing the way toward the future. It represents "great lights" and is our guiding star. We, too, have memories of God's good and merciful love that endures for ever. Israel's history is a former memory for us, too, of how God revealed himself, how he created a people of his own. Then God became man, one of us: he lived with us, he suffered with us, he died for us. He stays with us in the Sacrament and in the word. It is a history, a memory of God's goodness that assures us of his goodness: his love endures for ever. And then, in these two thousand years of the Church's history, there is always, again and again, the Lord's goodness. After the dark period of the Nazi and Communist persecution, God set us free; he showed that he is good, that he is powerful, that his mercy endures for ever. And, as in our common, collective history, this memory of God's goodness is present; it helps us and becomes for us a star of hope so that each one also has his personal story of salvation. We must truly treasure this story and, in order to trust, must keep ever present in our mind the memory of the great things he has also worked in my life: his mercy endures for ever. And if today I am immersed in the dark night, tomorrow he sets me free, for his mercy is eternal.

Let us return to the Psalm, because at the end it returns to the Creation. The Lord, it says, "gives food to all flesh, for his steadfast love endures for ever" (v. 25). The prayer of the Psalm concludes with an invitation to praise: "Give thanks to the God of heaven, for his steadfast love endures for ever." The Lord is our good and provident Father, who gives his children their heritage and lavishes life-giving food upon all. God who created the heavens and the earth and the great heavenly bodies, who entered human history to bring all his children to salvation, is the God who fills the universe with his presence of goodness, caring for life and providing bread. The invisible power of the Creator and Lord of which the Psalm sings is revealed in the humble sign of the bread he gives us, with which he enables us to live. And so it is that this daily bread symbolizes and sums up the love of God as Father and opens us to the fulfillment of the New Testament, to that "Bread of Life", the Eucharist, which accompanies us in our lives as believers, anticipating the definitive joy of the messianic banquet in Heaven.

Brothers and sisters, the praise and blessing of Psalm 136[135] has made us review the most important stages in the history of salvation, to reach the Paschal Mystery in which God's saving action reaches its culmination. Let us therefore celebrate with grateful joy the Creator, Savior, and faithful Father, who "so loved the world that he gave his only Son, that whoever believes in him should not perish but have eternal life" (Jn 3:16). In the fullness of time, the Son of God became man to give life, for the salvation of each one of us, and gave himself as bread in the Eucharistic mystery to enable us to enter his Covenant which makes us his children. May both God's merciful goodness and his sublime "steadfast love for ever" reach far afield.

I would therefore like to conclude this Catechesis by making my own the words that Saint John wrote in his First Letter and that we must always have in mind in our prayers: "See what love the Father has given us, that we should be called children of God; and so we are" (1 Jn 3:1).

17

Psalm 119 (118)

WEDNESDAY, 9 NOVEMBER 2011
Saint Peter's Square

Dear Brothers and Sisters,

In previous Catecheses we have meditated on several Psalms that are examples of typical forms of prayer: lamentation, trust, and praise. In today's Catechesis I would like to reflect on Psalm 119, according to the Hebrew tradition, Psalm 118 according to the Greco-Latin one. It is a very special Psalm, unique of its kind. This is, first of all, because of its length. Indeed, it is composed of 176 verses divided into twenty-two stanzas of eight verses each. Moreover, its special feature is that it is an "acrostic in alphabetical order"; in other words, it is structured in accordance with the Hebrew alphabet, which consists of twenty-two letters. Each stanza begins with a letter of this alphabet, and the first letter of the first word of each of the eight verses in the stanza begins with this letter. This is both original and, indeed, a demanding literary genre in which the author of the Psalm must have had to summon up all his skill.

However, what is most important for us is this Psalm's central theme. In fact, it is an impressive, solemn canticle on the *Torah* of the Lord, that is, on his Law, a term which in its broadest and most comprehensive meaning should be understood as a teaching, an instruction, a rule of life. The *Torah* is a revelation; it is a word of God that challenges the human being and elicits his response of trusting obedience and generous love. This Psalm is steeped in love for the word of God, whose beauty, saving power, and capacity for giving joy and life it celebrates, because the divine Law is not the heavy yoke of slavery but a liberating gift of grace that brings happiness. "I will delight in your statutes; I will not forget your word", the Psalmist declares (v. 16), and then: "Lead me in the path of your commandments, for I delight in it" (v. 35). And further: "Oh, how I love your law! It is my meditation all the day" (v. 97). The Law of the Lord, his word, is the center of the praying person's life; he finds comfort in it, he makes it the subject of meditation, he treasures it in his heart: "I have laid up your word in my heart, that I might not sin against you" (v. 11), and this is the secret of the Psalmist's happiness; and then, again, "the godless besmear me with lies, but with my whole heart I keep your precepts" (v. 69).

The Psalmist's faithfulness stems from listening to the word, from pondering on it in his inmost self, meditating on it, and cherishing it, just as did Mary, who "kept all these things, pondering them in her heart", the words that had been addressed to her and the marvelous events in which God revealed himself, asking her for the assent of her faith (cf. Lk 2:19, 51). And if the first verses of our Psalm begin by proclaiming "blessed" those "who walk in the law of the Lord" (v. 1b) and "who keep his testimonies" (v. 2a), it is once again the Virgin Mary who brings to completion the perfect figure of the believer, described by the Psalmist. It is she, in fact, who is the true "blessed", proclaimed such by Elizabeth because "she ... believed that there would be a fulfillment of what was spoken to her from the Lord" (Lk

1:45). Moreover, it was to her and to her faith that Jesus himself bore witness when he answered the woman who had cried: "Blessed is the womb that bore you" with "Blessed rather are those who hear the word of God and keep it!" (Lk 11:27–28). Of course, Mary is blessed because she carried the Savior in her womb, but especially because she accepted God's announcement and because she was an attentive and loving custodian of his Word.

Psalm 119 is thus woven around this Word of life and blessedness. If its central theme is the "word" and "Law" of the Lord, next to these terms in almost all the verses such synonyms recur as "precepts", "statutes", "commandments", "ordinances", "promises", "judgment"; and then so many verbs relating to them, such as observe, keep, understand, learn, love, meditate, and live. The entire alphabet unfolds through the twenty-two stanzas of this Psalm and also the whole vocabulary of the believer's trusting relationship with God; we find in it praise, thanksgiving, and trust, but also supplication and lamentation. However, they are always imbued with the certainty of divine grace and of the power of the word of God. Even the verses more heavily marked by grief and by a sense of darkness remain open to hope and are permeated by faith. "My soul cleaves to the dust; revive me according to your word" (v. 25), the Psalmist trustingly prays. "I have become like a wineskin in the smoke, yet I have not forgotten your statutes" (v. 83), is his cry as a believer. His fidelity, even when it is put to the test, finds strength in the Lord's word: "then shall I have an answer for those who taunt me, for I trust in your word" (v. 42), he says firmly; and even when he faces the anguishing prospect of death, the Lord's commandments are his reference point and his hope of victory: "They have almost made an end of me on earth; but I have not forsaken your precepts" (v. 87).

The Law of the Lord, the object of the passionate love of the Psalmist as well as of every believer, is a source of life. The desire to understand it, to observe it, and to direct the whole of one's being by it is the characteristic of every righteous person who is faithful to the Lord and who "on his law . . . meditates day and night", as Psalm 1 recites (v. 2). The Law of God is a way to be kept "in the heart", as the well-known text of the *Shema* in Deuteronomy says: "Hear, O Israel: And these words which I command you this day shall be upon your heart; and you shall teach them diligently to your children, and shall talk of them when you sit in your house, and when you walk by the way, and when you lie down, and when you rise" (6:4, 6–7).

The Law of God, at the center of life, demands that the heart listen. It is a listening that consists, not of servile, but, rather, of filial, trusting, and aware obedience. Listening to the word is a personal encounter with the Lord of life, an encounter that must be expressed in concrete decisions and become a journey and a "sequela". When Jesus is asked what one should do to inherit eternal life, he points to the way of observance of the Law but indicates what should be done to bring it to completion: "But you lack one thing; go, sell what you have, and give to the poor, and you will have treasure in heaven; and come, follow me!" (Mk 10:21ff.). Fulfillment of the Law is the following of Jesus, traveling on the road that Jesus took, in the company of Jesus.

Psalm 119 thus brings us to the encounter with the Lord and orients us to the Gospel. There is a verse in it on which I would now like to reflect: it is verse 57: "The Lord is my portion; I promise to keep his words." In other Psalms, too, the person praying affirms that the Lord is his "portion", his inheritance: "The Lord is my chosen portion and my cup", Psalm 16[15] says. "God is the strength of my heart and my portion for ever" is the protestation of faith of the faithful person in Psalm 73[72]: v. 26b, and again, in Psalm 142[141], the Psalmist cries to the Lord: "You are my refuge, my portion in the land of the living" (v. 5b).

This term "portion" calls to mind the event of the division of the Promised Land between the tribes of Israel, when no piece of land was assigned to the Levites because their "portion" was the Lord himself. Two texts of the Pentateuch, using the term in question, are explicit in this regard: "The Lord said to Aaron: 'You shall have no inheritance in their land, neither shall you have any *portion* among them; I am your *portion* and your inheritance among the people of Israel'", as the Book of Numbers (18:20) declares and as Deuteronomy reaffirms: "Therefore Levi has no *portion* or inheritance with his brothers; the Lord is his inheritance, as the Lord your God said to him" (Deut 10:9; cf. Deut 18:2; Josh 13:33; Ezek 44:28).

The priests, who belong to the tribe of Levi, cannot be landowners in the land that God was to bequeath as a legacy to his people, thus bringing to completion the promise he had made to Abraham (cf. Gen 12:1–7). The ownership of land, a fundamental element for permanence and for survival, was a sign of blessing because it presupposed the possibility of building a house, of raising children, of cultivating the fields, and of living on the produce of the earth. Well, the Levites, mediators of the sacred and of the divine blessing, unlike the other Israelites, could not own possessions, this external sign of blessing and source of subsistence. Totally dedicated to the Lord, they had to live on him alone, reliant on his provident love and on the generosity of their brethren without any other inheritance; since God was their portion, God was the land that enabled them to live to the full.

The person praying in Psalm 119 then applies this reality to himself: "The Lord is my portion." His love for God and for his word leads him to make the radical decision to have the Lord as his one possession and also to treasure his words as a precious gift more valuable than any legacy or earthly possession. There are two different ways in which our verse may be translated; it could also be translated as: "My portion, Lord, as I have said, is to preserve your words." The two translations are not contradictory but, on the contrary, complete each other: the Psalmist meant that his portion was the Lord but that preserving the divine words was also part of his inheritance, as he was to say later in v. 111: "Your testimonies are my heritage for ever; yea, they are the joy of my heart." This is the happiness of the Psalmist: like the Levites, he has been given the word of God as his portion, his inheritance.

Dear brothers and sisters, these verses are also of great importance for all of us. First of all, for priests, who are called to live on the Lord and his word alone with no other means of security, with him as their one possession and as their only source of true life. In this light, one understands the free choice of celibacy for the Kingdom of Heaven in order to rediscover it in its beauty and power. Yet these verses are also important for all the faithful, the People of God that belong to him alone, "a kingdom and priests" for the Lord (cf. 1 Pet 2:9; Rev 1:6, 5:10), called to the radicalism of the Gospel, witnesses of the life brought by Christ, the new and definitive "High Priest" who gave himself as a sacrifice for the salvation of the world (cf. Heb 2:17; 4:14–16; 5:5–10; 9, 11ff.). The Lord and his word: these are our "land" in which to live in communion and in joy.

Let us therefore permit the Lord to instill this love for his word in our hearts and to grant that we may always place him and his holy will at the center of our life. Let us ask that our prayers and the whole of our life be illuminated by the word of God, the lamp to light our footsteps and a light on our path, as Psalm 119 (cf. 105) says, so that we may walk safely in the land of men. And may Mary, who generously welcomed the Word, be our guide and comfort, the polestar that indicates the way to happiness. Then we, too, shall be able to rejoice in our prayers, like the praying person of Psalm 16, in the unexpected gifts of the Lord and in the undeserved legacy that fell to us:

> The Lord is my chosen portion and my cup . . .
> the lines have fallen for me in pleasant places;
> yea, I have a goodly heritage. (Ps 16:5, 6)

18

Psalm 110 (109)

WEDNESDAY, 16 NOVEMBER 2011
Saint Peter's Square

Dear Brothers and Sisters,

Today I would like to end my Catechesis on the prayer of the Book of Psalms by meditating on one of the most famous of the "royal Psalms", a Psalm that Jesus himself cited and that the New Testament authors referred to extensively and interpreted as referring to the Messiah, to Christ. It is Psalm 110 according to the Hebrew tradition, 109 according to the Greco-Latin one, a Psalm very dear to the ancient Church and to believers of all times. This prayer may at first have been linked to the enthronement of a Davidic king; yet its meaning exceeds the specific contingency of an historic event, opening to broader dimensions and thereby becoming a celebration of the victorious Messiah, glorified at God's right hand. The Psalm begins with a solemn declaration:

> The Lord says to my lord:
> "Sit at my right hand,
> till I make your enemies
> your footstool." (v. 1)

God himself enthrones the king in glory, seating him at his right, a sign of very great honor and of absolute privilege.

The king is thus admitted to sharing in the divine kingship, of which he is mediator to the people. The king's kingship is also brought into being in the victory over his adversaries whom God himself places at his feet. The victory over his enemies is the Lord's, but the king is enabled to share in it, and his triumph becomes a sign and testimony of divine power.

The royal glorification expressed at the beginning of the Psalm was adopted by the New Testament as a messianic prophecy. For this reason, the verse is among those most frequently used by New Testament authors, either as an explicit quotation or as an allusion. With regard to the Messiah, Jesus himself mentioned this verse in order to show that the Messiah was greater than David, that he was David's Lord (cf. Mt 22:41–45; Mk 12:35–37; Lk 20:41–44). And Peter returned to it in his discourse at Pentecost, proclaiming that this enthronement of the king was brought about in the Resurrection of Christ and that Christ was henceforth seated at the right hand of the Father, sharing in God's kingship over the world (cf. Acts 2:29–35). Indeed, Christ is the enthroned Lord, the Son of Man seated at the right hand of God and coming on the clouds of Heaven, as Jesus described himself during the trial before the Sanhedrin (cf. Mt 26:63–64; Mk 14:61–62; cf. also Lk 22:66–69). He is the true King who, with the Resurrection, entered into glory at the right hand of the Father (Rom 8:34; Eph 2:5; Col 3:1; Heb 8:1; 12:2), was made superior to angels, and seated in Heaven above every power with every adversary at his feet, until the time when the last enemy, death, is defeated by him once and for all (cf. 1 Cor 15:24–26; Eph 1:20–23; Heb 1:3–4; 2:5–8; 10:12–13; 1 Pet 3:22). And we immediately understand that this king, seated at the right hand of God, who shares in his kingship, is not one of those who succeeded David, but is actually the new David, the Son of God who triumphed over death and truly shares in God's glory. He is our king, who also gives us eternal life.

Hence an indissoluble relationship exists between the king celebrated by our Psalm and God. The two of them govern together as one, so that the Psalmist can say that it is God himself who extends the sovereign's scepter, giving him the task of ruling over his adversaries, as verse 2 says:

> The Lord sends forth from Zion your mighty scepter.
> Rule in the midst of your foes!

The exercise of power is an office that the king receives directly from the Lord, a responsibility which he must exercise in dependence and obedience, thereby becoming a sign, within the people, of God's powerful and provident presence. Dominion over his foes, glory, and victory are gifts received that make the sovereign a mediator of the Lord's triumph over evil. He subjugates his enemies, transforming them; he wins them over with his love.

For this reason, the king's greatness is celebrated in the following verse. In fact, the interpretation of verse 3 presents some difficulty. In the original Hebrew text, a reference was made to the mustering of the army to which the people generously responded, gathering round their sovereign on the day of his coronation. The Greek translation of the Septuagint, which dates back to between the second and third centuries B.C., refers, however, to the divine sonship of the king, to his birth or begetting on the part of the Lord. This is the interpretation that has been chosen by the Church, which is why the verse reads like this:

> Yours is princely power in the day of your birth,
> in holy splendor;
> before the daystar, like the dew,
> I have begotten you.

This divine oracle concerning the king would thus assert a divine procreation, steeped in splendor and mystery, a secret and inscrutable origin linked to the arcane beauty of dawn and to the miracle of dew that sparkles in the fields in the early morning light and makes them fertile. In this way, the figure of the king, indissolubly bound to the heavenly reality, who really comes from God, is outlined, the Messiah who brings divine life to the people and is the mediator of holiness and salvation. Here, too, we see that all this is achieved, not by the figure of a Davidic king, but by the Lord Jesus Christ, who really comes from God; he is the light that brings divine life to the world.

The first stanza of the Psalm ends with this evocative and enigmatic image. It is followed by another oracle, which unfolds a new perspective along the lines of a priestly dimension connected with kingship. Verse 4 says:

> The Lord has sworn
> and will not change his mind,
> "You are a priest for ever
> after the order of Melchizedek."

Melchizedek was the priest-king of Salem who had blessed Abraham and offered him bread and wine after the victorious military campaign the Patriarch led to rescue his nephew Lot from the hands of enemies who had captured him (cf. Gen 14). Royal and priestly power converge in the figure of Melchizedek. They are then proclaimed by the Lord in a declaration that promises eternity: the king celebrated in the Psalm will be a priest for ever, the mediator of the Lord's presence among his people, the intermediary of the blessing that comes from God, who, in liturgical action, responds to it with the human answer of blessing.

The Letter to the Hebrews makes an explicit reference to this verse (cf. 5:5–6, 10; 6:19–20), focusing on it the whole of chapter 7 and developing its reflection on Christ's priesthood. Jesus, as the Letter to the Hebrews tells us in the light of Psalm 110[109], is the true and definitive priest who brings to fulfillment and perfects the features of Melchizedek's priesthood.

Melchizedek, as the Letter to the Hebrews says, was "without father or mother or genealogy" (7:3a), hence not a priest according to the dynastic rules of Levitical priesthood. Consequently, he "continues a priest for ever" (7:3c), a prefiguration of Christ, the perfect High Priest who "has become a priest, not according to a legal requirement concerning bodily descent but by the power of an indestructible life" (7:16). In the Risen Lord Jesus who had ascended into Heaven where he is seated at the right hand of the Father, the prophecy of our Psalm is fulfilled and the priesthood of Melchizedek is brought to completion. This is because, rendered absolute and eternal, it became a reality that never fades (cf. 7:24). And the offering of bread and wine made by Melchizedek in Abraham's time is fulfilled in the Eucharistic action of Jesus, who offers himself in the bread and in the wine and, having conquered death, brings life to all believers. Since he is an eternal priest, "holy, blameless, unstained" (7:26), as the Letter to the Hebrews states further, "he is able for all time to save those who draw near to God through him, since he always lives to make intercession for them" (7:25).

After this divine pronouncement in verse 4, with its solemn oath, the scene of the Psalm changes and the poet, addressing the king directly, proclaims: "The Lord is at your right hand" (Psalm 110:5a). If in verse 1 it was the king who was seated at God's right hand as a sign of supreme prestige and honor, the Lord now takes his place at the right of the sovereign to protect him with this shield in battle and save him from every peril. The king was safe, God is his champion, and they fight together and defeat every evil.

Thus the last verses of the Psalm open with the vision of the triumphant sovereign. Supported by the Lord, having received both power and glory from him (cf. v. 2), he opposes his foes, crushing his adversaries and judging the nations. The scene is painted in strong colors to signify the drama of the battle and the totality of the royal victory. The sovereign, protected by the Lord, demolishes every obstacle and moves ahead safely to victory. He tells us: "Yes, there is widespread evil in the world; there is an ongoing battle between good and evil, and it seems as though evil is stronger. No, the Lord is stronger, Christ, our true King and Priest, for he fights with all God's power and in spite of all the things that make us doubt the positive outcome of history, Christ wins and good wins, love wins rather than hatred.

The evocative image that concludes our Psalm fits in here; it is also an enigmatic word:

> He will drink from the brook by the way;
> therefore he will lift up his head. (v. 7)

The king's figure stands out in the middle of the description of the battle. At a moment of respite and rest, he quenches his thirst at a stream, finding in it refreshment and fresh strength to continue on his triumphant way, holding his head high as a sign of definitive victory. It is clear that these deeply enigmatic words were a challenge for the Fathers of the Church because of the different interpretations they could be given. Thus, for example, Saint Augustine said: this brook is the onward flow of the human being, of humanity, and Christ did not disdain to drink of this brook, becoming man; and so it was that on entering the humanity of the human being, he lifted up his head and is now the Head of the mystical Body; he is our head; he is the definitive winner. (cf. *Enarrationes in Psalmos* CIX, 20: PL36, 1462).

Dear friends, following the lines of the New Testament translation, the Church's tradition has held this Psalm in high esteem as one of the most important messianic texts. And the Fathers made constant reference to it in a Christological key. The king of whom the Psalmist sang is definitively Christ, the Messiah who establishes the Kingdom of God and overcomes the powers of evil. He is the Word, begotten by the Father before every creature, before the dawn, the Son incarnate who died and rose and is seated in Heaven, the eternal priest who through the mystery of the bread and wine bestows forgiveness of sins and gives reconciliation with God, the king who lifts up his head, triumphing over death with his Resurrection. It would suffice to remember a passage, once again in Saint Augustine's commentary on this Psalm, where he writes:

> It was necessary to know the only begotten Son of God who was about to come among men, to adopt man, and to become a man by taking on his nature; he died, rose, and ascended into Heaven, he is seated at the right hand of the Father and fulfilled among the people all that he had promised.... All this, therefore, had to be prophesied; it had to be foretold, to be pointed out as destined to come about, so that by coming unexpectedly it would not give rise to

> fear but, by having been foretold, would then be accepted with faith, joy, and expectation. This Psalm fits into the context of these promises. It prophesies our Lord and Savior Jesus Christ in such reliable and explicit terms that we cannot have the slightest doubt that it is really Christ who is proclaimed in it. (Cf. *Enarrationes in Psalmos* CIX, 3: PL 36, 1447)

The paschal event of Christ thus becomes the reality to which the Psalm invites us to look, to look at Christ to understand the meaning of true kingship, to live in service and in the gift of self, in a journey of obedience and love "to the end" (cf. Jn 13:1 and 19:30). In praying with this Psalm, let us therefore ask the Lord to enable us to proceed on his paths, in the following of Christ, the Messiah King, ready to climb with him the mount of the Cross to attain glory with him and to contemplate him seated at the right hand of the Father, a victorious king and a merciful priest who gives forgiveness and salvation to all men and women. And we, too, by the grace of God made "a chosen race, a royal priesthood, a holy nation" (cf. 1 Pet 2:9), will be able to draw joyfully from the wells of salvation (cf. Is 12:3) and proclaim to the whole world the marvels of the One who "called you out of darkness into his marvelous light" (cf. 1 Pt 2:9).

Dear friends, in these recent Catecheses I wanted to present to you certain Psalms, precious prayers that we find in the Bible and that reflect the various situations of life and the various states of mind that we may have with regard to God. I would then like to renew to you all the invitation to pray with the Psalms, even becoming accustomed to using the Liturgy of the Hours of the Church, Lauds in the morning, Vespers in the evening, and Compline before retiring. Our relationship with God cannot but be enriched with greater joy and trust in the daily journey toward him.

19

Prayer through the Whole Life of Jesus

WEDNESDAY, 30 NOVEMBER 2011
Paul VI Audience Hall

Dear Brothers and Sisters,

In our previous Catecheses we have reflected on several examples of prayer in the Old Testament. Today I would like to begin to look at Jesus, at his prayer, which flows through the whole of his life like a secret channel that waters existence, relationships, and actions and guides them, with progressive firmness, to the total gift of self in accordance with the loving plan of God the Father. Jesus is also our Teacher in prayer, indeed, he is our active and fraternal support on every occasion that we address the Father. Truly, "prayer", as it is summed up in a heading in the *Compendium of the Catechism of the Catholic Church*, "is fully revealed and realized in Jesus" (nos. 541–547). Let us also look at him in our forthcoming Catecheses.

The prayer that followed the baptism in the River Jordan to which he submitted is an especially important moment on his journey. Luke the Evangelist noted that after receiving baptism from John the Baptist together with all the people, he was praying a very personal, extended prayer. "When all the people were baptized, and when Jesus also had been baptized and was praying, the heaven was opened, and the

Holy Spirit descended upon him" (Lk 3:21–22). The fact that he "was praying", in conversation with the Father, illuminated the act he had carried out along with so many of his people who had flocked to the banks of the Jordan. By praying, he gave his action, baptism, an exclusively personal character.

The Baptist had launched a forceful appeal to live truly as "children to Abraham", being converted to goodness and bearing fruit worthy of this change (cf. Lk 3:7–9). And a large number of Israelites had felt impelled to act, as Mark the Evangelist recalled, writing: "There went out to him [to John] all the country of Judea, and all the people of Jerusalem; and they were baptized by him in the River Jordan, confessing their sins" (Mk 1:5). The Baptist was bringing something really new: to undergo baptism was to mark a decisive turning point, leaving behind forms of conduct linked to sin and starting a new life. Jesus, too, accepted this invitation; he joined the grey multitude of sinners waiting on the banks of the Jordan. However, a question also wells up in us, as it did in the early Christians: why did Jesus voluntarily submit to this baptism of penance and conversion? He had no sins to confess; he had not sinned, hence he was in no need of conversion. So what accounts for his action? The Evangelist Matthew records the amazement of the Baptist, who stated: "I need to be baptized by you, and do you come to me?" (Mt 3:14), and Jesus' response: "Let it be so now; for thus it is fitting for us to fulfill all righteousness" (v. 15). The word "righteousness" in the biblical world means the acceptance of God's will without reserve. Jesus showed his closeness to that part of his people who, following the Baptist, recognized that it was not enough merely to consider themselves children of Abraham and wanted to do God's will, wanted to commit themselves to ensuring that their behavior was a faithful response to the Covenant God had offered through Abraham. Therefore, by entering the River Jordan, Jesus, without sin, showed his solidarity with those who recognize their sins, who choose to repent and to change their lives; Jesus made it clear that being part of the People of God means entering into a perspective of newness of life, of life in accordance with God.

In this action, Jesus anticipated the Cross; he began his ministry by taking his place among sinners, by taking upon his shoulders the burden of the whole of mankind, and by doing the Father's will. Recollected in prayer, Jesus showed his profound bond with the Father who is in Heaven; he experienced his fatherhood, understood the demanding beauty of his love, and, in conversation with the Father, received the confirmation of his mission. The words that resounded from Heaven (cf. Lk 3:22) anticipated a reference to the Paschal Mystery, the Cross, and the Resurrection. The divine voice referred to him as "my beloved Son", recalling Isaac, the beloved son whom Abraham his father was prepared to sacrifice, in accordance with God's command (cf. Gen 22:1–14). Jesus was not only *the son of David*, of royal, messianic lineage, or *the Servant* with whom God was well pleased; he was also the *only begotten Son*, beloved, like Isaac, whom God the Father gave for the world's salvation. At the moment when, through prayer, Jesus was experiencing the depth of his own sonship and God's fatherhood (cf. Lk 3:22b), the Holy Spirit, whom he was to pour out after being raised on the Cross (cf. Jn 1:32–34; 7:37–39), descended upon him (cf. Lk 3:22a) and guided him in his mission, that he might illuminate the Church's action. In prayer, Jesus lived in uninterrupted contact with the Father in order to fulfill completely his plan of love for mankind.

Against the background of this extraordinary prayer, Jesus lived his entire life in a family deeply tied to the religious tradition of the people of Israel. This is demonstrated by the references we find in the Gospels: his circumcision (cf. Lk 2:21) and his presentation in the temple (cf. Lk 2:22–24), as well as his education and training at Nazareth, in the holy house (cf. Lk 2:39–40 and 2:51–52). This was "about thirty years" (Lk 3:23), a long period of hidden daily life, even though it included experiences of participation with the community in moments of religious expression, such as pilgrimages to Jerusalem (cf. Lk 2:41). In recounting the episode of the twelve-year-old Jesus in the temple, sitting among the teachers (cf. Lk 2:42–52), Luke the Evangelist makes us understand that Jesus, who was praying after his baptism in the Jordan, had a long-standing habit of intimate prayer to God the Father. This habit was rooted in the traditions, in the manner of his family, and in his own crucial experiences within it. The twelve-year-old's answer to Mary and Joseph already suggests the divine Sonship which the heavenly voice expressed after his baptism: "How is it that you sought me? Did you not know that I must be in my Father's house?" to do his bidding (Lk 2:49). Jesus did not begin to pray after emerging from the waters of the Jordan, but continued in his ongoing, customary relationship with the Father; and it was in this close union with the Father that he stepped out of the hidden life in Nazareth into his public ministry.

Jesus' teaching on prayer certainly derives from the approach to prayer that he acquired in his family, but its deep, essential origins are found in his being the Son of God and in his unique relationship with God the Father. The *Compendium of the Catechism of the Catholic Church* answers the question: "*From whom did Jesus learn how to pray?*" in this way: "Jesus, with his human heart, learned how to pray from his Mother and from the Jewish tradition. But his prayer sprang from a more secret source because he is the eternal Son of God who in his holy humanity offers his perfect filial prayer to his Father" (no. 541).

In the Gospel narrative, the settings of Jesus' prayer are always placed half-way between insertion into his people's tradition and the newness of a unique personal relationship with God. The "lonely place" (cf. Mk 1:35; Lk 5:16), to which he often withdrew, "the hills" he climbs in order to pray (cf. Lk 6:12; 9:28), "the night" that affords him solitude (cf. Mk 1:35; 6:46–47; Lk 6:12) recall moments in the process of God's revelation in the Old Testament, pointing out the continuity of his saving plan. Yet, at the same time, they mark moments of special importance for Jesus, who fits consciously into this plan, completely faithful to the Father's will.

In our prayer, too, we must learn, increasingly, to enter this history of salvation of which Jesus is the summit, to renew before God our personal decision to open ourselves to his will, to ask him for the strength to conform our will to his will, throughout our life, in obedience to his design of love for us.

Jesus' prayer penetrates all the phases of his ministry and all his days. Difficulties do not obstruct it. The Gospels, on the contrary, allow us a glimpse of Jesus' habit of spending part of the night in prayer. Mark the Evangelist tells of one of these nights, after the tiring day of the multiplication of the loaves, and writes: "Immediately he made his disciples get into the boat and go before him to the other side, to Bethsaida, while he dismissed the crowd. And after he had taken leave of them, he went into the hills to pray. And when evening came, the boat was out on the sea, and he was alone on the land" (Mk 6:45–47). When decisions became urgent and complicated, his prayers grew longer and more intense. Just before Jesus chose the Twelve Apostles, for example, Luke emphasizes the nocturnal duration of Jesus' preparatory prayer: "In those days he went out into the hills to pray; and all night he continued in prayer to God. And when it was day, he called his disciples, and chose from them twelve, whom he named apostles" (Lk 6:12–13).

In looking at Jesus' prayers, a question must arise within us: how do I pray? How do we pray? How much time do I give to my relationship with God? Are people today given sufficient education and formation in prayer? And who can teach it? In the Apostolic Exhortation *Verbum Domini* I spoke of the importance of the prayerful reading of Sacred Scripture. In gathering together what emerged at the Assembly of the Synod of Bishops, I placed a special emphasis on the specific form of *lectio divina*. Listening, meditating, and being silent before the Lord who speaks is an art which is learned by practicing it with perseverance. Prayer, of course, is a gift which nevertheless asks to be accepted; it is a work of God but demands commitment and continuity on our part. Above all, continuity and constancy are important. Jesus' exemplary experience itself shows that his prayer, enlivened by the fatherhood of God and by communion with the Spirit, was deepened and prolonged in faithful practice, up to the Garden of Olives and to the Cross. Today Christians are called to be witnesses of prayer precisely because our world is often closed to the divine horizon and to the hope that brings the encounter with God. In deep friendship with Jesus and living in him and with him the filial relationship with the Father, through our constant and faithful prayer we can open windows on God's Heaven. Indeed, by taking the way of prayer, attaching no importance to human things, we can help others to take it. For Christian prayer, too, it is true that, in journeying on, new paths unfold.

Dear brothers and sisters, let us train ourselves in an intense relationship with God, with prayer that is not occasional but constant, full of faith, capable of illuminating our lives, as Jesus taught us. And let us ask him to enable us to communicate to people who are close to us, to those whom we meet on our way, the joy of the encounter with the Lord, Light for our existence.

20

The "Jewel" of the "Cry of Exultation"

WEDNESDAY, 7 DECEMBER 2011
Paul VI Audience Hall

Dear Brothers and Sisters,

The Evangelists Matthew and Luke (cf. Mt 11:25–30 and Lk 10:21–22) have handed down to us a "jewel" of Jesus' prayer that is often called the "Cry of Exultation" or the "Cry of Messianic Exultation". It is a prayer of thanksgiving and praise, as we have heard. In the original Greek of the Gospels, the word with which this jubilation begins and which expresses Jesus' attitude in addressing the Father is *exomologoumai*, which is often translated with "I praise" (cf. Mt 11:25 and Lk 10:21). However, in the New Testament writings, this term indicates mainly two things: the first is "to confess" fully—for example, John the Baptist asked those who went to him to be baptized "to recognize their every sin" (cf. Mt 3:6); the second thing is "to be in agreement". Therefore, the words with which Jesus begins his prayer contain his *full recognition* of the Father's action and, at the same time, his *total, conscious, and joyful agreement* with this way of acting, with the Father's plan. The "Cry of Exultation" is the apex of a journey of prayer in which

Jesus' profound and close communion with the life of the Father in the Holy Spirit clearly emerges and his divine sonship is revealed.

Jesus addresses God by calling him "Father". This word expresses Jesus' awareness and certainty of being "the Son" in intimate and constant communion with him, and this is the central focus and source of every one of Jesus' prayers. We see it clearly in the last part of the hymn, which illuminates the entire text. Jesus said: "All things have been delivered to me by my Father; and no one knows who the Son is except the Father, or who the Father is except the Son and any one to whom the Son chooses to reveal him" (Lk 10:22). Jesus was therefore affirming that only "the Son" truly knows the Father. All the knowledge that people have of each other—we all experience this in our human relationships—entails involvement, a certain inner bond between the one who knows and the one who is known, at a more or less profound level: we cannot know anyone without a communion of being. In the "Cry of Exultation"—as in all his prayers—Jesus shows that true knowledge of God presupposes communion with him. Only by being in communion with the other can I begin to know him; and so it is with God: only if I am in true contact, if I am in communion with him, can I also know him. True knowledge, therefore, is reserved to the "Son", the Only Begotten One who is in the bosom of the Father since eternity (cf. Jn 1:18), in perfect unity with him. The Son alone truly knows God, since he is in an intimate communion of being; only the Son can truly reveal who God is.

The name "Father" is followed by a second title, "Lord of heaven and earth". With these words, Jesus sums up faith in creation and echoes the first words of Sacred Scripture:

"In the beginning God created the heavens and the earth" (Gen 1:1). In praying, he recalls the great biblical narrative of the history of God's love for man that begins with the act of creation. Jesus fits into this love story; he is its culmination and its fulfillment. Sacred Scripture is illumined through his experience of prayer and lives again in its fullest breadth: the proclamation of the mystery of God and the response of man transformed. Yet, through the expression: "Lord of heaven and earth", we can also recognize that in Jesus, the Revealer of the Father, the possibility for man to reach God is reopened.

Let us now ask ourselves: to whom does the Son want to reveal God's mysteries? At the beginning of the Hymn, Jesus expresses his joy because the Father's will is to keep these things hidden from the learned and the wise and to reveal them to little ones (cf. Lk 10:21). Thus in his prayer, Jesus manifests his communion with the Father's decision to disclose his mysteries to the simple of heart: the Son's will is one with the Father's. Divine revelation is not brought about in accordance with earthly logic, which holds that cultured and powerful people possess important knowledge and pass it on to simpler people, to little ones. God used a quite different approach: those to whom his communication was addressed were, precisely, "babes". This is the Father's will, and the Son shares it with him joyfully. The *Catechism of the Catholic Church* says: "His exclamation, 'Yes, Father!' expresses the depth of his heart, his adherence to the Father's 'good pleasure,' echoing his mother's 'Fiat' at the time of his conception and prefiguring what he will say to the Father in his agony. The whole prayer of Jesus is contained in this loving adherence of his human heart to the 'mystery of the will' of the Father (Eph 1:9)" (no. 2603). The invocation that we address to God in the "Our Father" derives from this: "Thy will be done on earth as it is in heaven": together with Christ and in Christ, we, too, ask to enter into harmony with the Father's will, thereby also becoming his children. Thus Jesus, in this "Cry of Exultation", expresses his will to involve in his own filial knowledge of God all those whom the Father wishes to become sharers in it; and those who welcome this gift are the "little ones".

But what does "being little" and simple mean? What is the "littleness" that opens man to filial intimacy with God so as to receive his will? What must the fundamental attitude of our prayer be? Let us look at "The Sermon on the Mount", in which Jesus says: "Blessed are the pure in heart, for they shall see God" (Mt 5:8). It is purity of heart that permits us to recognize the Face of God in Jesus Christ; it is having a simple heart like the heart of a child, free from the presumption of those who withdraw into themselves, thinking they have no need of anyone, not even God.

It is also interesting to notice the occasion on which Jesus breaks into this hymn to the Father. In Matthew's Gospel narrative, it is joyful because, in spite of opposition and rejection, there are "little ones" who accept his word and open themselves to the gift of faith in him. The "Cry of Exultation" is in fact preceded by the contrast between the praise of John the Baptist—one of the "little ones" who recognized God's action in Jesus Christ (cf. Mt 11:2–19)—and the reprimand for the disbelief of the lake cities "where most of his mighty works had been performed" (cf. Mt 11:20–24). Hence Matthew saw the "Exultation" in relation to the words with which Jesus noted the effectiveness of his word and action: "Go and tell John what you hear and see: the blind receive their sight and the lame walk, lepers are cleansed and the deaf hear, and the dead are raised up, and the poor have good news of the Gospel preached to them. And blessed is he who takes no offense at me" (Mt 11:4–6).

Saint Luke also presented the "Cry of Exultation" in connection with a moment of development in the proclamation of the Gospel. Jesus sent out the "seventy-two" others (Lk 10:1), and they departed fearful of the possible failure of their mission. Luke also emphasized the rejection encountered in the cities where the Lord had preached and had worked miracles. Nonetheless, the seventy-two disciples returned full of joy because their mission had met with success; they realized that human infirmities are overcome with the power of Jesus' word. Jesus shared their pleasure: "in that same hour", at that very moment, he rejoiced.

There are still two elements that I would like to underline. Luke the Evangelist introduces the prayer with the annotation: Jesus "rejoiced in the Holy Spirit" (Lk 10:21). Jesus rejoiced from the depths of his being, in what counted most: his unique communion of knowledge and love with the Father, the fullness of the Holy Spirit. By involving us in his sonship, Jesus invites us, too, to open ourselves to the light of the Holy Spirit, since—as the Apostle Paul affirms—"we do not know how to pray as we ought, but the Spirit himself intercedes for us with sighs too deep for words . . . according to the will of God" (Rom 8:26–27), and reveals the Father's love to us. In Matthew's Gospel, following the "Cry of Exultation", we find one of Jesus' most heartfelt appeals: "Come to me, all who labor and are heavy laden, and I will give you rest" (Mt 11:28). Jesus asks us to go to him, for he is true Wisdom, to him who is "gentle and lowly in heart". He offers us "his yoke", the way of the wisdom of the Gospel, which is neither a doctrine to be learned nor an ethical system but rather a Person to follow:

he himself, the only begotten Son in perfect communion with the Father.

Dear brothers and sisters, we have experienced for a moment the wealth of this prayer of Jesus. With the gift of his Spirit we, too, can turn to God in prayer with the confidence of children, calling him by the name Father, "Abba". However, we must have the heart of little ones, of the "poor in spirit" (Mt 5:3), in order to recognize that we are not self-sufficient, that we are unable to build our lives on our own but need God, that we need to encounter him, to listen to him, to speak to him. Prayer opens us to receiving the gift of God, his wisdom, which is Jesus himself, in order to do the Father's will in our lives and thus to find rest in the hardships of our journey.

21

The Prayer of Jesus Linked to His Miraculous Healing Action

WEDNESDAY, 14 DECEMBER 2011
Paul VI Audience Hall

Dear Brothers and Sisters,

Today I would like to reflect with you on the prayer of Jesus linked to his miraculous healing action. Various situations are presented in the Gospels in which Jesus prays while he contemplates the beneficial and healing work of God the Father, who acts through him. This is a form of prayer which, once again, demonstrates his unique relationship of knowledge and communion with the Father, while Jesus lets himself be involved with deep human participation in the hardships of his friends, for example, those of Lazarus and his family or of the many poor and sick people to whom he seeks to give practical help.

A significant case is the healing of the deaf mute (cf. Mk 7:32–37). Mark the Evangelist's account—which we have just heard—shows that Jesus' healing action is connected with the intense relationship he had both with his neighbor—the sick man—and with the Father. The scene of the miracle is described carefully, in these words: "taking him aside from the multitude privately, he put his fingers into his ears, and he spat and touched his tongue; and looking up to heaven, he sighed, and said to him, '*Ephphatha*', that is 'Be opened'" (Mk 7:33–34). Jesus wanted the healing to take place "aside from the multitude". This does not seem to be due solely to the fact that the miracle must be kept hidden from people to prevent them from making any restrictive or distorted interpretation of the Person of Jesus. The decision to take the sick man aside ensures that at the moment of healing, Jesus and the deaf mute are on their own, brought together in a unique relationship. With a single gesture, the Lord touches the sick man's ears and tongue, that is, the specific sites of his infirmity. The intensity of Jesus' attention is also demonstrated in the unusual treatment that was part of the healing. He uses his fingers and even his saliva. And the fact that the Evangelist records the original word spoken by the Lord, '*Ephphatha*', in other words, "be opened", highlights the unusual character of the scene.

The central point of this episode, however, is the fact that when Jesus was about to work the healing, he directly sought his relationship with the Father. Indeed, the account relates that, "looking up to heaven, he sighed" (v. 34). Jesus' attention and treatment of the sick man are linked by a profound attitude of prayer addressed to God. Moreover, his sighing is described with a verb which, in the New Testament, indicates the aspiration to something good that is still lacking (cf. Rom 8:23). Thus, as a whole, the narrative shows that it was his human involvement with the sick man that prompted Jesus to pray. His unique relationship with the Father and his identity as the only begotten Son surface once again. God's healing and beneficial action become present in him, through his Person. It is not by chance that the people's last remark after the miracle has been performed is reminiscent of the evaluation of the Creation at the beginning of the Book of Genesis: "He has done all things well" (Mk 7:37). Prayer clearly entered the healing action of Jesus as he looked up to heaven. The power that healed the deaf mute was certainly elicited by compassion for him but came from recourse to the Father. These two relationships interact: the human relationship of compassion with the man enters into the relationship with God and, thus, becomes healing.

In the Johannine narrative of the raising of Lazarus, this same dynamic is attested by an even greater proof (cf. Jn 11:1–44) Here, too, are interwoven, on the one hand, Jesus' bond with a friend and with his suffering and, on the other, his filial relationship with the Father. Jesus' human participation in Lazarus' case has some special features. His friendship with Lazarus is repeatedly mentioned throughout the account as well as his relationship with Martha and Mary, the sisters of Lazarus. Jesus himself says: "Our friend Lazarus has fallen asleep, but I go to awake him out of sleep" (Jn 11:11). Jesus' sincere affection for his friend is also highlighted by Lazarus' sisters as well as by the Jews (cf. Jn 11:3; 11:36). It is expressed in Jesus' deep distress at seeing the grief of Martha and Mary and of all Lazarus' friends, and he finds relief by bursting into tears—so profoundly human—on approaching the tomb: "When Jesus saw her [Martha] weeping, and the Jews who came with her also weeping, he was deeply moved in spirit and troubled; and he said, 'Where have you laid him?' They said to him, 'Lord, come and see.' Jesus wept" (Jn 11:33–35).

This bond of friendship and Jesus' participation and distress at the sorrow of Lazarus' relatives and acquaintances are connected throughout the narrative to a continuous, intense relationship with the Father. The event, from the outset, is interpreted by Jesus in relation to his own identity and mission and to the glorification that awaits him. In fact, on hearing of Lazarus' illness, he comments: "The illness is not unto death; it is for the glory of God, so that the Son of God may be glorified by means of it" (Jn 11:4). Jesus also hears the news of his friend's death with deep human sadness but always with a clear reference to his relationship with God and with the mission that God has entrusted to him; he says: "Lazarus is dead; and for your sake I am glad that I was not there, so that you may believe" (Jn 11:14–15). The moment of Jesus' explicit prayer to the Father at the tomb was the natural outlet for all that had happened, which took place in the double key of his friendship with Lazarus and his filial relationship with God. Here too, the two relationships go hand in hand. "And Jesus lifted up his eyes and said, 'Father, I thank you that you have heard me'" (Jn 11:41): it was a *eucharist.* The sentence shows that Jesus did not cease, even for an instant, his prayer of petition for Lazarus' life. This prayer continued; indeed, it reinforced his ties with his friend and, at the same time strengthened Jesus' decision to remain in communion with the Father's will, with his plan of love, in which Lazarus' illness and death were to be considered as a place for the manifestation of God's glory.

Dear brothers and sisters, in reading this account, each one of us is called to understand that in our prayers of petition to the Lord, we must not expect an immediate fulfillment of what we ask, of our own will. Rather, we must entrust ourselves to the Father's will, interpreting every event in the perspective of his glory, of his plan of love, which to our eyes is often mysterious. For this reason, in our prayers, petition, praise, and thanksgiving must be joined together, even when it seems to us that God is not responding to our real expectations. Abandoning ourselves to God's love, which always precedes and accompanies us, is one of the basic attitudes for our dialogue with him. On Jesus' prayer in the account of the raising of Lazarus, the *Catechism of the Catholic Church* comments: "Jesus' prayer, characterized by thanksgiving, reveals to us how to ask: before the gift is given, Jesus commits himself to the One who in giving gives himself. The Giver is more precious than the gift; he is the 'treasure'; in him abides his Son's heart; the gift is given 'as well' (cf. Mt 6:21, 33)" (no. 2604). To me this seems very important: before the gift is given, committing ourselves to the One who gives. The Giver is more precious than the gift. For us, too, therefore, over and above what God bestows on us when we call on him, the greatest gift that he can give us is his friendship, his presence, and his love. He is the precious treasure to ask for and to preserve for ever.

The prayer that Jesus prays as the rock is rolled away from the entrance to Lazarus' tomb thus has a special and unexpected development. In fact, after thanking God the Father, he adds: "I knew that you hear me always, but I have said this on account of the people standing by, that they may believe that you sent me" (Jn 11:42). With his prayer, Jesus wanted to lead people back to faith, to total trust in God and in his will. And he wanted to show that this God who so loved man and the world that he gave his only begotten Son (cf. Jn 3:16) is the God of Life, the God who brings hope and can reverse humanly impossible situations. Therefore, a believer's trusting prayer is a living testimony to God's presence in the world, to his concern for mankind, to his action with a view to bringing about his plan of salvation.

Jesus' two prayers on which we have meditated just now and which accompany the healing of the deaf mute and the raising of Lazarus reveal that the deep connection between the love of God and love of one's neighbor must also come into our own prayer. In Jesus, true God and true man, attention to others, especially if they are needy and suffering, compassion at the sight of the sorrow of a family who were his friends, led him to address the Father in that fundamental relationship which directed his entire life. However, the opposite is also true: communion with the Father, constant dialogue with him, spurred Jesus to be uniquely attentive to practical human situations so as to bring God's comfort and love to them. Human relationships lead us toward the relationship with God, and the relationship with God leads us back to our neighbor.

Dear brothers and sisters, our prayer opens the door to God, who teaches us to come out of ourselves constantly in order to make us capable of being close to others, to bring them comfort, hope, and light, especially at moments of trial. May the Lord grant us to be capable of ever more intense prayer, in order to strengthen our personal relationship with God the Father, to open our heart to the needs of those beside us, and to feel the beauty of being "sons in the Son", together with a great many brothers and sisters.

22

Prayer and the Holy Family of Nazareth

WEDNESDAY, 28 DECEMBER 2011
Paul VI Audience Hall

Dear Brothers and Sisters,

Today's meeting is taking place in the atmosphere of Christmas, imbued with deep joy at the Birth of the Savior. We have just celebrated this mystery whose echo ripples through the Liturgy of all these days. It is a Mystery of Light that all people in every era can relive with faith and prayer. It is through prayer itself that we become capable of drawing close to God with intimacy and depth. Therefore, bearing in mind the theme of prayer that I am developing in the Catecheses in this period, I would like to invite you to reflect today on the way that prayer was part of the life of the Holy Family of Nazareth. Indeed, the house of Nazareth is a school of prayer where one learns to listen to, meditate on, and penetrate the profound meaning of the manifestation of the Son of God, following the example of Mary, Joseph, and Jesus.

The Discourse of the Servant of God Paul VI during his Visit to Nazareth is memorable. The Pope said that at the school of the Holy Family we "understand why we must maintain a spiritual discipline, if we wish to follow the teaching of the Gospel and become disciples of Christ". He added: "In the first place it teaches us silence. Oh! If only esteem for silence, a wonderful and indispensable spiritual atmosphere, could be reborn within us! Whereas we are deafened by the din, the noise and discordant voices in the frenetic, turbulent life of our time. O silence of Nazareth! Teach us to be steadfast in good thoughts, attentive to our inner life, ready to hear God's hidden inspiration clearly and the exhortations of true teachers" (*Discourse in Nazareth*, 5 January 1964).

We can draw various ideas about prayer and the relationship with God and with the Holy Family from the Gospel narratives of the infancy of Jesus. We can begin with the episode of the Presentation of Jesus in the temple. Saint Luke tells how, "when the time came for their purification according to the law of Moses", Mary and Joseph "brought him up to Jerusalem to present him to the Lord" (2:22). Like every Jewish family that observed the Law, Jesus' parents went to the temple to consecrate their firstborn son to God and to make the sacrificial offering. Motivated by their fidelity to the precepts of the Law, they set out from Bethlehem and went to Jerusalem with Jesus, who was only forty days old. Instead of a year-old lamb, they presented the offering of simple families, namely, two turtledoves. The Holy Family's pilgrimage was one of faith, of the offering of gifts—a symbol of prayer—and of the encounter with the Lord whom Mary and Joseph already perceived in their Son, Jesus.

Mary was a peerless model of contemplation of Christ. The face of the Son belonged to her in a special way because he had been knit together in her womb and had taken a human likeness from her. No one has contemplated Jesus as diligently as Mary. The gaze of her heart was already focused on him at the moment of the Annunciation, when she conceived him through the action of the Holy Spirit; in the following months, she gradually became aware of his presence, until, on the day of his birth, her eyes could look with motherly tenderness upon the face of her son as she wrapped him in swaddling clothes and laid him in the manger. Memories of Jesus, imprinted on her mind and on her heart, marked every instant of Mary's existence. She lived with her eyes fixed on Christ and cherished his every word. Saint Luke says: "Mary kept all these things, pondering them in her heart" (2:19) and thus describes Mary's approach to the mystery of the Incarnation, which was to extend throughout her life: keeping these things, pondering on them in her heart. Luke is the Evangelist who acquaints us with Mary's heart, with her faith (cf. 1:45), her hope, and her obedience (cf. 1:38), and, especially, with her interiority and prayer (cf. 1:46–56), her free adherence to Christ (cf. 1:55). And all this proceeded from the gift of the Holy Spirit who overshadowed her (cf. 1:35), just as he was to come down on the Apostles in accordance with Christ's promise (cf. Acts 1:8). This image of Mary which Saint Luke gives us presents Our Lady as a model for every believer who cherishes and compares Jesus' words with his actions, a comparison which is always progress in the knowledge of Jesus. After Blessed Pope John Paul II's example (cf. Apostolic Letter *Rosarium Virginis Mariae*), we can say that the prayer of the Rosary is modeled precisely on Mary, because it consists in contemplating the mysteries of Christ in spiritual union with the Mother of the Lord. Mary's ability to live by God's gaze is, so to speak, contagious. The first to experience this was Saint Joseph. His humble and sincere love for his betrothed and his decision to join his life to Mary's attracted and introduced him, "a just man" (Mt 1:19), to a special intimacy with God. Indeed, with Mary and later, especially, with Jesus, he began a new way of relating to God, accepting him in his life, entering his project of salvation, and doing his will. After trustfully complying with the Angel's instructions—"Do not fear to take Mary your wife" (Mt 1:20)—he took Mary to himself and shared his life with her; he truly gave the whole of himself to Mary and to Jesus, and this led him to perfect his response to the vocation he had received. As we know, the Gospel has not recorded any of Joseph's words: his is a silent and faithful, patient and hard-working presence. We may imagine that he, too, like his wife and in close harmony with her, lived the years of Jesus' childhood and adolescence savoring, as it were, his presence in their family. Joseph fulfilled every aspect of his paternal role. He, together with Mary, must certainly have taught Jesus to pray. In particular, Joseph himself must have taken Jesus to the Synagogue for the rites of the Sabbath as well as to Jerusalem for the great feasts of the people of Israel. Joseph, in accordance with the Jewish tradition, would have led the prayers at home both every day—in the morning, in the evening, at meals—and on the principal religious feasts. In the rhythm of the days he spent at Nazareth, in the simple home and in Joseph's workshop, Jesus learned to alternate prayer and work as well as to offer God his labor in earning the bread the family needed.

And lastly, there is another episode that sees the Holy Family of Nazareth gathered together in an event of prayer. When Jesus was twelve years old, as we have heard, he went with his parents to the temple of Jerusalem. This episode fits into the context of pilgrimage, as Saint Luke stresses: "His parents went to Jerusalem every year at the feast of the Passover. And when he was twelve years old, they went up according to custom" (2:41–42). Pilgrimage is an expression of religious devotion that is nourished by and at the same time nourishes prayer. Here, it is the Passover pilgrimage, and the Evangelist points out to us that the family of Jesus made this pilgrimage every year in order to take part in the rites in the Holy City. Jewish families, like Christian families, pray in the intimacy of the home, but they also pray together with the community, recognizing that they belong to the People of God, journeying on; and the pilgrimage expresses exactly this state of the People of God on the move. Easter is the center and culmination of all this and involves both the family dimension and that of liturgical and public worship.

In the episode of the twelve-year-old Jesus, the first words of Jesus are also recorded: "How is it that you sought me? Did you not know that I must be in my Father's house?" (2:49). After three days spent looking for him, his parents found him in the temple, sitting among the teachers, listening to them and asking them questions (cf. 2:46). His answer to the question of why he had done this to his father and mother was that he had only done what the Son should do, that is, to be with his Father. Thus he showed who is the true Father, what is the true home, and that he had done nothing unusual or disobedient. He had stayed where the Son ought to be, that is, with the Father, and he stressed who his Father was. The term "Father" therefore dominates the tone of this answer, and the Christological mystery appears in its entirety. Hence, this word unlocks the mystery; it is the key to the mystery of Christ, who is the Son, and also the key to our mystery as Christians, who are sons and daughters in the Son. At the same time, Jesus teaches us to be children by being with the Father in prayer. The Christological mystery, the mystery of Christian existence, is closely linked to, founded on, prayer. Jesus was one day to teach his disciples to pray, telling them: when you pray, say "Father". And, naturally, do not just say the word; say it with your life, learn to say it meaningfully with your life: "Father"; and in this way you will be true sons in the Son, true Christians.

It is important at this point, when Jesus was still fully integrated in the life of the Family of Nazareth, to note what effect it must have had in the hearts of Mary and Joseph to hear this word "Father" on Jesus' lips. It is also important to reveal, to emphasize, who the Father is and to hear this word on his lips in his awareness of being the only begotten Son, who, for this very reason, chose to stay on for three days in the temple, which is the "Father's house". We may imagine that from this time the life of the Holy Family must have been even more full of prayer, since from the heart of Jesus the boy—then an adolescent and a young man—this deep meaning of the relationship with God the Father would not cease to spread and to be echoed in the hearts of Mary and Joseph. This episode shows us the real situation, the atmosphere of being with the Father. So it was that the Family of Nazareth became the first model of the Church in which, around the presence of Jesus and through his mediation, everyone experiences the filial relationship with God the Father, which also transforms interpersonal, human relationships.

Dear friends, because of these different aspects that I have outlined briefly in the light of the Gospel, the Holy Family is the icon of the domestic Church, called to pray together. The family is the domestic Church and must be the first school of prayer. It is in the family that children, from the tenderest age, can learn to perceive the meaning of God, thanks to the teaching and example of their parents: to live in an atmosphere marked by God's presence. An authentically Christian education cannot dispense with the experience of prayer. If one does not learn how to pray in the family, it will later be difficult to bridge this gap. And so I would like to address to you the invitation to pray together as a family at the school of the Holy Family of Nazareth and thereby really to become of one heart and soul, a true family.

23

The Prayer of Jesus at the Last Supper

WEDNESDAY, 11 JANUARY 2012
Paul VI Audience Hall

Dear Brothers and Sisters,

During our journey of reflection on Jesus' prayer as it is presented in the Gospels, I would like today to meditate on the particularly solemn moment of his prayer at the Last Supper.

The temporal and emotional background of the festive meal at which Jesus takes leave of his friends is the imminence of his death, which he feels is now at hand. For some time Jesus had been talking about his Passion and had also been seeking to involve his disciples increasingly in this prospect. The Gospel according to Mark tells that from the time when he set out for Jerusalem, in the villages of distant Caesarea Philippi, Jesus had begun "to teach them that the Son of man must suffer many things and be rejected by the elders and the chief priests and the scribes, and be killed, and after three days rise again" (Mk 8:31). In addition, in the very days when he was preparing to say goodbye to the disciples, the life of the people was marked by the imminence of the Passover, that is, the commemoration of Israel's liberation from Egypt. This liberation, lived in the past and expected in the present and in the future, is experienced again in family celebrations of the Passover. The Last Supper fits into this context, but with a basic innovation. Jesus looks at his Passion, death, and Resurrection with full awareness. He wishes to spend with his disciples this Supper, which has a quite special character and is different from other meals; it is his Supper, in which he gives something entirely new: himself. In this way, Jesus celebrates his Pasch, anticipating his Cross and his Resurrection.

This new element is highlighted for us in the account of the Last Supper in the Gospel of John, who does not describe it as the Passover meal for the very reason that Jesus was intending to inaugurate something new, to celebrate his Pasch, which is of course linked to the events of the Exodus. Moreover, according to John, Jesus died on the Cross at the very moment when the Passover lambs were being sacrificed in the temple.

What, then, is the key to this Supper? It is in the gestures of breaking bread, of distributing it to his followers, and of sharing the cup of wine, with the words that accompany them, and in the context of prayer in which they belong; it is the institution of the Eucharist, it is the great prayer of Jesus and of the Church. However, let us now take a closer look.

First of all, the New Testament traditions of the institution of the Eucharist (cf. 1 Cor 11:23–25; Lk 22:14–20; Mk 14:22–25; Mt 26:26–29) point to the prayer that introduces Jesus' acts and words over the bread and over the wine by using two parallel and complementary verbs. Paul and Luke speak of *eucaristia*/thanksgiving: "And he took bread, and when *he had given thanks* he broke it and gave it to them" (Lk 22:19). Mark and Matthew, however, emphasize instead the aspect of *eulogia*/blessing: "he took bread, and *blessed*, and broke it, and gave it to them" (Mk 14:22).

Both these Greek terms, *eucaristeìn* and *eulogeìn*, refer to the Hebrew *berakha*, that is, the great prayer of thanksgiving and blessing of Israel's tradition which inaugurated the important feasts. The two different Greek words indicate the two intrinsic and complementary orientations of this prayer. *Berakha*, in fact, means primarily thanksgiving and praise for the gift received that rise to God: at the Last Supper of Jesus, it is a matter of bread—made from the wheat that God causes to sprout and grow in the earth—and wine, produced from the fruit that ripens on the vine. This prayer of praise and thanksgiving that is raised to God returns as a blessing that comes down from God upon the gift and enriches it. Thanking and praising God thus become blessing, and the offering given to God returns to man blessed by the Almighty. The words of the institution of the Eucharist fit into this context of prayer; in them the praise and blessing of the *berakha* become the blessing and transformation of the bread and wine into the Body and Blood of Jesus.

Before the words of the institution come the actions: the breaking of the bread and the offering of the wine. The one who breaks the bread and passes the cup is, first of all, the head of the family, who welcomes his relatives at table; but these gestures are also those of hospitality, of the welcome in convivial communion of the stranger who does not belong to the house. These very gestures, in the Supper with which Jesus takes leave of his followers, acquire a completely new depth. He gives a visible sign of welcome to the banquet in which God gives himself. Jesus offers and communicates himself in the bread and in the wine.

But how can all this happen? How can Jesus give himself at that moment? Jesus knows that his life is about to be taken from him in the torture of the Cross, the capital punishment of slaves, which Cicero described as *mors turpissima crucis* [a most cruel and disgraceful death]. With the gift of the bread and of the wine that he offers at the Last Supper, Jesus anticipates his death and his Resurrection, bringing about what he had said in his Good Shepherd Discourse: "I lay down my life, that I may take it again. No one takes it from me, but I lay it down of my own accord. I have power to lay it down, and I have power to take it again; this charge I have received from my Father" (Jn 10:17–18). He therefore offers in anticipation the life that will be taken from him and in this way transforms his violent death into a free act of giving himself for others and to others. The violence he suffered is transformed into an active, free, and redemptive sacrifice.

Once again, in prayer, begun in accordance with the ritual forms of the biblical tradition, Jesus shows his identity and his determination to fulfill his mission of total love to the very end and of offering in obedience to the Father's will. The profound originality of the gift of himself to his followers, through the Eucharistic memorial, is the culmination of the prayer that distinguishes his farewell supper with those who are his own. In contemplating Jesus' actions and words on that night, we see clearly that it is in this close and constant relationship with the Father that he carries out his act of bequeathing to his followers and to each one of us the sacrament of love, the "*Sacramentum caritatis*". The words: "Do this in remembrance of me" (1 Cor 11:24, 25) ring out twice in the Upper Room. With the gift of himself, he celebrates his Pasch, becoming the true Lamb that brings the whole of the ancient worship to fulfillment. For this reason, Saint Paul, speaking to the Christians of Corinth, says: "Christ [our Pasch], our Paschal Lamb, has been sacrificed. Let us, therefore, celebrate the festival . . .

with the unleavened bread of sincerity and truth" (1 Cor 5:7–8).

Luke the Evangelist has retained a further precious element of the events of the Last Supper that enables us to see the moving depth of Jesus' prayer for his own on that night: his attention to each one. Starting with the prayer of thanksgiving and blessing, Jesus arrives at the Eucharistic gift, the gift of himself, and, while he is giving the crucial sacramental reality, he addresses Peter. At the end of the meal, he says: "Simon, Simon, behold, Satan demanded to have you, that he might sift you like wheat, but I have prayed for you that your faith may not fail; and when you have turned again, strengthen your brethren" (Lk 22:31–32). Jesus' prayer, when his disciples are about to be put to the test, helps them to overcome their weakness, their difficulty in understanding that the way of God passes through the Paschal Mystery of the death and Resurrection, anticipated in the offering of the bread and the wine. The Eucharist is the food of pilgrims that also becomes strength for those who are weary, worn-out, and bewildered. And the prayer was especially for Peter, so that once he had turned again he might strengthen his brethren in the faith. Luke the Evangelist recalls that it was the very gaze of Jesus in seeking Peter's face at the moment when he had just denied him three times which gave him the strength to continue following in his footsteps: "And immediately, while he was still speaking, the cock crowed. And the Lord turned and looked at Peter. And Peter remembered the word of the Lord" (Lk 22:60–61).

Dear brothers and sisters, by participating in the Eucharist, we experience in an extraordinary manner the prayer that Jesus prayed and prays ceaselessly for every person so that the evil which we all encounter in life may not get the upper hand and that the transforming power of Christ's death and Resurrection may act within us. In the Eucharist, the Church responds to Jesus' commandment: "Do this in remembrance of me" (Lk 22:19; cf. 1 Cor 11:24–26); she repeats the prayer of thanksgiving and praise and, with it, the words of the transubstantiation of the bread and wine into the Body and Blood of the Lord. Our Eucharists are a way of being drawn into this moment of prayer, of being united ever anew to Jesus' prayer. From the outset, the Church has understood the words of consecration to be part of the *prayer prayed together with Jesus*; to be a central part of the praise filled with gratitude, through which the fruits of the earth and the work of man are given to us anew by God as the Body and Blood of Jesus, as the self-giving of God himself in his Son's self-emptying love (cf. *Jesus of Nazareth*, Part Two [San Francisco: Ignatius Press, 2011], p. 128). Participating in the Eucharist, nourishing ourselves with the Flesh and Blood of the Son of God, we join our prayers to that of the Paschal Lamb on his supreme night, so that our life may not be lost despite our weakness and our unfaithfulness, but be transformed.

Dear friends, let us ask the Lord that, after being duly prepared, also with the sacrament of Penance, our participation in his Eucharist, indispensable to Christian life, may always be the highest point in all our prayer. Let us ask that we, too, profoundly united in his offering to the Father, may transform our own crosses into a free and responsible sacrifice of love for God and for our brethren.

24

The Priestly Prayer of Jesus

WEDNESDAY, 25 JANUARY 2012
Paul VI Audience Hall

Dear Brothers and Sisters,

In today's Catechesis let us focus our attention on the prayer that Jesus raises to the Father in the "Hour" of his exaltation and glorification (cf. Jn 17:1–26). As the *Catechism of the Catholic Church* says: "Christian Tradition rightly calls this prayer the 'priestly' prayer of Jesus. It is the prayer of our high priest, inseparable from his sacrifice, from his passing over (Passover) to the Father to whom he is wholly 'consecrated'" (no. 2747).

The extreme richness of Jesus' prayer can be understood especially if we set it against the backdrop of the Jewish feast of expiation, *Yom Kippur*. On that day, the high priest makes expiation first for himself and then for the category of priests and, lastly, for the whole community of the people. The purpose is to restore to the People of Israel, after a year's transgressions, the awareness of their reconciliation with God, the awareness that they are the Chosen People, a "holy people", among the other peoples. The prayer of Jesus, presented in Chapter 17 of the Gospel according to John, returns to the structure of this feast. On that night, Jesus addresses the Father at the moment when he is offering himself. He, priest and victim, prays for himself, for the Apostles, and for all those who will believe in him and for the Church of all the time (cf. Jn 17:20).

The prayer that Jesus prays for himself is the request for his glorification, for his "exaltation" in his "Hour". In fact, it is more than a prayer of petition, more than the declaration of his full willingness to enter, freely and generously, into the plan of God the Father, which is fulfilled in his being handed over and in his death and Resurrection. This "Hour" began with Judas' betrayal (cf. 13:31) and was to end in the ascension of the Risen Jesus to the Father (Jn 20:17). Jesus comments on Judas' departure from the Upper Room with these words: "Now is the Son of man glorified, and in him God is glorified" (Jn 13:31). It is not by chance that he begins his priestly prayer saying: "Father, the hour has come; glorify your Son that the Son may glorify you" (Jn 17:1). The glorification that Jesus asks for himself as High Priest is the entry into full obedience to the Father, an obedience that leads to his fullest filial condition: "And now, Father, glorify me in your own presence with the glory which I had with you before the world was made" (Jn 17:5). This readiness and this request are the first act of the new priesthood of Jesus, which is a total gift of himself on the Cross, and on the Cross itself—the supreme act of love—he is glorified, because love is the true glory, the divine glory.

The second moment of this prayer is the intercession that Jesus makes for the disciples who have been with him. They are those of whom Jesus can say to the Father: "I have manifested your name to the men whom you gave me out of the world; yours they were, and you gave them to me, and they have kept your word" (Jn 17:6). This "manifesting God's name to men" is the fulfillment of a new presence of the

Father among the people, among mankind. This "manifesting" is not only a *word*, but is *reality* in Jesus; God is with us, and so his name—his presence with us, his being one of us—is "fulfilled". This manifestation is thus realized in the Incarnation of the Word. In Jesus, God enters human flesh; he becomes close in a new and unique way. And this presence culminates in the sacrifice that Jesus makes in his Pasch of death and Resurrection.

At the center of this prayer of intercession and of expiation in favor of the disciples is the request for *consecration*; Jesus says to the Father: "They are not of the world, even as I am not of the world. Sanctify them in the truth; your word is truth. As you did send me into the world, so I have sent them into the world. And for their sake I consecrate myself, that they also may be consecrated in truth" (Jn 17:16–19). I ask: what does "consecrate" mean in this case? First of all, it must be said that really only God is "consecrated" or "holy". "To consecrate", therefore, means "to transfer" a reality—a person or a thing—to become the property of God. And two complementary aspects are present in this: on the one hand, removing them from ordinary things, segregating, "setting them apart" from the context of personal human life so that they may be totally given to God; and, on the other, this segregation, this transferal into God's sphere, has the very meaning of "sending", of mission: precisely because he is given to God, the reality, the consecrated person, exists "for" others, is given to others. Giving to God means existing no longer for oneself, but for everyone. Whoever, like Jesus, is segregated from the world and set apart for God with a view to a task is, for this very reason, fully available to all. For the disciples, the task will be to continue Jesus' mission, to be given to God and thereby to be on mission for all. The Risen One, appearing to his disciples on Easter evening, was to say to them: "Peace be with you. As the Father has sent me, even so I send you" (Jn 20:21).

The third part of this priestly prayer extends to the end of time. In it Jesus turns to the Father in order to intercede for all those who will be brought to the faith through the mission inaugurated by the Apostles and continued in history: "I do not pray for these only, but also for those who believe in me through their word." Jesus prays for the Church of all time; he also prays for us (Jn 17:20). The *Catechism of the Catholic Church* comments: "Jesus fulfilled the work of the Father completely; his prayer, like his sacrifice, extends until the end of time. The prayer of this hour fills the end-times and carries them toward their consummation" (no. 2749).

The central request of the priestly prayer of Jesus dedicated to his disciples of all epochs is that of the future unity of those who will believe in him. This unity is not a worldly product. It comes exclusively from the divine unity and reaches us from the Father, through the Son, and in the Holy Spirit. Jesus invokes a gift that comes from Heaven and has its effect—real and perceptible—on earth. He prays "that they may all be one; even as you, Father, are in me, and I in you, that they also may be in us, so that the world may believe that you have sent me" (Jn 17:21). Christian unity, on the one hand, is a secret reality that is in the heart of believers. But, at the same time, it must appear with full clarity in history; it must appear so that the world may believe; it has a very practical and concrete purpose: it must appear so that all may really be one. The unity of future disciples, in being united with Jesus—whom the Father sent into the world—is also the original source of the efficacy of the Christian mission in the world.

"We can say that the founding of the Church takes place" in the priestly prayer of Jesus. In this very place, in the act of the Last Supper, Jesus creates the Church. "For what else is the Church, if not the community of disciples who ... through faith in Jesus Christ as the one sent by the Father" receives its unity and is involved in Jesus' mission to save the world, leading it to knowledge of God? Here we really find a true definition of the Church. "The Church is born from Jesus' prayer. But this prayer is more than words; it is the act by which he 'sanctifies' himself, that is to say, he 'sacrifices' himself for the life of the world" (cf. *Jesus of Nazareth*, Part II, p. 101). Jesus prays that his disciples may be one. By virtue of this unity, received and preserved, the Church can walk "in the world" without being "of the world" (cf. Jn 17:16) and can live the mission entrusted to her so that the world may believe in the Son and in the Father who sent him. Therefore the Church becomes the place in which the mission of Christ itself continues: to lead the "world" out of man's alienation from God and out of himself, out of sin, so that it may return to being the world of God.

Dear brothers and sisters, we have grasped a few elements of the great richness of the priestly prayer of Jesus, which I invite you to read and to meditate on so that it may guide us in dialogue with the Lord and teach us to pray. Let us too, therefore, in our prayers, ask God to help us to enter more fully into the design he has for each one of us. Let us ask to be "consecrated" to him, to belong to him more and more, to be able to love others more and more, those who are near and far; let us ask to be able always to open our prayer to the dimensions of the world, not closing it in the request for help with our problems, but remembering our neighbor before the Lord, learning the beauty of interceding for others; let us ask him for the gift of visible unity among all believers in Christ—we have invoked it forcefully in this Week of Prayer for Christian Unity—let us pray to be ever ready to answer anyone who asks us to account for the hope that is in us (cf. 1 Pt 3:15).

25

Jesus in Gethsemane

WEDNESDAY, 1 FEBRUARY 2012
Paul VI Audience Hall

Dear Brothers and Sisters,

Today I would like to talk about Jesus' prayer in the Garden of Olives at Gethsemane. The scenario of the Gospel narrative of this prayer is particularly significant. Jesus sets out for the Mount of Olives after the Last Supper while he is praying together with his disciples. The Evangelist Mark says: "when they had sung a hymn, they went out to the Mount of Olives" (Mk 14:26). This is probably an allusion to singing one of the *Hallel* Psalms, with which thanks are given to God for the liberation of the People from slavery and his help is asked for the ever new difficulties and threats of the present. The walk to Gethsemane is punctuated by Jesus' remarks that convey a sense of his impending death and proclaim the imminent dispersion of the disciples.

Having reached the grove on the Mount of Olives, that night too Jesus prepares for personal prayer. However, this time something new happens: it seems that he does not want to be left alone. Jesus would often withdraw from the crowd and from the disciples themselves "to a lonely place" (Mk 1:35), or he would go up "into the hills", Saint Mark says (cf. Mk 6:46). Instead, at Gethsemane he invites Peter,

James, and John to stay closer to him. They are the disciples he called upon to be with him on the Mount of the Transfiguration (cf. Mk 9:2–13). This closeness of the three during his prayer in Gethsemane is important. On that night, too, Jesus was going to pray to the Father "apart", for his relationship with the Father is quite unique: it is the relationship of the only begotten Son. Indeed, one might say that especially on that night no one could really have come close to the Son, who presented himself to the Father with his absolutely unique and exclusive identity. Yet, although Jesus arrives "alone" at the place in which he is to stop and pray, he wants at least three disciples to be near him, to be in a closer relationship with him. This is a spacial closeness, a plea for solidarity at the moment in which he feels death approaching, but above all it is closeness in prayer, in a certain way to express harmony with him at the moment when he is preparing to do the Father's will to the very end; and it is an invitation to every disciple to follow him on the Way of Cross.

Mark the Evangelist recounts: "he took with him Peter and James and John, and began to be greatly distressed and troubled. And he said to them '*My soul is very sorrowful*, even to death; remain here, and watch'" (14:33–34). In the words he addresses to the three, Jesus once again expresses himself in the language of the Psalms: "*My soul is very sorrowful*", an expression borrowed from Psalm 43 (cf. Ps 43[42]:5). The firm determination "unto death" thus calls to mind a situation lived by many of those sent by God in the Old Testament and which is expressed in their prayers. Indeed, following the mission entrusted to them frequently means encountering hostility, rejection, and persecution. Moses is dramatically aware of the trial he is undergoing while guiding the people through the desert and says to

God: "I am not able to carry all this people alone, the burden is too heavy for me. If you will deal thus with me, rather kill me at once, kill me if I have found favor in your sight, that I may not see my wretchedness" (cf. Num 11:14–15). Elijah, too, finds doing his duty to God and to his People difficult. The first Book of Kings recounts: "he himself went a day's journey into the wilderness, and came and sat under a broom tree; and he asked that he might die, saying, 'It is enough; now, O Lord, take away my life; for I am no better than my fathers'" (19:4). What Jesus says to the three disciples whom he wants near him during his prayer at Gethsemane shows that he feels fear and anguish in that "Hour", experiencing his last profound loneliness precisely while God's plan is being brought about. Moreover, Jesus' fear and anguish sum up the full horror of man in the face of his own death, the certainty that it is inescapable and a perception of the burden of evil that touches our lives.

After the invitation to stay with him to watch and pray, which he addresses to the three, Jesus speaks to the Father "alone". Mark the Evangelist tells us that "going a little farther, he fell on the ground and prayed that, if it were possible, the hour might pass from him" (14:35). Jesus fell prostrate on the ground: a position of prayer that expresses obedience to the Father and abandonment in him with complete trust. This gesture is repeated at the beginning of the celebration of the Passion, on Good Friday, as well as in monastic profession and in the ordination of deacons, priests, and bishops in order to express, in prayer, corporally too, complete entrustment to God, trust in him. Jesus then asks the Father, if this be possible, to obtain that this hour pass from him. It is not only man's fear and anguish in the face of death, but it is the devastation of the Son of God, who perceives the terrible mass of evil that he must take upon himself to overcome it, to deprive it of power. Dear friends, in prayer we, too, should be able to lay before God our labors, the suffering of certain situations, of certain days, the daily commitment to following him, to being Christian, and also the weight of the evil that we see within ourselves and around us, so that he may give us hope and make us feel his closeness and give us a little light on the path of life.

Jesus continues his prayer: "*Abba*, Father, all things are possible to you; remove this cup from me; yet not what I will, but what you will" (Mk 14:36). In this invocation, there are three revealing passages. At the beginning, we have the double use of the word with which Jesus addresses God: "*Abba*! Father!" (Mk 14:36a). We know well that the Aramaic word *Abbà* is the term that children use to address their father and, hence, that it expresses Jesus' relationship with God, a relationship of tenderness, affection, trust, and abandonment. The second element is found in the central part of the invocation: awareness of the Father's omnipotence: "all things are possible to you", which introduces a request in which, once again, the drama of Jesus' human will appears as he faces death and evil: "remove this cup from me!" However, there is the third expression in Jesus' prayer, and it is the crucial one, in which the human will adheres to the divine will without reserve. In fact, Jesus ends by saying forcefully: "yet not what I will but what you will" (Mk 14:36c). In the unity of the Divine Person of the Son, the human will finds its complete fulfillment in the total abandonment of the I to the You of the Father, called Abba. Saint Maximus the Confessor says that ever since the moment of the creation of man and woman, the human will has been oriented to the divine will and that it is precisely in the "yes" to God that the human will is fully free and finds its fulfillment. Unfortunately, because of sin, this "yes" to God is transformed into opposition: Adam and Eve thought that the "no" to God was the crowning point of freedom, of being fully themselves. On the Mount of Olives, Jesus brings the human will back to the unreserved "yes" to God; in him the natural will is fully integrated in the orientation that the Divine Person gives it. Jesus lives his life in accordance with the center of his Person: his being the Son of God. His human will is drawn into the I of the Son, who abandons himself totally to the Father. Thus Jesus tells us that it is only by conforming our own will to the divine one that human beings attain their true height, that they become "divine"; only by coming out of ourselves, only in the "yes" to God, is Adam's desire—and the desire of us all—fulfilled: the desire to be completely free. It is what Jesus brings about at Gethsemane: in transferring the human will into the divine will, the true man is born and we are redeemed.

The *Compendium of the Catholic Church* teaches concisely: "The prayer of Jesus during his agony in the garden of Gethsemane and his last words on the cross reveal the depth of his filial prayer. Jesus brings to completion the loving plan of the Father and takes upon himself all the anguish of humanity and all the petitions and intercessions of the history of salvation. He presents them to the Father, who accepts them and answers them beyond all hope by raising his Son from the dead" (no. 543). Truly "nowhere else in sacred Scripture do we gain so deep an insight into the inner mystery of Jesus as in the prayer on the Mount of Olives" (*Jesus of Nazareth*, Part Two [San Francisco: Ignatius Press, 2011], p. 157).

Dear brothers and sisters, every day in the prayer of the *Our Father* we ask the Lord: "thy will be done, on earth as it is in heaven" (Mt 6:10). In other words, we recognize that there is a will of God with us and for us, a will of God for our life that must become every day, increasingly, the reference of our willing and of our being; we recognize, moreover, that "heaven" is where God's will is done and where the "earth" becomes "heaven", a place where love, goodness, truth, and divine beauty are present only if, on earth, God's will is done. In Jesus' prayer to the Father on that terrible and marvelous night in Gethsemane, the "earth" became "heaven"; the "earth" of his human will, shaken by fear and anguish, was taken up by his divine will in such a way that God's will was done on earth. And this is also important in our own prayers: we must learn to entrust ourselves more to divine Providence, to ask God for the strength to come out of ourselves to renew our "yes" to him, to say to him "thy will be done", so as to conform our will to his. It is a prayer we must pray every day because it is not always easy to entrust ourselves to God's will, repeating the "yes" of Jesus, the "yes" of Mary. The Gospel accounts of Gethsemane regretfully show that the three disciples, chosen by Jesus to be close to him, were unable to watch with him, sharing in his prayer, in his adherence to the Father, and they were overcome by sleep.

Dear friends, let us ask the Lord to enable us to keep watch with him in prayer, to follow the will of God every day even if he speaks of the Cross, to live in ever greater intimacy with the Lord, in order to bring a little bit of God's "heaven" to this "earth".

26

The Prayer of Jesus in the Face of Death (Mark and Matthew)

WEDNESDAY, 8 FEBRUARY 2012
Paul VI Audience Hall

Dear Brothers and Sisters,

Today I would like to reflect with you on the prayer of Jesus when death was imminent, pausing to think about everything Saint Mark and Saint Matthew tell us. The two Evangelists record the prayer of the dying Jesus not only in Greek, in which their accounts are written, but, because of the importance of these words, also in a mixture of Hebrew and Aramaic. In this way they have passed down not only the content but also the sound that this prayer had on Jesus' lips: let us really listen to Jesus' words as they were. At the same time, the Evangelists describe to us the attitude of those present at the crucifixion who did not understand—or did not want to understand—this prayer.

Saint Mark wrote, as we have heard: "when the sixth hour had come, there was darkness over the whole land until the ninth hour. And at the ninth hour Jesus cried with a loud voice, '*Eloi, Eloi, lama sabachthani*?' which means, 'My God, my God, why have you forsaken me?'" (15:33–34). In the structure of the account, the prayer, Jesus' cry, is raised at the end of the three hours of darkness that shrouded all the earth from midday until three o'clock in the afternoon. These three hours of darkness are in turn the continuation of a previous span of time, also of three hours, that began with the crucifixion of Jesus. The Evangelist Mark, in fact, tells us that "it was the third hour, when they crucified him" (15:25). From all the times given in the narrative, Jesus' six hours on the Cross are divided into two parts of equal length.

The mockery of various groups which displays their scepticism and confirms their disbelief fits into the first three hours, from nine o'clock in the morning until midday. Saint Mark writes: "Those who passed by derided him" (15:29); "So also the chief priests mocked him to one another with the scribes" (15:31); "those who were crucified with him also reviled him" (15:32). In the following three hours, from midday until "the ninth hour" [three o'clock in the afternoon], the Evangelist spoke only of the darkness that had come down over the entire earth; only darkness fills the whole scene without any references to people's movements or words. While Jesus is drawing ever closer to death, there is nothing but darkness that covers "the whole land". The cosmos also takes part in this event: the darkness envelops people and things, but even at this moment of darkness God is present, he does not abandon them. In the biblical tradition, darkness has an ambivalent meaning: it is a sign of the presence and action of evil, but also of a mysterious presence and action of God, who can triumph over every shadow. In the Book of Exodus, for example, we read "The Lord said to Moses: 'Lo, I am coming to you in a thick cloud'" (19:9); and, further: "the people stood afar off, while Moses drew near to the thick darkness where God was" (20:21). And in his discourses in Deuteronomy, Moses recounts: "And you came near and stood at the foot of the mountain, while the mountain burned with fire to the heart of heaven wrapped in darkness, cloud, and gloom" (4:11); you "heard the voice out of the midst of the darkness, while the mountain was burning with fire" (5:23). In the scene of the crucifixion of Jesus, the darkness engulfs the earth and the Son of God immerses himself in the shadows of death in order to bring life with his act of love.

Returning to Saint Mark's narrative, in the face of the insults of various categories of people, in the face of the pall of darkness that shrouds everything, at the moment when he faces death, Jesus, with the cry of his prayer, shows that with the burden of suffering and death in which there seems to be abandonment, the absence of God, Jesus is utterly certain of the closeness of the Father, who approves this supreme act of love, the total gift of himself, although the voice from on high is not heard, as it was on other occasions. In reading the Gospels, we realize that in other important passages on his earthly existence, Jesus had also seen the explanatory voice of God associated with the signs of the Father's presence and approval of his journey of love. Thus in the event that follows the Baptism in the Jordan, at the opening of the heavens, the words of the Father had been heard: "Thou art my beloved Son, with thee I am well pleased" (Mk 1:11). Then in the Transfiguration, the sign of the cloud was accompanied with these words: "this is my beloved Son; listen to him" (Mk 9:7). Conversely, at the approach of the death of the Crucified One, silence falls, no voice is heard, but the Father's loving gaze is fixed on his Son's gift of love.

However, what is the meaning of Jesus' prayer, of the cry he addresses to the Father: "My God, my God, why have you forsaken me?": doubt about his mission, about the Father's presence? Might there not be in this prayer the knowledge that he had been forsaken? The words that Jesus addresses to the Father are the beginning of Psalm 22[21], in which the Psalmist expresses to God his being torn between feeling forsaken and the certain knowledge of God's presence in his People's midst. He, the Psalmist, prays: "O my God, I cry by day, but you do not answer; and by night, but find no rest. Yet you are holy, enthroned on the praises of Israel" (vv. 3–4). The Psalmist speaks of this "cry" in order to express the full suffering of his prayer to God, seemingly absent: in the moment of anguish, his prayer becomes a cry.

This also happens in our relationship with the Lord: when we face the most difficult and painful situations, when it seems that God does not hear, we must not be afraid to entrust the whole weight of our overburdened hearts to him; we must not fear to cry out to him in our suffering; we must be convinced that God is close, even if he seems silent.

Repeating from the Cross the first words of Psalm 22[21] "*Eli, Eli, lama sabachthani*?"—"My God my God, why have you forsaken me?" (Mt 27:46); uttering the words of the Psalm, Jesus prays at the moment of his ultimate rejection by men, at the moment of abandonment; yet he prays, with the Psalm, in the awareness of God's presence, even in that hour when he is feeling the human drama of death. However, a question arises within us: how is it possible that such a powerful God does not intervene to save his Son from this terrible trial? It is important to understand that Jesus' prayer is not the cry of one who meets death with despair, nor is it the cry of one who knows he has been forsaken. At this moment, Jesus makes his own the whole of Psalm 22[21], the Psalm of the suffering People of Israel. In this way, he takes upon himself not only the sin of his people, but also that of all men and women who are suffering from the oppression of evil, and, at the same time, he places all this before God's own heart, in the certainty that his cry will be heard in the Resurrection: "The cry of extreme anguish is at the same time the certainty of an answer from God, the certainty of salvation—not only for Jesus himself, but for 'many'" (*Jesus of Nazareth*, Part Two [San Francisco: Ignatius Press, 2011], pp. 213–14). In this prayer of Jesus are contained his extreme trust and his abandonment into God's hands, even when God seems absent, even when he seems to be silent, complying with a plan incomprehensible to us. In the *Catechism of the Catholic Church* we read: "in the redeeming love that always united him to the Father, he assumed us in the state of our waywardness of sin, to the point that he could say in our name from the cross: 'My God, my God, why have you forsaken me?'" (no. 603). His is a suffering in communion with us and for us, which derives from love and already bears within it redemption, the victory of love.

The bystanders at the foot of the Cross of Jesus fail to understand, thinking that his cry is a supplication addressed to Elijah. In the scene, they seek to assuage his thirst in order to prolong his life and to find out whether Elijah will truly come to his aid, but with a loud cry Jesus' earthly life, as well as their wish, come to an end. At the supreme moment, Jesus gives vent to his heart's grief but, at the same time, makes clear the meaning of the Father's presence and his consent to the Father's plan for the salvation of mankind. We, too, have to face ever anew the "today" of suffering, of God's silence—we express it so often in our prayers—but we also find ourselves facing the "today" of the Resurrection, of the response of God, who took upon himself our sufferings, to carry them together with us and to give us the firm hope that they will be overcome (cf. Encyclical Letter *Spe Salvi*, nos. 35–40).

Dear friends, let us lay our daily crosses before God in our prayers in the certainty that he is present and hears us. Jesus' cry reminds us that in prayer we must surmount the barriers of our "ego" and our problems and open ourselves to the needs and suffering of others. May the prayer of Jesus dying on the Cross teach us to pray lovingly for our many brothers and sisters who are oppressed by the weight of daily life, who are living through difficult moments, who are in pain, who have no word of comfort; let us place all this before God's heart, so that they, too, may feel the love of God who never abandons us.

27

The Prayer of Jesus in the Imminence of Death (Luke)

WEDNESDAY, 15 FEBRUARY 2012
Paul VI Audience Hall

Dear Brothers and Sisters,

At our school of prayer last Wednesday, I spoke of Jesus' prayer on the Cross, taken from Psalm 22[21]: "My God, my God, why have you forsaken me?" I would now like to continue to meditate on the prayer of Jesus on the Cross in the imminence of death. Today, I would like to reflect on the account we find in Saint Luke's Gospel. The Evangelist has passed down to us three words spoken by Jesus on the Cross, two of which—the first and the third—are prayers explicitly addressed to the Father. The second, instead, consists of the promise made to the so-called "good thief", crucified with him; indeed, in response to the thief's entreaty, Jesus reassures him: "Truly, I say to you, today you will be with me in Paradise" (Lk 23:43). Thus, in Luke's narrative, the two prayers that the dying Jesus addresses to the Father and his openness to the supplication addressed to him by the repentant sinner are evocatively interwoven. Jesus calls on the Father and at the same time listens to the prayer of this man who is often called *latro poenitens*, "the repentant thief".

Let us reflect on these three prayers of Jesus. He prays the first one immediately after being nailed to the Cross, while the soldiers are dividing his garments between them as a wretched reward for their service. In a certain sense, the process of the crucifixion ends with this action. Saint Luke writes: "When they came to the place which is called The Skull, there they crucified him, and the criminals, one on the right and one on the left. And Jesus said, 'Father, forgive them; for they know not what they do.' And they cast lots to divide his garments" (23:33–34). The first prayer that Jesus addresses to the Father is a prayer of intercession; he asks for forgiveness for his executioners. Jesus is thereby doing in person what he taught in the Sermon on the Mount when he said: "I say to you that hear, Love your enemies, do good to those who hate you" (Lk 6:27); and he also promised to those who are able to forgive: "your reward will be great, and you will be sons of the Most High" (v. 35). Now, from the Cross he not only pardons his executioners, but he addresses the Father directly, interceding for them.

Jesus' attitude finds a moving "imitation" in the account of the stoning of Saint Stephen, the first martyr. Indeed, Stephen, now nearing his end, "knelt down and cried with a loud voice, 'Lord, do not hold this sin against them.' And when he had said this, he fell asleep" (Acts 7:60): these were his last words. The comparison between Jesus' prayer for forgiveness and that of the protomartyr is significant. Saint Stephen turns to the Risen Lord and requests that his killing—an action described clearly by the words "this sin"—not be held against those who stoned him. Jesus on the Cross addresses the Father and not only asks forgiveness for those who crucify him but also offers an interpretation of what is happening. According to what he says, in fact, the men who are crucifying him "know not what they do" (Lk 23:34). He therefore postulates ignorance, "not knowing", as a reason for his request for the Father's forgiveness, because it leaves the door open to conversion, as, moreover, happens in the words that the centurion was to speak at Jesus' death: "Certainly this man was innocent" (v. 47), he was the Son of God. "It remains a source of comfort for all times and for all people that both in the case of those who genuinely did not know (his executioners) and in the case of those who did know (the people who condemned him), the Lord makes their ignorance the motive for his plea for forgiveness: he sees it as a door that can open us to conversion" (*Jesus of Nazareth*, Part Two [San Francisco: Ignatius Press, 2011], p. 208).

The second word spoken by Jesus on the Cross recorded by Saint Luke is a word of hope; it is his answer to the prayer of one of the two men crucified with him. The good thief comes to his senses before Jesus and repents; he realizes he is facing the Son of God, who makes the very Face of God visible, and begs him; "Jesus, remember me when you come in your kingly power" (v. 42). The Lord's answer to this prayer goes far beyond the request: in fact, he says: "Truly, I say to you, today you will be with me in Paradise" (v. 43). Jesus knows that he is entering into direct communion with the Father and reopening to man the way to God's paradise. Thus, with this response, he gives the firm hope that God's goodness can also touch us, even at the very last moment of life, and that sincere prayer, even after a wrong life, encounters the open arms of the good Father who awaits the return of his son.

However, let us consider the last words of the dying Jesus. The Evangelist tells us: "it was now about the sixth hour, and there was darkness over the whole land until the ninth hour, while the sun's light failed; and the curtain of the temple was torn in two. Then Jesus, crying with a loud voice, said, 'Father, into your hands I commit my spirit!' And having said this he breathed his last" (vv. 44–46). Certain aspects of this narrative differ from the scene as described in Mark and in Matthew. The three hours of darkness in Mark are not described, whereas in Matthew they are linked with a series of different apocalyptic events, such as the quaking of the earth, the opening of the tombs, the dead who are raised (cf. Mt 27:51–53). In Luke, the hours of darkness are caused by the eclipse of the sun, but the veil of the temple is torn at that moment. In this way, Luke's account presents two signs, in a certain way parallel, in the heavens and in the temple. The heavens lose their light, the earth sinks, while in the temple, a place of God's presence, the curtain that protects the sanctuary is rent in two. Jesus' death is characterized explicitly as a cosmic and a liturgical event; in particular, it marks the beginning of a new form of worship, in a temple not built by men because it is the very Body of Jesus who died and rose which gathers peoples together and unites them in the sacrament of his Body and his Blood.

At this moment of suffering, Jesus' prayer, "Father into your hands I commit my spirit", is a loud cry of supreme and total entrustment to God. This prayer expresses the full awareness that he has not been abandoned. The initial invocation—"Father"—recalls his first declaration as a twelve-year-old boy. At that time he had stayed for three days in the temple of Jerusalem, whose veil was now torn in two. And when his parents had told him of their anxiety, he had answered: "How is it that you sought me? Did you not know that I must be in my Father's house?" (Lk 2:49). From the beginning to the end, what fully determines Jesus' feelings, words, and actions is his unique relationship with the Father. On the Cross he lives to the full, in love, this filial relationship he has with God which gives life to his prayer.

The words spoken by Jesus after his invocation, "Father", borrow a sentence from Psalm 31[30]: "into your hand I commit my spirit" (Ps 31[30]:6). Yet these words are not a mere citation but, rather, express a firm decision: Jesus "delivers" himself to the Father in an act of total abandonment. These words are a prayer of "entrustment"—total trust in God's love. Jesus' prayer as he faces death is dramatic, as it is for every man, but, at the same time, it is imbued with that deep calmness which is born from trust in the Father and from the desire to commend oneself totally to him. In Gethsemane, when he began his final struggle and his most intense prayer and was about to be "delivered into the hands of men" (Lk 9:44), his sweat had become "like great drops of blood falling down upon the ground" (Lk 22:44). Nevertheless, his heart was fully obedient to the Father's will, and because of this "an angel from heaven" came to strengthen him (cf. Lk 22:42–43). Now, in his last moments, Jesus turns to the Father, telling him into whose hands he really commits his whole life. Before starting out on his journey toward Jerusalem, Jesus had insisted to his disciples: "Let these words sink into your ears; for the Son of man is to be delivered into the hands of men" (Lk 9:44). Now that life is about to depart from him, he seals his last decision in prayer: Jesus let himself be delivered "into the hands of men", but it is into the hands of the Father that he places his spirit; thus—as the Evangelist John affirms—all was finished, the supreme act of love was carried to the end, to the limit and beyond the limit.

Dear brothers and sisters, the words of Jesus on the Cross at the last moments of his earthly life offer us demanding instructions for our prayers, but they also open us to serene trust and firm hope. Jesus, who asks the Father to forgive those who are crucifying him, invites us to take the difficult step of also praying for those who wrong us, who have injured us, ever able to forgive, so that God's light may illuminate their hearts; and he invites us to live in our prayers the same attitude of mercy and love with which God treats us; "forgive us our trespasses and forgive those who trespass against us", we say every day in the Lord's prayer. At the same time, Jesus, who at the supreme moment of death entrusts himself totally to the hands of God the Father, communicates to us the certainty that, however harsh the trial, however difficult the problems, however acute the suffering may be, we shall never fall from God's hands, those hands that created us, that sustain us, and that accompany us on our way through life, because they are guided by an infinite and faithful love.

28

Silence and Prayer: Jesus, the Master of Prayer

WEDNESDAY, 7 MARCH 2012
Saint Peter's Square

Dear Brothers and Sisters,

In the preceding series of Catecheses I have spoken of Jesus' prayer, and I would not like to conclude this reflection without briefly considering the topic of Jesus' silence, so important in his relationship with God.

In the Post-Synodal Apostolic Exhortation *Verbum Domini*, I spoke of the role that silence plays in Jesus' life, especially on Golgotha: "Here we find ourselves before 'the word of the cross' (cf. 1 Cor 1:18). The word is muted; it becomes mortal silence, for it has 'spoken' exhaustively, holding back nothing of what it had to tell us" (no. 12). Before this silence of the Cross, Saint Maximus the Confessor puts this phrase on the lips of the Mother of God: "Wordless is the Word of the Father, who made every creature which speaks; lifeless are the eyes of the one at whose word and whose nod all living things move!" (*Life of Mary*, no. 89: *Testi mariani del primo millennio*, 2 [Rome, 1989], p. 253).

The Cross of Christ not only demonstrates Jesus' silence as his last word to the Father but reveals that God also *speaks* through *silence*:

> The silence of God, the experience of the distance of the almighty Father, is a decisive stage in the earthly journey of the Son of God, the Incarnate Word. Hanging from the wood of the cross, he lamented the suffering caused by that silence: "My God, my God, why have you forsaken me?" (Mk 15:34; Mt 27:46). Advancing in obedience to his very last breath, in the obscurity of death, Jesus called upon the Father. He commended himself to him at the moment of passage, through death, to eternal life: "Father, into your hands I commend my spirit" (Lk 23:46). (Post-Synodal Apostolic Exhortation *Verbum Domini*, no. 21)

Jesus' experience on the Cross profoundly reveals the situation of the person praying and the culmination of his prayer: having heard and recognized the word of God, we must also come to terms with the silence of God, an important expression of the same divine Word.

The dynamic of words and silence which marks Jesus' prayer throughout his earthly existence, especially on the Cross, also touches our own prayer life in two directions. The first is the one that concerns the acceptance of the word of God. Inward and outward silence are necessary if we are to be able to hear this word. And in our time this point is particularly difficult for us. In fact, ours is an era that does not encourage recollection; indeed, one sometimes gets the impression that people are frightened of being cut off, even for an instant, from the torrent of words and images that mark and fill the day. It was for this reason that in the above-mentioned Exhortation *Verbum Domini* I recalled our need to learn the value of silence: "Rediscovering the centrality of God's word in the life of the Church also means rediscovering a sense of recollection and inner repose. The great patristic tradition teaches us that the mysteries of Christ all involve silence. Only in silence can the word of God find a home in us, as it did in Mary, woman of the word and, inseparably, woman of silence" (no. 66). This principle—that without silence one does not hear, does not listen, does not receive a word—applies especially to personal prayer as well as to our liturgies: to facilitate authentic listening, they must also be rich in moments of silence and of non-verbal reception. Saint Augustine's observation is still valid: *Verbo crescente, verba deficient*—"when the word of God increases, the words of men fail" (cf. *Sermo* 288, 5: PL 38, 1307; *Sermo* 120, 2: PL 38, 677). The Gospels often present Jesus, especially at times of crucial decisions, withdrawing to lonely places, away from the crowds and even from the disciples in order to pray in silence and to live his filial relationship with God. Silence can carve out an inner space in our very depths to enable God to dwell there, so that his word will remain within us and love for him take root in our minds and hearts and inspire our life. Hence the first direction: relearning silence, openness to listening, which opens us to the other, to the word of God.

However, there is also a second important connection between silence and prayer. Indeed, it is not only our silence that disposes us to listen to the word of God; in our prayers we often find we are confronted by God's silence, we feel, as it were, let down; it seems to us that God neither listens nor responds. Yet God's silence, as was also the case for Jesus, does not indicate his absence. Christians know well that the Lord is present and listens, even in the darkness of pain, rejection, and loneliness. Jesus reassures his disciples and each one of us that God is well acquainted with our needs at every moment of our life. He teaches the disciples: "In praying do not heap up empty phrases as the Gentiles do; for they think that they will be heard for their many words. Do not be like them, for your Father knows what you need before you ask him" (Mt 6:7–8): an attentive, silent, and open heart is more important than many words. God knows us in our inmost depths, better than we ourselves do, and loves us; and knowing this must suffice. In the Bible, Job's experience is particularly significant in this regard. In a short time this man lost everything: relatives, possessions, friends, and health. It truly seems that God's attitude toward him was one of abandonment, of total silence. Yet in his relationship with God, Job speaks to God, cries out to God; in his prayers, in spite of all, he keeps his faith intact and, in the end, discovers the value of his experience and of God's silence. And thus he can finally conclude, addressing the Creator: "I had heard of you by the hearing of the ear, but now my eye sees you" (Job 42:5): almost all of us know God only through hearsay, and the more open we are to his silence and to our own silence, the more we truly begin to know him. This total trust that opens us to the profound encounter with God developed in silence. Saint Francis Xavier prayed to the Lord, saying: I do not love you because you can give me paradise or condemn me to hell, but because you are my God. I love you because You are You.

As we reach the end of the reflections on Jesus' prayer, certain teachings of the *Catechism of the Catholic Church* spring to mind: "The drama of prayer is fully revealed to us in the Word who became flesh and dwells among us. To seek to understand his prayer through what his witnesses proclaim to us in the Gospel is to approach the holy Lord Jesus as Moses approached the burning bush: first to contemplate him in prayer, then to hear how he teaches us to pray, in order to know how he hears our prayer" (no. 2598). So, how does Jesus teach us to pray? We find a clear answer in the *Compendium of the Catechism of the Catholic Church*: "Jesus teaches us to pray not only with the *Our Father*"—certainly the high point of his instruction on how to pray—"but also when he prays. In this way he teaches us, in addition to the content, the dispositions necessary for every true prayer: purity of heart that seeks the Kingdom and forgives one's enemies, bold and filial faith that goes beyond what we feel and understand, and watchfulness that protects the disciple from temptation" (no. 544).

In going through the Gospels we have seen that concerning our prayers the Lord is conversation partner, friend, witness, and teacher. The newness of our dialogue with God is revealed in Jesus: the filial prayer that the Father expects of his children. And we learn from Jesus that constant prayer helps us to interpret our life, make our decisions, recognize and accept our vocation, discover the talents that God has given us, and do his will daily, the only way to fulfill our life.

Jesus' prayer points out to us, all too often concerned with operational efficacy and the practical results we achieve, that we need to pause, to experience moments of intimacy with God, "detaching ourselves" from the everyday commotion in order to listen, to go to the "root" that sustains and nourishes life. One of the most beautiful moments of Jesus' prayer is precisely when—in order to deal with the illnesses, hardships, and limitations of those who are conversing with him—he turns to the Father in prayer and thereby teaches those around him where to seek the source of hope and salvation. I have already recalled as a moving example Jesus' prayer at the tomb of Lazarus. The Evangelist John recounts: "So they took away the stone. And Jesus lifted up his eyes and said, 'Father, I thank you that you have heard me. I knew that you hear me always, but I have said this on account of the people standing by, that they may believe that you sent me.' When he had said this, he cried with a loud voice, 'Lazarus, come out'" (Jn 11:41–43). However, Jesus reaches the most profound depths in prayer to the Father at the moment of his Passion and his death when he says the extreme "yes" to God's plan and shows how the human will finds its fulfillment precisely in full adherence to the divine will rather than in opposition to it. In Jesus' prayer, in his cry to the Father on the Cross, are summed up "all the troubles, for all time, of humanity enslaved by sin and death, all the petitions and intercessions of salvation history.... Here the Father accepts them and, beyond all hope, answers them by raising his Son. Thus is fulfilled and brought to completion the drama of prayer in the economy of creation and salvation" (*Catechism of the Catholic Church*, no. 2606). Dear brothers and sisters, let us trustingly ask the Lord to grant that we live the journey of our filial prayer learning daily from the only-begotten Son, who became man for our sake, what should be our way of addressing God. Saint Paul's words on Christian life in general also apply to our prayers: "I am sure that neither death, nor life, nor angels, nor principalities, nor things present, nor things to come, nor powers, nor height, nor depth, nor anything else in all creation, will be able to separate us from the love of God in Christ Jesus our Lord" (Rom 8:38–39).

29

Mary and Prayer

WEDNESDAY, 14 MARCH 2012
Saint Peter's Square

Dear Brothers and Sisters,

With today's Catechesis, I would like to begin to talk about prayer in the Acts of the Apostles and in the Letters of Saint Paul. Saint Luke, as we know, presented us with one of the four Gospels, dedicated to the earthly life of Jesus, but he also left us what has been described as the first book on the history of the Church, the Acts of the Apostles. In these two books, one of the recurring elements is precisely prayer, from the prayer of Jesus to that of Mary, of the disciples, of the women, and of the Christian community. The initial path of the Church is punctuated above all by the action of the Holy Spirit, who transforms the Apostles into witnesses of the Risen One to the point of bloodshed, and by the rapid spread of the word of God to the East and to the West. Before the proclamation of the Gospel spreads, however, Luke reports the episode of the Ascension of the Risen One (cf. Acts 1:6–9). The Lord hands over to the disciples the plan of their life, devoted to evangelization, and says: "You shall receive power when the Holy Spirit has come upon you; and you shall be my witnesses in Jerusalem and in all Judea and Samaria and to the end of the earth" (Acts 1:8). In Jerusalem, the Apostles, who have remained eleven in number after the treachery of Judas Iscariot, have gathered in the house to pray, and it is precisely in prayer that they await the gift promised by the Resurrected Christ: the Holy Spirit.

In this context of waiting, situated between the Ascension and Pentecost, Saint Luke mentions Mary, the Mother of Jesus, and her family (v. 14) for the last time. He devoted the beginning of his Gospel to Mary, from the Annunciation by the angel to the birth and childhood of the Son of God made man. With Mary begins the earthly life of Jesus, and with Mary, too, the first steps of the Church begin; in both moments, the atmosphere is one of listening to God, of recollection. This is why I would like to pause today with the prayerful presence of the Virgin in the group of disciples who are the nascent Church. Mary discreetly followed the whole path of her Son in the course of his public life up to the foot of the Cross, and she continues at present to follow, with silent prayer, the path of the Church. At the time of the Annunciation, in the house at Nazareth, Mary receives the angel of God; she is attentive to his words; she welcomes them and responds to the divine plan by manifesting her full availability: "Behold, I am the handmaid of the Lord; let it be to me according to your word" (Lk 1:38). Mary, precisely because of her interior attitude of listening, is capable of interpreting her own history, recognizing with humility that it is the Lord who is acting. In visiting her cousin Elizabeth, she breaks into a prayer of praise and joy, the celebration of divine grace, which has filled her heart and her life, making her the Mother of the Lord (cf. Lk 1:46–55). Praise, thanksgiving, joy: in the canticle of the *Magnificat*, Mary looks not only at what God has worked in her but also at what he has continually accomplished in history. Saint Ambrose, in a famous commentary on the *Magnificat*, invites us to have the same spirit in prayer and writes: "May the soul of Mary dwell in every soul, that it might glorify the Lord; may the spirit of Mary dwell in every spirit, that it might exult in God" (*Expositio Evangelii secundum Lucam* 2, 26: PL 15, 1561).

She is also present in the Cenacle, in Jerusalem, in the "upper room, where [the disciples of Jesus] were staying" (cf. Acts 1:13). In an atmosphere of listening and prayer, the doors open and the disciples begin to proclaim Christ the Lord to all peoples, teaching them to observe all that he commanded (cf. Mt 28:19–20). The stages of Mary's path, from the house in Nazareth via the Cross, where her Son entrusted her to the Apostle John, to the house in Jerusalem, are marked by the capacity to preserve an atmosphere of persevering recollection in order to meditate on each event in the silence of her heart, before God (cf. Lk 2:19–51), and, in meditation before God, also to understand the will of God and to become capable of accepting it interiorly. The presence of the Mother of God with the Eleven, after the Ascension, is not, then, a mere historical reference to some past thing; rather it assumes a significance of great value, because she shares with them what is most precious: the living memory of Jesus, in prayer; she shares that mission of Jesus: to preserve the memory of Jesus and in that way to preserve his presence.

The last mention of Mary in the two writings of Saint Luke takes place on Saturday: the day of God's rest after the Creation, the day of silence after the death of Jesus and the day of waiting for his Resurrection. And the tradition of commemorating the Holy Virgin on Saturday is rooted in this episode. Between the Ascension of the Risen One and the first Christian Pentecost, the Apostles and the Church gather with Mary to await with her the gift of the Holy Spirit, without which one cannot become a witness. She who has already received it in order to bring forth the incarnate Word shares with the whole Church the anticipation of this same gift so that in the heart of each believer "Christ [may] be formed" (cf. Gal 4:19). If there is no Church without Pentecost, neither is there a Pentecost without the Mother of Jesus, for she lived in a unique way what the Church experiences every day under the action of the Holy Spirit. Saint Chromatius of Aquila thus comments on the statement by the Acts of the Apostles: "The Church thus gathers in the room on the upper floor with Mary, the Mother of Jesus, and with his brothers. So one cannot speak of the Church if Mary, the Mother of the Lord, is not present. . . . The Church of Christ is there where the Incarnation of Christ is preached by the Virgin; and where the Apostles, who are the brothers of the Lord, preach, there one hears the Gospel" (*Sermo* 30, 1: SC 164, 135).

The Second Vatican Council wished to emphasize in a particular way this link that is manifested in a visible way in the prayer Mary and the Apostles shared in common, in the same place, in waiting for the Holy Spirit. The dogmatic constitution *Lumen gentium* affirms: "But since it has pleased God not to manifest solemnly the mystery of the salvation of the human race before He would pour forth the Spirit promised by Christ, we see the apostles before the day of Pentecost 'persevering with one mind in prayer with the women and Mary the Mother of Jesus, and with His brethren' (Acts 1:14), and Mary by her prayers imploring the gift of the Spirit, who had already overshadowed her in the Annunciation" (no. 59). The privileged place of Mary is the Church in which she is "hailed as a pre-eminent and singular member and as its type and excellent exemplar in faith and charity" (no. 53).

To venerate the Mother of Jesus in the Church, then, means to learn from her to be a community that prays: this is one of the essential observations of the first description of the Christian community given in the Acts of the Apostles (cf. 2:42). Often prayer is dictated by situations of difficulty, by personal problems that lead one to appeal to the Lord in order to find light, comfort, and help. Mary invites us to expand the dimensions of prayer, to turn to God not only in need and not only for oneself, but in a unanimous, persevering, faithful way, with "one heart and soul" (cf. Acts 4:32).

Dear friends, human life goes through various transitional phases, which are often difficult and demanding, which require urgent decisions, renunciations, and sacrifices. The Mother of Jesus was placed by the Lord in decisive moments of salvation history, and she always knew how to respond with complete availability, the fruit of a profound bond with God that had matured in assiduous and intense prayer. Between the Friday of the Passion and the Sunday of the Resurrection, it was to her that the Beloved Disciple, and with him the whole community of disciples, was entrusted (cf. Jn 19:26). Between the Ascension and Pentecost, she was *with* and *in* the Church in prayer (cf. Acts 1:14). Mother of God and Mother of the Church, Mary fulfills this motherhood until the end of history. Let us entrust to her each stage of our personal and ecclesial history, not least that of our final departure. May Mary teach us the necessity of prayer and show us that it is only through a constant, intimate, wholly loving bond with her Son that we can leave "our house", ourselves, with courage in order to reach the ends of the earth and proclaim everywhere the Lord Jesus, Savior of the world.

30

Prayer and the Christian Community

WEDNESDAY, 18 APRIL 2012

Saint Peter's Square

Dear Brothers and Sisters,

After the great celebrations let us now return to the Catecheses on Prayer. At the Audience before Holy Week we reflected on the figure of the Blessed Virgin Mary and her prayerful presence among the Apostles while they were waiting for the descent of the Holy Spirit. The Church took her first steps in an atmosphere of prayer. Pentecost is not an isolated episode because the Holy Spirit's presence and action never cease to guide and encourage the Christian community as it journeys on.

Indeed, in addition to recounting the event of the great outpouring in the Upper Room which occurred fifty days after Easter (cf. Acts 2:1–13), Saint Luke mentions in the Acts of the Apostles other extraordinary occasions on which the Holy Spirit burst in and which recur in the Church's history. And today I would like to reflect on what has been defined as the "little Pentecost", which took place at the height of a difficult phase in the life of the nascent Church. The Acts of the Apostles tell that after the healing of a paralytic at the temple of Jerusalem (cf. Acts 3:1–10), Peter and John were arrested (cf. Acts 4:1) for proclaiming Jesus'

Resurrection to all the people (cf. Acts 3:11–26). They were released after a hasty trial, joined their brethren, and told them what they had been obliged to undergo on account of the witness they had borne to Jesus, the Risen One. At that moment, Luke says, "they lifted their voices together to God" (Acts 4:24). Here Saint Luke records the Church's most extensive prayer in the New Testament, at the end of which, as we have heard, "the place in which they were gathered together was shaken; and they were all filled with the Holy Spirit and spoke the word of God with boldness" (Acts 4:31).

Before reflecting on this beautiful prayer, let us take note of an important basic attitude: when the first Christian community is confronted by dangers, difficulties, and threats, it does not attempt to work out how to react, find strategies, and defend itself or what measures to adopt; rather, when it is put to the test, the community starts to pray and makes contact with God. And what are the features of this prayer? It is a unanimous, concordant prayer of the entire community which reacts to persecution because of Jesus. In the original Greek, Saint Luke uses the word "*homothumadon*"—"all these with one accord", "in agreement", a term that appears in other parts of the Acts of the Apostles to emphasize this persevering, harmonious prayer (cf. Acts 1:14; 2:46). This harmony was the fundamental element of the first community and must always be fundamental to the Church. Thus it was not only the prayer prayed by Peter and John, who were in danger, but the prayer of the entire community, since what the two Apostles were experiencing concerned, not them alone, but the whole of the Church. In facing the persecution it suffered for the cause of Jesus, not only was the community neither frightened nor divided but it was also deeply united in prayer, as one person, to invoke the Lord. I would say that this is the first miracle which is worked when because of their faith believers are put to the test. Their unity, rather than being jeopardized, is strengthened because it is sustained by steadfast prayer. The Church must not fear the persecutions to which she has been subjected throughout her history but must always trust, like Jesus at Gethsemane, in the presence, help, and power of God, invoked in prayer.

Let us take a further step: what does the Christian community ask God at this moment of trial? It does not ask for the safety of life in the face of persecution or that the Lord get even with those who imprisoned Peter and John; it asks only that it be granted "to speak [his] word with all boldness" (Acts 4:29); in other words, it prays that it may not lose the courage of faith, the courage to proclaim faith. First, however, it seeks to understand in depth what has occurred, to interpret events in the light of faith, and it does so precisely through the word of God which enables us to decipher the reality of the world. In the prayer it raises to the Lord, the community begins by recording and invoking God's omnipotence and immensity: "Sovereign Lord, who did make the heaven and the earth and the sea and everything in them" (Acts 4:24). It is the invocation to the Creator: we know that all things come from him, that all things are in his hands. It is knowledge of this which gives us certainty and courage: everything comes from him, everything is in his hands.

The prayer then goes on to recognize how God acted in the past—so it begins with the creation and continues through history—how he was close to his people, showing himself to be a God concerned with man, a God who did not withdraw, who did not abandon man, his creature; and here Psalm 2 is explicitly cited. It is in this light that the difficult situation the Church was going through at the time should be read. Psalm 2 celebrates the enthronement of the King of Judaea, but refers prophetically to the Coming of the Messiah, against whom human rebellion, persecution and abuse can do nothing: "Why do the nations conspire, and the people plot in vain? The kings of the earth set themselves, and the rulers take counsel together, against the Lord and his anointed" (Ps 2:1–2; cf. Acts 4:25). The Psalm about the Messiah already stated this prophetically, and this uprising of the powerful against God's power is characteristic throughout history.

It is precisely by reading Sacred Scripture, which is the word of God, that the community can say to God in prayer: "truly in this city there were gathered together against your holy servant Jesus, whom you did anoint, . . . to do whatever your hand and your plan had predestined to take place" (Acts 4:27). What happened is interpreted in the light of Christ, which is also the key to understanding persecution, and the Cross, which is always the key to the Resurrection. The opposition to Jesus, his Passion, and his death are reinterpreted through Psalm 2, as the actuation of God the Father's project for the world's salvation. And here we also find the meaning of the experience of persecution through which the first Christian community was living. This first community is not a mere association but a community that lives in Christ, so what happens to it is part of God's plan. Just as it happened to Jesus, the disciples also meet with opposition, misunderstanding, and persecution. In prayer, meditation on Sacred Scripture in the light of Christ's mystery helps us to interpret the reality present within the history of salvation which God works in the world, always in his own way. This is precisely why the request to God that the first Christian community of Jerusalem formulated in a prayer does not ask to be protected or to be spared trials and hardship. It is not a prayer for success but only to be able to proclaim the word of God with "*parrhesia*", that is, with boldness, freedom, and courage (cf. Acts 4:29).

Then there is the additional request that this proclamation may be guided by God's hand so that healing, signs, and wonders may be performed (cf. Acts 4:30), in other words, that God's goodness may be visible as a power that transforms reality, that changes peoples' hearts, minds, and lives and brings the radical newness of the Gospel. At the end of the prayer, Saint Luke notes, "the place in which they were gathered together was shaken; and they were all filled with the Holy Spirit and spoke the word of God with boldness" (Acts 4:31). The place shook, that is, faith has the power to transform the earth and the world. The same Spirit who spoke through Psalm 2 in the prayer of the Church bursts into the house and fills the hearts of all those who have invoked the Lord. This is the fruit of the unanimous prayer that the Christian community raises to God: the outpouring of the Spirit, a gift of the Risen One that sustains and guides the free and courageous proclamation of God's word, which impels the disciples of the Lord to go out fearlessly to take the Good News to the ends of the world.

We too, dear brothers and sisters, must be able to ponder the events of our daily life in prayer, in order to seek their deep meaning. And like the first Christian community, let us too let ourselves be illuminated by the word of God, so that, through meditation on Sacred Scripture, we can learn to see that God is present in our life, present also and especially in difficult moments, and that all things—even those that are incomprehensible—are part of a superior plan of love in which the final victory over evil, over sin, and over death is truly that of goodness, of grace, of life, and of God.

Just as prayer helped the first Christian community, prayer also helps us to interpret our personal and collective history in the most just and faithful perspective, that of God. And let us too renew our request for the gift of the Holy Spirit, which warms hearts and enlightens minds, in order to recognize how the Lord hears our prayers, in accordance with his will of love and not with our own ideas. Guided by the Spirit of Jesus Christ, we will be able to live with serenity, courage, and joy every situation in life and with Saint Paul boast: "we rejoice in our sufferings, knowing that suffering produces endurance, and endurance produces character, and character produces hope", that hope which "does not disappoint us, because God's love has been poured into our hearts through the Holy Spirit who has been given to us" (Rom 5:3–5).

31

The Primacy of Prayer and the Word of God (Acts 6:1–7)

WEDNESDAY, 25 APRIL 2012
Saint Peter's Square

Dear Brothers and Sisters,

In our last Catechesis I explained that from the outset the Church has had to face unexpected situations on her journey, new issues and emergencies to which she has sought to respond in the light of faith, letting herself be guided by the Holy Spirit. Today I would like to pause to reflect on another of these situations, on a serious problem that the first Christian community of Jerusalem was obliged to face and to solve, as Saint Luke tells us in the sixth chapter of the Acts of the Apostles, concerning pastoral charity to lonely people and those in need of assistance and help. This is not a secondary matter for the Church and at that time risked creating divisions in the Church; the number of disciples, in fact, continued to increase, but the Greek-speaking began to complain about those who spoke Hebrew because their widows were left out of the daily distribution (cf. Acts 6:1).

To face this urgent matter, which concerned a fundamental aspect of community life, namely, charity to the weak, the poor, and the defenseless and justice, the Apostles summoned the entire group of disciples. In that moment of pastoral emergency the Apostles' discernment stands out. They were facing the primary need to proclaim God's word in accordance with the Lord's mandate, but—even if this was a priority of the Church—they considered with equal gravity the duty of charity and justice, that is, the duty to help widows and poor people and, in response to the commandment of Jesus: love one another as I have loved you (cf. Jn 15:12, 17), to provide lovingly for their brothers and sisters in need. So it was that difficulties arose in the two activities that must coexist in the Church—the proclamation of the word, the primacy of God, and concrete charity, justice—and it was necessary to find a solution so that there would be room for both, for their necessary relationship. The Apostles' reflection is very clear; they say, as we heard: "It is not right that we should give up preaching the word of God to serve tables. Therefore, brethren, pick out from among you seven men of good repute, full of the Spirit and of wisdom, whom we may appoint to this duty. But we will devote ourselves to prayer and to the ministry of the word" (Acts 6:2–4).

Two points stand out: first, since that moment a ministry of charity has existed in the Church. The Church must not only proclaim the word but must also put the word—which is charity and truth—into practice. And, the second point: these men must not only enjoy a good reputation but also they must be filled with the Holy Spirit and with wisdom; in other words, they cannot merely be organizers who know what "to do", but must "act" in a spirit of faith with God's enlightenment, with wisdom of heart. Hence their role—although it is above all a practical one—has nonetheless also a spiritual function. Charity and justice are not only social but also spiritual actions, accomplished in the light of the Holy Spirit. We can thus say that the Apostles confronted this situation with great responsibility. They took the following decision: seven men were chosen; the Apostles prayed the Holy Spirit to grant them strength and then laid their hands on the seven so that they might dedicate themselves in a special way to this ministry of charity.

Thus in the life of the Church, the first steps she took, in a certain way, reflected what had happened in Jesus' public life at Martha and Mary's house in Bethany. Martha was completely taken up with the service of hospitality to offer to Jesus and his disciples; Mary, on the contrary, devoted herself to listening to the Lord's word (cf. Lk 10:38–42). In neither case were the moments of prayer, of listening to God, and daily activity, the exercise of charity, in opposition. Jesus' reminder, "Martha, Martha, you are anxious and troubled about many things; one thing is needful. Mary has chosen the good portion, which shall not be taken away from her" (Lk 10:41–42), and, likewise, the Apostles' reflection: "We will devote ourselves to prayer and to the ministry of the word" (Acts 6:4), show the priority we must give to God. I do not wish here to enter into the interpretation of this Martha-Mary passage. In any case, activity undertaken to help one's neighbor, "the other", is not to be condemned, but it is essential to stress the need for it to be imbued also with the spirit of contemplation. Moreover, Saint Augustine says that this reality of Mary is a vision of our situation from heaven, so on earth we can never possess it completely, but a little anticipation must be present in all our activities. Contemplation of God must also be present. We must not lose ourselves in pure activism but always let ourselves also be penetrated in our activities by the light of the word of God and thereby learn true charity, true service to others, which does not need many things—it certainly needs the necessary things—but needs above all our heartfelt affection and the light of God.

In commenting on the episode of Martha and Mary, Saint Ambrose urges his faithful and us too: "Let us too seek to have what cannot be taken from us, dedicating diligent, not distracted, attention to the Lord's word. The seeds of the heavenly word are blown away if they are sown along the roadside. May the wish to know be an incentive to you too, as it was to Mary; this is the greatest and most perfect act." And he added that "attention to the ministry must not distract from knowledge of the heavenly word" through prayer (*Expositio Evangelii secundum Lucam* VII, 85: PL 15, 1720). Saints have therefore experienced a profound unity of life between prayer and action, between total love for God and love for their brethren. Saint Bernard, who is a model of harmony between contemplation and hard work, in his book *De consideratione*, addressed to Pope Innocent II to offer him some reflections on his ministry, insists precisely on the importance of inner recollection, of prayer to defend oneself from the dangers of being hyperactive, whatever our condition and whatever the task to be carried out. Saint Bernard says that all too often too much work and a frenetic life-style end by hardening the heart and causing the spirit to suffer (cf. II, 3).

His words are a precious reminder to us today, used as we are to evaluating everything with the criterion of productivity and efficiency. The passage from the Acts of the Apostles reminds us of the importance—without a doubt a true and proper ministry is created—of devotion to daily activities which should be carried out with responsibility and dedication and also our need for God, for his guidance, for his light, which gives us strength and hope. Without daily prayer lived with fidelity, our acts are empty, they lose their profound soul and are reduced to being mere activism which in the end leaves us dissatisfied. There is a beautiful invocation of the Christian tradition to be recited before any other activity which says: "*Actiones nostras, quæsumus, Domine, aspirando præveni et adiuvando prosequere, ut cuncta nostra oratio et operatio a te semper incipiat, et per te coepta finiatur*"; that is, "Inspire our actions, Lord, and accompany them with your help, so that our every word and action may always begin and end in you." Every step in our life, every action, of the Church too, must be taken before God, in the light of his word.

In last Wednesday's Catechesis I emphasized the unanimous prayer of the first Christian community in times of trial and explained how in prayer itself, in meditation on Sacred Scripture, it was able to understand the events that were happening. When prayer is nourished by the word of God, we can see reality with new eyes, with the eyes of faith and the Lord, who speaks to the mind and the heart and gives new light to the journey at every moment and in every situation. We believe in the power of the word of God and of prayer. Even the difficulties that the Church was encountering as she faced the problem of service to the poor, the issue of charity, was overcome in prayer, in the light of God, of the Holy Spirit. The Apostles did not limit themselves to ratifying the choice of Stephen and the other men, but "they prayed and laid their hands upon them" (Acts 6:6). The Evangelist was once again to recall these gestures on the occasion of the election of Paul and Barnabas, where we read: "after fasting and praying they laid their hands on them and sent them off" (Acts 13:3). He confirms again that the practical service of charity is a spiritual service. Both these realities must go hand in hand.

With the act of the laying on of hands, the Apostles conferred a special ministry on seven men so that they might be granted the corresponding grace. The emphasis on prayer—"after praying"—they say, is important because it highlights the gesture's spiritual dimension; it is not merely a question of conferring an office as happens in a public organization, but it is an ecclesial event in which the Holy Spirit appropriates seven men chosen by the Church, consecrating them in the Truth that is Jesus Christ: he is the silent protagonist, present during the imposition of hands so that the chosen ones may be transformed by his power and sanctified in order to face the practical challenges, the pastoral challenges. And the emphasis on prayer also reminds us that the response to the Lord's choice and the allocation of every ministry in the Church stem solely from a close relationship with God, nurtured daily.

Dear brothers and sisters, the pastoral problem that induced the Apostles to choose and to lay their hands on seven men charged with the service of charity, so that they themselves might be able to devote themselves to prayer and to preaching the word, also indicates to us the primacy of prayer and of the word of God which, however, then result in pastoral action. For pastors, this is the first and most valuable form of service for the flock entrusted to them. If the lungs of prayer and of the word of God do not nourish the breath of our spiritual life, we risk being overwhelmed by countless everyday things: prayer is the breath of the soul and of life. And there is another precious reminder that I would like to underscore: in the relationships with God, in listening to his word, in dialogue with God, even when we may be in the silence of a church or of our room, we are united in the Lord to a great many brothers and sisters in faith, like an ensemble of musical instruments which, in spite of their individuality, raise to God one great symphony of intercession, of thanksgiving and praise.

32

The Prayer of the First Christian Martyr (Acts 7:53–60)

WEDNESDAY, 2 MAY 2012
Saint Peter's Square

Dear Brothers and Sisters,

In our recent Catecheses we have seen how through personal and community prayer the interpretation of and meditation on Sacred Scripture open us to listening to God, who speaks to us and instills light in us so that we may understand the present. Today, I would like to talk about the testimony and prayer of the Church's first martyr, Saint Stephen, one of the seven men chosen to carry out the service of charity for the needy. At the moment of his martyrdom, recounted in the Acts of the Apostles, the fruitful relationship between the word of God and prayer is once again demonstrated.

Stephen is brought before the council, before the Sanhedrin, where he is accused of declaring that "this Jesus of Nazareth will destroy this place, [the temple] and will change the customs which Moses delivered to us" (Acts 6:14). During his public life Jesus had effectively foretold the destruction of the temple of Jerusalem: you will "destroy this temple, and in three days I will raise it up" (Jn 2:19). But, as the

Evangelist John remarked, "he spoke of the temple of his body. When therefore he was raised from the dead, his disciples remembered that he had said this; and they believed the Scripture and the word which Jesus had spoken" (Jn 2:21–22).

Stephen's speech to the council, the longest in the Acts of the Apostles, develops on this very prophecy of Jesus, who is the new temple, inaugurates the new worship, and, with his immolation on the Cross, replaces the ancient sacrifices. Stephen wishes to demonstrate how unfounded is the accusation leveled against him of subverting the Mosaic Law and describes his view of salvation history and of the covenant between God and man. In this way he reinterprets the whole of the biblical narrative, the itinerary contained in Sacred Scripture, in order to show that it leads to the "place" of the definitive presence of God that is Jesus Christ and, in particular, his Passion, death, and Resurrection. In this perspective Stephen also interprets his being a disciple of Jesus, following him even to martyrdom. Meditation on Sacred Scripture thus enables him to understand his mission, his life, his present. Stephen is guided in this by the light of the Holy Spirit and by his close relationship with the Lord, so that the members of the Sanhedrin saw that his face was "like the face of an angel" (Acts 6:15). This sign of divine assistance is reminiscent of Moses' face, which shone after his encounter with God when he came down from Mount Sinai (cf. Ex 34:29–35; 2 Cor 3:7–8).

In his discourse, Stephen starts with the call of Abraham, a pilgrim bound for the land pointed out to him by God which he possessed only at the level of a promise. He then speaks of Joseph, sold by his brothers but helped and liberated by God, and continues with Moses, who becomes an instrument of God in order to set his people free but also and several times comes up against his own people's rejection. In these events narrated in Sacred Scripture to which Stephen demonstrates he listens religiously, God always emerges, who never tires of reaching out to man in spite of frequently meeting with obstinate opposition. And this happens in the past, in the present, and in the future. So it is that throughout the Old Testament he sees the prefiguration of the life of Jesus himself, the Son of God made flesh, who—like the ancient Fathers—encounters obstacles, rejection, and death. Stephen then refers to Joshua, David, and Solomon, whom he mentions in relation to the building of the temple of Jerusalem, and ends with the word of the Prophet Isaiah (66:1–2): "Heaven is my throne, and earth my footstool. What house will you build for me, says the Lord, or what is the place of my rest? Did not my hand make all these things?" (Acts 7:49–50). In his meditation on God's action in salvation history, by highlighting the perennial temptation to reject God and his action, he affirms that Jesus is the Righteous One foretold by the prophets; God himself has made himself uniquely and definitively present in him: Jesus is the "place" of true worship. Stephen does not deny the importance of the temple for a certain period, but he stresses that "the Most High does not dwell in houses made with hands" (Acts 7:48). The new, true temple in which God dwells is his Son, who has taken human flesh; it is the humanity of Christ, the Risen One, who gathers the peoples together and unites them in the sacrament of his Body and his Blood. The description of the temple as "not made by human hands" is also found in the theology of Saint Paul and in the Letter to the Hebrews; the Body of Jesus, which he assumed in order to offer himself as a sacrificial victim for the expiation of sins, is the new temple of God, the place of the presence of the living God; in him, God and man, God and the world are truly in touch: Jesus takes upon himself all the sins of mankind in order to bring it into the love of God and to "consummate" it in this love. Drawing close to the Cross, entering into communion with Christ, means entering this transformation. And this means coming into contact with God, entering the true temple.

Stephen's life and words are suddenly cut short by the stoning, but his martyrdom itself is the fulfillment of his life and message: he becomes one with Christ. Thus his meditation on God's action in history, on the divine word which in Jesus found complete fulfillment, becomes participation in the very prayer on the Cross. Indeed, before dying, Stephen cries out: "Lord Jesus, receive my spirit" (Acts 7:59), making his own the words of Psalm 31[30]:6 and repeating Jesus' last words on Calvary: "Father, into your hands I commit my spirit" (Lk 23:46). Lastly, like Jesus, he cries out with a loud voice facing those who are stoning him: "Lord, do not hold this sin against them" (Acts 7:60). Let us note that if, on the one hand, Stephen's prayer echoes Jesus', on the other, it is addressed to someone else, for the entreaty is to the Lord himself, namely, to Jesus, whom he contemplates in glory at the right hand of the Father: "Behold, I see the heavens opened, and the Son of man standing at the right hand of God" (v. 56).

Dear brothers and sisters, Saint Stephen's witness gives us several instructions for our prayers and for our lives. Let us ask ourselves: where did this first Christian martyr find the strength to face his persecutors and to go so far as to give himself? The answer is simple: from his relationship with God, from his communion with Christ, from meditation on the history of salvation, from perceiving God's action which reached its crowning point in Jesus Christ. Our prayers, too, must be nourished by listening to the word of God, in communion with Jesus and his Church.

A second element: Saint Stephen sees the figure and mission of Jesus foretold in the history of the loving relationship between God and man. He—the Son of God—is the temple that is not "made with hands" in which the presence of God the Father became so close as to enter our human flesh to bring us to God, to open the gates of heaven. Our prayer, therefore, must be the contemplation of Jesus at the right hand of God, of Jesus as the Lord of our, or my, daily life. In him, under the guidance of the Holy Spirit, we too can address God and be truly in touch with God, with the faith and abandonment of children who turn to a Father who loves them infinitely.

33

Prayer and Saint Peter

WEDNESDAY, 9 MAY 2012
Saint Peter's Square

Dear Brothers and Sisters,

Today I would like to touch upon the last episode in the life of Saint Peter recorded in the Acts of the Apostles, his imprisonment by order of Herod Agrippa and his release through the marvelous intervention of the angel of the Lord on the eve of his trial in Jerusalem (cf. Acts 12:1–17).

The narrative is once again marked by the prayer of the Church. Saint Luke writes: "So Peter was kept in prison; but earnest prayer for him was made to God by the church" (Acts 12:5). And, after Peter miraculously left the prison, on the occasion of his visit to the house of Mary, the mother of John also called Mark, it tells us "many were gathered together and were praying" (Acts 12:12). Between these two important observations, which illustrate the attitude of the Christian community in the face of danger and persecution is recounted the detainment and release of Peter, which involved the entire night. The strength of the unceasing prayer of the Church rises to God, and the Lord listens and performs an unheard of and unexpected deliverance, sending his angel.

The account reminds us of the great elements during Israel's deliverance from captivity in Egypt, the Hebrew Passover. As happened in that major event, here also, the angel of the Lord performs the primary action that frees Peter. And the actions of the Apostle—who is asked to rise quickly, put on his belt, and gird his loins—repeat those of the Chosen People on the night of their deliverance through God's intervention, when they were invited to eat the lamb quickly with their belts fastened, sandals on their feet, and their staffs in their hands, ready to leave the country (cf. Ex 12:11). Thus, Peter could exclaim: "Now I am sure that the Lord has sent his angel and rescued me from the hand of Herod" (Acts 12:11). The angel recalls not only the deliverance of Israel from Egypt but also the Resurrection of Christ. The Acts of the Apostles recount: "and behold, an angel of the Lord appeared, and a light shone in the cell; and he struck Peter on the side and woke him" (Acts 12:7). The light that fills the prison cell and also the same action to awaken the Apostle refer to the liberating light of the Passover of the Lord that triumphs over the darkness of night and evil. Finally, the invitation to "Wrap your mantle around you and follow me" (Acts 12:8) echoes the words of the initial call of Jesus in our hearts (cf. Mk 1:17), repeated after the Resurrection on Lake Tiberias, where on two occasions the Lord says to Peter, "Follow me" (Jn 21:19,22). It is a pressing call to follow him. Only by coming out of ourselves to walk with the Lord and by doing his will can we live in true freedom.

I would also like to highlight another aspect of Peter's attitude in prison. In fact, we note that while the Christian community is praying earnestly for him, Peter "was sleeping" (Acts 12:6). In a critical situation of serious danger, it is an attitude that might seem strange but, instead, denotes tranquility and faith. He trusts God. He knows he is surrounded by the solidarity and prayers of his own people and completely abandons himself into the hands of the Lord. So it must be with our prayer, assiduous, in solidarity with others, fully trusting that God knows us in our depths and takes care of us to the point that Jesus says "even the hairs of your head are all numbered. Fear not, therefore" (Mt 10:30–31). Peter lives through that night of imprisonment and release from prison as a moment of his discipleship with the Lord, who overcomes the darkness of night and frees him from the chains of slavery and the threat of death. His is a miraculous release, marked by various accurately described steps, guided by the angel, despite the monitoring of the guards, through the first and second guard posts, up to the iron gate that leads into the city, with the gate opening by itself in front of them (cf. Acts 12:10). Peter and the angel of the Lord make their way together down a stretch of the street until, coming back to himself, the Apostle realizes that the Lord has really freed him and, after having reflected on the matter, goes to the house of Mary, the mother of Mark, where many disciples are gathered in prayer. Once again the community's response to difficulty and danger is to trust in God, strengthening the relationship with him.

Here it seems useful to recall another difficult situation that the early Christian community experienced. Saint James speaks of it in his Letter. It is a community in crisis, in difficulty, not so much because of persecution, but because of the jealousies and contentions within it (cf. Jas 3:14–16). The Apostle wonders about the reason for this situation. He finds two primary motives. The first is that they let themselves be carried away by their emotions, by the dictates of their own interests, by selfishness (cf. Jas 4:1–2a). The second is the lack of prayer—"you do not ask" (Jas

4:2b)—or the presence of a kind of a prayer that cannot qualify as such—"You ask and do not receive, because you ask wrongly, to spend it on your passions" (Jas 4:3). This situation would change, according to Saint James, if the community all spoke together with God, truly praying assiduously and unanimously. In fact, even talk about God runs the risk of losing inner strength and testimony dries up if they are not animated, sustained, and accompanied by prayer, by the continuity of a living dialogue with the Lord. An important reminder also for us and our communities, both the small ones like the family and the bigger ones like the parish, the diocese, and the entire Church. And it makes me think that they prayed in this community of Saint James, but prayed wrongly, solely for their own passions. We must always learn again how to pray properly, truly pray, moving toward God and not toward our own good.

On the other hand, the community that is concerned about Peter's imprisonment is a community that truly prays the entire night, deeply united. And it is overwhelming joy that fills the hearts of all when the Apostle unexpectedly knocks at the door. It is joy and amazement in light of the actions of the God who listens. Thus, from the Church arises the prayer for Peter, and to the Church he returns to tell "how the Lord had brought him out of the prison" (Acts 12:17). In that Church where he is set as a rock (cf. Mt 16:18), Peter recounts his "Passover" of liberation. He experiences true freedom in following Jesus. He is enveloped in the radiant light of the Resurrection and can therefore testify to the point of martyrdom that the Lord is risen and "has sent his angel and rescued me from the hand of Herod" (Acts 12:11). The martyrdom he was to suffer in Rome will definitively unite him with Christ, who had told him: when you are old, another will take you where you do not want to go, to show by what kind of death he was to glorify God (cf. Jn 21:18–19).

Dear brothers and sisters, the episode of the liberation of Peter as told by Luke tells us that the Church, each of us, goes through the night of trial. But it is unceasing vigilance in prayer that sustains us. I too, from the first moment of my election as the Successor of Saint Peter, have always felt supported by your prayer, by the prayers of the Church, especially in moments of great difficulty. My heartfelt thanks. With constant and faithful prayer the Lord releases us from the chains, guides us through every night of imprisonment that can gnaw at our hearts. He gives us the peace of heart to face the difficulties of life, persecution, opposition, and even rejection. Peter's experience shows us the power of prayer. And the Apostle, though in chains, feels calm in the certainty of never being alone. The community is praying for him. The Lord is near him. He indeed knows that Christ's "power is made perfect in weakness" (2 Cor 12:9). Constant and unanimous prayer is also a precious tool to overcome any trial that may arise on life's journey, because it is being deeply united to God that allows us also to be united to others.

34

The Holy Spirit as the Master of Prayer

WEDNESDAY, 16 MAY 2012

Saint Peter's Square

Dear Brothers and Sisters,

In recent Catecheses we reflected on prayer in the Acts of the Apostles; today I would like to begin to speak about prayer in the Letters of Saint Paul, the Apostle to the Gentiles. First of all, I would like to note that it is by no accident that his Letters open and close with expressions of prayer: at the beginning, thanksgiving and praise; and at the end, the hope that the grace of God may guide the path of the community to whom the Letter is addressed. Between the opening formula: "I thank my God through Jesus Christ" (Rom 1:8), and his final wish: "The grace of the Lord Jesus be with you all" (1 Cor 16:23), the Apostle's letters unfold. Saint Paul's prayer is one which manifests itself in a great many ways that move from thanksgiving to blessing, from praise to petitions and intercessions, from hymns to supplication. He uses a variety of expressions which demonstrate how prayer concerns and penetrates every one of life's situations, whether they be personal or of the communities whom he is addressing.

One element that the Apostle would have us understand is that prayer should not be seen simply as a good deed done by us to God, our own action. It is, above all, a gift, the fruit of the living presence, the life-giving presence of the Father and of Jesus Christ in us. In the Letter to the Romans, he writes: "Likewise the Spirit helps us in our weakness; for we do not know how to pray as we ought, but the Spirit himself intercedes for us with sighs too deep for words" (8:26). And we know how true it is when the Apostle says: "we do not know how to pray as we ought." We want to pray, but God is distant; we do not have the words, the language, to speak with God, not even the thought. We can only open ourselves, set our time at the disposal of God, waiting for him to help us enter into true dialogue. The Apostle says: this very lack of words, this absence of words, even the desire to enter into contact with God is a prayer that the Holy Spirit not only understands, but carries, interprets, to God. It is precisely our weakness which becomes, through the Holy Spirit, true prayer, true contact with God. The Holy Spirit is almost the interpreter who makes God and us ourselves understand what we want to say.

In prayer we experience, more so than in other dimensions of life, our weakness, our poverty, our creatureliness, because we stand before the omnipotence and the transcendence of God. And the more we progress in listening and in dialogue with God, for prayer becomes the daily breath of our soul, the more we perceive the meaning of our limits, not just before the concrete situations of every day, but in our relationship with the Lord, too. Growing within us is the need to trust, to trust ever more in him; we understand that "we do not know how to pray as we ought" (Rom 8:26). And it is the Holy Spirit who helps us in our incapacity, who illuminates our minds and warms our hearts, guiding us to turn to God. For Saint Paul, prayer is above all the work of the Spirit in our humanity, taking charge of our weakness and transforming us from men attached to the material world into spiritual men. In the First Letter to the Corinthians he writes: "Now we have received not the spirit of the world, but the Spirit which is from God, that we might understand the gifts bestowed on us by God. And we impart this in words not taught by human wisdom but taught by the Spirit, interpreting spiritual truths to those who possess the Spirit" (2:12–13). By his dwelling in our human frailty, the Holy Spirit changes us, intercedes for us, leads us toward the heights of God (cf. Rom 8:26).

With this presence of the Holy Spirit, our union with Christ is realized, for it is the Spirit of the Son of God in whom we are made children. Saint Paul speaks of the Spirit of Christ (cf. Rom 8:9), and not only of the Spirit of God. Clearly: if Christ is the Son of God, his Spirit is also the Spirit of God, and thus if the Spirit of God, the Spirit of Christ, has already become very close to us in the Son of God and the Son of man, the Spirit of God too becomes a human spirit and touches us; we can enter into the communion of the Spirit. It is as if he said that not only God the Father was made visible in the Incarnation of the Son, but also the Spirit of God is manifest in the life and action of Jesus, of Jesus Christ who lived, was crucified, died, and rose again. The Apostle reminds us that "No one can say 'Jesus is Lord' except by the Holy Spirit" (1 Cor 12:3). Therefore, the Spirit directs our heart toward Jesus Christ, in such a way that "it is no longer we who live, but Christ who lives in us" (cf. Gal 2:20). In his *De sacramentis*, reflecting on the Eucharist, Saint Ambrose says: "Whoever is drunk of the Spirit is rooted in Christ" (5, 3, 12: PL 16, 450).

And now I would like to underline three consequences in Christian life when we let work within us, not the spirit of the world, but the Spirit of Christ as the interior principle of our entire action.

First, with prayer animated by the Spirit we are enabled to abandon and overcome every form of fear and slavery, living the authentic freedom of the children of God. Without prayer which every day nourishes our being in Christ, in an intimacy which progressively grows, we find ourselves in the state described by Saint Paul in his Letter to the Romans: we do, not the good we want, but the evil we do not want (cf. Rom 7:19). And this is the expression of the alienation of human beings, of the destruction of our freedom, the circumstances of our being because of original sin: we want the good that we do not do, and we do what we do not want to do: evil. The Apostle wants to make us understand that it is not primarily our will that frees us from these conditions, nor even the law, but the Holy Spirit. And since "where the Spirit of the Lord is, there is freedom" (2 Cor 3:17), in prayer we experience the freedom given by the Spirit: an authentic freedom, which is freedom from evil and sin for the good and for life, for God. The freedom of the Spirit, Saint Paul continues, is never identified with licentiousness or with the possibility to choose evil, but rather with "the fruit of the Spirit . . . love, joy, peace, patience, kindness, goodness, faithfulness, gentleness, self-control" (Gal 5:22–23a). This is true freedom: actually to be able to follow our desire for good, for true joy, for communion with God and to be free from the oppression of circumstances that pull us in other directions.

A second consequence occurs in our life when we let work within us the Spirit of Christ and when the very relationship with God becomes so profound that no other reality or situation affects it. We understand that with prayer we are not liberated from trials and suffering, but we can live through them in union with Christ, with his suffering, in the hope of also participating in his glory (cf. Rom 8:17). Many times, in our prayer, we ask God to be freed from physical and spiritual evil, and we do it with great trust. However, often we have the impression of not being heard, and we may well feel discouraged and fail to persevere. In reality, there is no human cry that is not heard by God, and it is precisely in constant and faithful prayer that we comprehend with Saint Paul that "the sufferings of this present time are not worth comparing with the glory that is to be revealed to us" (Rom 8:18). Prayer does not exempt us from trial and suffering; indeed—Saint Paul says—we "groan inwardly as we wait for adoption as sons, the redemption of our bodies" (Rom 8:23). He says that prayer does not exempt us from suffering, but prayer does permit us to live through it and face it with a new strength, with the confidence of Jesus, who—according to the Letter to the Hebrews—"In the days of his flesh, ... offered up prayers and supplications, with loud cries and tears, to him [God] who was able to save him from death, and he was heard for his godly fear" (5:7). The answer of God the Father to the Son, to his loud cries and tears, was not freedom from suffering, from the Cross, from death, but a much greater fulfillment, an answer much more profound; through the Cross and death God responded with the Resurrection of the Son, with new life. Prayer animated by the Holy Spirit leads us, too, to live every day a journey of life with its trials and sufferings, with the fullness of hope, with trust in God who answers us as he answered the Son.

And, the third consequence, the prayer of the believer opens also to the dimensions of mankind and of all creation, in the expectation that "creation waits with eager longing for the revealing of the sons of God" (Rom 8:19).

This means that prayer, sustained by the Spirit of Christ speaking in the depths of each one of us, does not stay closed in on itself. It is never just prayer for me, but opens itself to sharing the suffering of our time, of others. It becomes intercession for others, and thus deliverance from myself, a channel of hope for all creation, the expression of that love of God which is poured into our hearts through the Spirit whom he has given to us (cf. Rom 5:5). And precisely this is a sign of true prayer, which does not end in us, but opens itself to others and thus delivers me and, thus, helps in the redemption of the world.

Dear brothers and sisters, Saint Paul teaches us that in our prayer we must open ourselves to the presence of the Holy Spirit, who prays in us with sighs too deep for words, in order to lead us to adhere to God with all our heart and with all our being. The Spirit of Christ becomes the strength of our "weak" prayers, the light of our "darkened" prayer, the fire of our "barren" prayer, giving us true inner freedom, teaching us to live facing the trials of existence, in the certainty of not being alone, opening us to the horizons of mankind and of creation, which "has been groaning in travail" (Rom 8:22).

35

The Spirit and the "Abba" of Believers (Gal 4:6–7; Rom 8:14–17)

WEDNESDAY, 23 MAY 2012
Saint Peter's Square

Dear Brothers and Sisters,

Last Wednesday I explained what Saint Paul says about the Holy Spirit being the great master of prayer who teaches us to address God with the affectionate words that children use, calling him: "Abba, Father". This is what Jesus did; even in the most dramatic moment of his earthly life, he never lost his trust in the Father and always called on him with the intimacy of the beloved Son. In Gethsemane, when he feels the anguish of his approaching death, his prayer is: "Abba, Father, all things are possible to you; remove this cup from me; yet not what I will, but what you will" (Mk 14:36).

Since the very first steps on her journey, the Church has taken up this invocation and made it her own, especially in the prayer of the "Our Father", in which we say every day: "Our Father ... Thy will be done, on earth as it is in heaven!" (Mt 6:9–10). We find it twice in the Letters of Saint Paul. The Apostle, as we have just heard, addresses these words to the Galatians: "And because you are sons,

God has sent the Spirit of his Son into our hearts, crying, 'Abba! Father!'" (Gal 4:6). And, at the center of that hymn to the Holy Spirit which is the eighth chapter of the Letter to the Romans, Saint Paul declares: "For you did not receive the spirit of slavery to fall back into fear, but you have received the spirit of sonship. When we cry: 'Abba! Father!' it is the Spirit himself . . ." (Rom 8:15–16a). Christianity is not a religion of fear but of trust and of love for the Father who loves us. Both these crucial affirmations speak to us of the sending forth and reception of the Holy Spirit, the gift of the Risen One which makes us sons in Christ, the Only-Begotten Son, and places us in a filial relationship with God, a relationship of deep trust, like that of children; a filial relationship like that of Jesus, even though its origin and quality are different. Jesus is the eternal Son of God who took flesh; we instead become sons in him, in time, through faith and through the sacraments of Baptism and Confirmation. Thanks to these two sacraments, we are immersed in the Paschal Mystery of Christ. The Holy Spirit is the precious and necessary gift that makes us children of God, that brings about that adoption as sons to which all men are called because, as the divine blessing in the Letter to the Ephesians explains, God, in Christ, "chose us in him before the foundation of the world, that we should be holy and blameless before him. He destined us in love to be his [adopted] sons through Jesus Christ" (Eph 1:4–5a).

Perhaps men today fail to perceive the beauty, greatness, and profound consolation contained in the word "father" with which we can turn to God in prayer because today the father figure is often not sufficiently present and all too often is not sufficiently positive in daily life. The father's absence, the problem of a father who is not present in a child's life, is a serious problem of our time. It therefore becomes difficult to understand what it means to say that God is really our Father. From Jesus himself, from his filial relationship with God, we can learn what "father" really means and what is the true nature of the Father who is in heaven. Critics of religion have said that speaking of the "Father", of God, is a projection of our ancestors onto heaven. But the opposite is true: in the Gospel Christ shows us who is the father, and, as he is a true father, we can understand true fatherhood and even learn true fatherhood. Let us think of Jesus' words in the Sermon on the Mount where he says: "But I say to you, love your enemies and pray for those who persecute you, so that you may be sons of your Father who is in heaven" (Mt 5:44–45). It is the very love of Jesus, the Only-Begotten Son—who goes even to the point of giving himself on the Cross—that reveals to us the true nature of the Father: he is Love, and in our prayers as children we too enter this circuit of love, the love of God that purifies our desires, our attitudes marked by closure, self-sufficiency, and the typical selfishness of the former man.

We could therefore say that God in being Father has two dimensions. First of all, God is our Father because he is our Creator. Each one of us, each man and each woman, is a miracle of God, is wanted by him, and is personally known by him. When the Book of Genesis says that man is created in the image of God (cf. 1:27), it tries to express this precise reality: God is our Father, for him we are not anonymous, impersonal beings but have a name. And a phrase in the Psalms always moves me when I pray it: "Your hands have made and fashioned me", says the Psalmist (Ps 119[118]:73). In this beautiful image each one of us can express his personal relationship with God. "Your hands have fashioned me. You thought of me and created and wanted me." Nonetheless, this is still not enough. The Spirit of Christ opens us to a second dimension of God's fatherhood, beyond creation, since Jesus is the "Son" in the full sense of "one in being with the Father", as we profess in the Creed. Becoming a man like us, with his Incarnation, death, and Resurrection, Jesus in his turn accepts us in his humanity and even in his being Son, so that we too may enter into his specific belonging to God. Of course, our being children of God does not have the fullness of Jesus. We must increasingly become so throughout the journey of our Christian existence, developing in the following of Christ and in communion with him so as to enter ever more intimately into the relationship of love with God the Father which sustains our life. It is this fundamental reality that is disclosed to us when we open ourselves to the Holy Spirit and he makes us turn to God saying "Abba!", Father. We have truly preceded creation, entering into adoption with Jesus; united, we are really in God and are his children in a new way, in a new dimension.

Now I would like to return to Saint Paul's two passages on this action of the Holy Spirit in our prayers on which we are reflecting. Here, too, are two passages that correspond with each other but contain a different nuance. In the Letter to the Galatians, in fact, the Apostle says that the Spirit cries: "Abba! Father!" in us. In the Letter to the Romans, he says that it is we who cry: "Abba! Father!" And Saint Paul wants to make us understand that Christian prayer is never one way, never happens in one direction from us to God; it is never merely "an action of ours" but, rather, is the expression of a reciprocal relationship in which God is the first to act; it is the Holy Spirit who cries in us, and we are able to cry because the impetus comes from the Holy Spirit. We would not be able to pray were the desire for God, for being children of God, not engraved in the depths of our heart. Since he came into existence, *homo sapiens* has always been in search of God and endeavors to speak with God because God has engraved himself in our hearts. The first initiative therefore comes from God, and with Baptism, once again God acts in us, the Holy Spirit acts in us; he is the prime initiator of prayer so that we may really converse with God and say "Abba" to God. Hence his presence opens our prayers and our lives; it opens on to the horizons of the Trinity and of the Church.

We realize in addition—this is the second point—that the prayer of the Spirit of Christ in us and ours in him is not solely an individual act but an act of the entire Church. In praying, our heart is opened; we enter into communion not only with God but actually with all the children of God, because we are one body. When we address the Father in our inner room in silence and in recollection, we are never alone. Those who speak to God are not alone. We are within the great prayer of the Church; we are part of a great symphony that the Christian community in all the parts of the earth and in all epochs raises to God. Naturally, the musicians and instruments differ—and this is an element of enrichment—but the melody of praise is one and in harmony. Every time, then, that we shout or say: "Abba! Father!" it is the Church, the whole communion of people in prayer, that supports our invocation, and our invocation is an invocation of the Church. This is also reflected in the wealth of charisms and of the ministries and tasks that we carry out in the community. Saint Paul writes to the Christians of Corinth: "There are varieties of gifts, but the same Spirit; and there are varieties of service, but the same Lord; and there are varieties of working, but it is the same God who inspires them all in everyone" (1 Cor 12:4–6). Prayer guided by the Holy Spirit, who makes us say: "Abba! Father!" with Christ and in Christ, inserts us into the great mosaic of the family of God in which each one has a place and an important role, in profound unity with the whole.

One last remark: we also learn to cry "Abba! Father!" with Mary, Mother of the Son of God. The consummation of the fullness of time, of which Saint Paul speaks in his Letter to the Galatians (cf. 4:4), is brought about at the moment when Mary says "yes", the moment of her full adherence to God's will: "Behold, I am the handmaid of the Lord" (Lk 1:38).

Dear brothers and sisters, let us learn to savor in our prayers the beauty of being friends, indeed children of God, of being able to call on him with the trust that a child has for the parents who love him. Let us open our prayers to the action of the Holy Spirit so that he may cry to God in us: "Abba! Father!" and so that our prayers may transform and constantly convert our way of thinking and our action to bring us ever more closely into line with Jesus Christ, the Only-Begotten Son of God.

36

In Jesus Christ, the Faithful "Yes" of God and the "Amen" of the Church (2 Cor 1:3–14, 19–20)

WEDNESDAY, 30 MAY 2012
Saint Peter's Square

Dear Brothers and Sisters,

In this series of Catecheses we are meditating on prayer in the Letters of Saint Paul, and we are endeavoring to see Christian prayer as a true and personal encounter with God the Father, in Christ, and through the Holy Spirit. At this meeting today the faithful "yes" of God and the trusting "amen" of believers enter into dialogue, and I would like to emphasize this dynamic by reflecting on the Second Letter to the Corinthians. Saint Paul sends this passionate Letter to a Church which has called his apostolate into question on several occasions and opens his heart so that those to whom he is writing may be reassured of his fidelity to Christ and to the Gospel. This Second Letter to the Corinthians begins with one of the most exalted prayers of blessing in the New Testament. It says "Blessed be the God and Father of our Lord Jesus Christ, the Father of mercies and God of all comfort, who comforts us in all our affliction, so that we may be able to comfort those who are in any affliction, with the comfort with which we ourselves are comforted by God" (2 Cor 1:3–4).

Indeed, Paul lived amidst great trials; he had to pass through much difficulty and affliction, but he never gave in to discouragement. He was sustained by the grace and closeness of the Lord Jesus Christ, for whom he had become an apostle and a witness, putting his whole life into Jesus' hands. For this very reason, Paul begins this Letter with a prayer of blessing and thanksgiving to God, since in his life as an Apostle of Christ he never, not even for a single moment, felt deprived of the support of the merciful Father, the God of all comfort. His suffering was appalling, as he says in this very Letter, but in all these situations, when it seemed that there was no way out, he received consolation and comfort from God. He was also persecuted for proclaiming Christ and even thrown into prison, but he always felt inwardly free, enlivened by Christ's presence and keen to proclaim the word of hope of the Gospel. So it was that he wrote from prison to Timothy, his faithful collaborator. In chains, he wrote, "the word of God is not fettered. Therefore I endure everything for the sake of the elect, that they also may obtain the salvation which in Christ Jesus goes with eternal glory" (2 Tim 2:9b–10). In suffering for Christ, he experiences God's consolation. He writes: "For as we share abundantly in Christ's sufferings, so through Christ we share abundantly in comfort too" (2 Cor 1:5).

So, in the prayer of blessing that introduces the Second Letter to the Corinthians, the theme of affliction stands out next to the theme of consolation. This should not be understood merely as comfort but especially as an encouragement and an exhortation not to let oneself be overcome by trials and tribulations. The invitation is to live every situation united to Christ, who takes upon his shoulders the whole burden of the world's suffering and sin in order to bring light, hope, and redemption. So it is that Jesus makes us capable in our turn of consoling those experiencing every sort of affliction. Profound union with Christ in prayer and trust in his presence lead to the readiness to share in the suffering and troubles of our brethren. Saint Paul writes: "Who is weak, and I am not weak? Who is made to fall, and I am not indignant?" (2 Cor 11:29). This sharing is not born simply from kindness or solely from human generosity or an altruistic spirit; rather, it stems from the consolation of the Lord, from the steadfast support of the "transcendent power [that] belongs to God and not to us" (2 Cor 4:7).

Dear brothers and sisters, our life and our journey are frequently marked by difficulty, misunderstanding, and suffering. We all know it. In a faithful relationship with the Lord, in constant, daily prayer, we too can feel tangibly the consolation that comes from God. And this strengthens our faith, because it enables us to have an actual experience of God's "yes" to man, to us, to me, in Christ. It makes us feel the fidelity of his love, which even extended to the gift of his Son on the Cross. Saint Paul says, "for the Son of God, Jesus Christ, whom we preached among you, Silvanus and Timothy and I, was not Yes and No; but in him it is always Yes. For all the promises of God find their Yes in him. That is why we utter the Amen through him, to the glory of God" (2 Cor 1:19–20). The "yes" of God is not halved, it is not somewhere between "yes" and "no", but is a sound and simple "yes". And we respond to this "yes" with our own "yes", with our "amen", and so we are sure of the "yes" of God.

Faith is not primarily a human action but rather a freely given gift of God which is rooted in his faithfulness, in his "yes", which makes us understand how to live our life, loving him and our brethren. The whole history of salvation is a gradual revelation of this faithfulness of God, in spite of our infidelity and negation, in the certainty that "the gifts and the call of God are irrevocable!" as the Apostle declares in his Letter to the Romans (11:29).

Dear brothers and sisters, God's way of acting—very different from ours—gives us comfort, strength, and hope because God does not withdraw his "yes". In the face of stressful human relations, even in the family, we often fail to persevere in freely given love, which demands commitment and sacrifice. Instead, God does not grow tired of us; he never wearies of being patient with us and, with his immense mercy, always leads the way and reaches out to us first: his "yes" is absolutely reliable. In the event of the crucifixion, he offers us the measure of his love which does not count the cost and knows no bounds. Saint Paul writes in his Letter to Titus: "the goodness and loving kindness of God our Savior appeared" (Tit 3:4). And because this "yes" is renewed every day, "it is God who . . . has commissioned us; he has put his seal upon us and given us his Spirit in our hearts as a guarantee" (2 Cor 1:21b–22).

Indeed, it is the Holy Spirit who makes God's "yes" in Jesus Christ constantly present and alive and creates in our hearts the desire to follow him so as to enter totally into his love, one day, when we will receive a dwelling-place in heaven not built by human hands. There is no one who has not been touched and called into question by this faithful love, which is also capable of waiting even for all those who continue to respond with the "no" of rejection or of the hardening of their hearts. God waits for us, he always seeks us out, he wants to welcome us into communion with him in order to give to each one of us fullness of life, hope, and peace.

The Church's "amen" is grafted onto God's faithful "yes", which resonates in every action of the Liturgy. "Amen" is the answer of faith that always concludes our personal and community prayers and expresses our "yes" to God's project. We often respond to prayers with our "amen" out of habit, without grasping its deep meaning. The word derives from *'aman*, which in Hebrew and in Aramaic means "to make permanent", "to consolidate", and, consequently, "to be certain", "to tell the truth". If we look at Sacred Scripture, we see that this "amen" is said at the end of the Psalms of blessing and praise, such as, for example, Psalm 41 [40]: "But you have upheld me because of my integrity, and set me in your presence for ever. Blessed be the Lord, the God of Israel, from everlasting to everlasting! Amen and Amen" (vv. 12–13).

Or else it expresses adherence to God at the moment when the People of Israel return full of joy from the Babylonian Exile and say their "yes", their "amen" to God and to his Law. In the Book of Nehemiah it is told that after this return, "Ezra opened the book [of the Law] in the sight of all the people; for he was above all the people; and when he opened it all the people stood. And Ezra blessed the Lord, the great God; and all the people answered, 'Amen, Amen', lifting up their hands" (Neh 8:5–6).

From the outset, therefore, the "amen" of the Jewish liturgy became the "amen" of the first Christian communities. Indeed, the book of the Christian Liturgy par excellence, the Revelation to John begins with the "amen" of the Church: "To him who loves us and has freed us from our sins by his blood and made us a kingdom, priests to his God and Father, to him be glory and dominion for ever and ever. Amen" (Rev 1:5b–6). This is what it says in the first chapter of the Book of Revelation. And the same book ends with the invocation "Amen. Come, Lord Jesus!" (Rev 22:20).

Dear friends, prayer is the encounter with a living Person to listen to and with whom to converse; it is the meeting with God that renews his unshakeable fidelity, his "yes" to man, to each one of us, to give us his consolation in the storms of life and to enable us to live, united to him, a life full of joy and goodness, which will find fulfillment in eternal life.

In our prayers, we are called to say "yes" to God, to respond with this "amen" of adherence, of faithfulness to him throughout our life. We can never achieve this faithfulness by our own efforts; it is not only the fruit of our daily striving; it comes from God and is founded on the "yes" of Christ, who said: my food is to do the will of the Father (cf. Jn 4:34). It is into this "yes" that we must enter, into this "yes" of Christ, into adherence to God's will, in order to reach the point of saying with Saint Paul that it is not we who live but Christ himself who lives in us. Then the "amen" of our personal and community prayers will envelop and transform the whole of our life into a life of God's consolation, a life immersed in eternal and steadfast love.

37

Contemplation and the Power of Prayer (2 Cor 12:1–10)

WEDNESDAY, 13 JUNE 2012
Paul VI Audience Hall

Dear Brothers and Sisters,

The daily encounter with the Lord and regular acceptance of the sacraments enable us to open our mind and heart to his presence, his words, and his action. Prayer is not only the breath of the soul, but, to make use of a metaphor, it is also the oasis of peace from which we can draw the water that nourishes our spiritual life and transforms our existence. God draws us toward him, offering us enlightenment and consolation and enabling us to scale the mountain of holiness so that we may be ever closer to him. This is the personal experience to which Saint Paul refers in Chapter 12 of his Second Letter to the Corinthians, on which I wish to reflect today. In the face of those who contested the legitimacy of his apostolate, he does not actually list the communities he has founded, the miles he has covered; he does not limit himself to recalling the difficulty and opposition he has confronted in order to proclaim the Gospel; he points to his relationship with the Lord, a relationship so intense as also to be marked by moments of ecstasy, of profound contemplation (cf. 2 Cor 12:1); hence he boasts, not of his achievements, his strength, or his activities and successes but, rather, of what God has worked in and through him. Indeed, with great modesty he tells of the moment when he lived the special experience of being caught up to heaven by God. He recalls that fourteen years before he sent the Letter he "was caught up to the third heaven" (v. 2). With the language and ways of someone who is telling something that cannot be told, Saint Paul also speaks of that event in the third person. He says that a man was caught up into God's "garden", into Paradise. The Apostle's contemplation is so profound and so intense that he does not even remember the content of the revelation he received; yet he clearly remembers the date and the circumstances in which the Lord grasped him in such a complete way and attracted him to himself, just as he had on the road to Damascus at the time of his conversion (cf. Phil 3:12).

Saint Paul continues, saying that precisely to prevent pride from going to his head in the greatness of the revelations he received, he has been given a "thorn" (2 Cor 12:7), an affliction, and insistently begs the Risen One to free him of the messenger of Satan, of this painful thorn in the flesh. Three times, he says, he beseeched the Lord to remove this trial. And it is in this situation that in deep contemplation of God, in which "he heard things that cannot be told, which man may not utter" (v. 4), he receives an answer to his entreaty. The Risen One addresses to him clear and reassuring words: "My grace is sufficient for you, for my power is made perfect in weakness" (v. 9).

Paul's commentary on these words may leave us amazed, but it shows that he understood what it means truly to be an apostle of the Gospel. In fact, he exclaims: "I will all the more gladly boast of my weaknesses, that the power of Christ may rest upon me. For the sake of Christ, then, I am content with weaknesses, insults, hardships, persecutions, and calamities; for when I am weak, then I am strong" (vv. 9b–10); in other words, he does not boast of his own actions but of the activity of Christ, who acts precisely through his weakness. Let us reflect a little longer on this event that occurred during the years in which Saint Paul lived in silence and contemplation, before he began to travel in the West to proclaim Christ, because this attitude of profound humility and trust before God's manifestation of himself is also fundamental to our prayer and to our life, to our relationship with God and to our weaknesses.

First of all, what are the weaknesses about which the Apostle is talking? What is this "thorn" in the flesh? We do not know, and he does not tell us, but his attitude enables us to realize that every difficulty in following Christ and witnessing to his Gospel may be overcome by opening oneself with trust to the Lord's action. Saint Paul is well aware that he is an "unworthy servant" (Lk 17:10)—it is not he who has done great things; it is the Lord—an "earthen vessel" (2 Cor 4:7), in which God places the riches and power of his grace. In this moment of concentrated contemplative prayer, Saint Paul understands clearly how to face and how to live every event, especially suffering, difficulty, and persecution. The power of God, who does not abandon us or leave us on our own but becomes our support and strength, is revealed at the very moment when we experience our own weakness. Of course, Paul would have preferred to be freed from this "thorn", from this affliction; but God says: "No, you are in need of it. You will have sufficient grace to resist it and to do what must be done." This also applies to us. The Lord does not free us from evils, but helps us to mature in sufferings, difficulties, and persecutions. Faith, therefore, tells us that if we abide in God, "though our outer nature is wasting away, our inner nature is being renewed every day", in trials (cf. v. 16). The Apostle communicates to the Christians of Corinth and to us, too, that "this slight momentary affliction is preparing for us an eternal weight of glory beyond all comparison" (v. 17). In fact, humanly speaking, the burden of his difficulties was not light, it was very heavy; but in comparison with God's love, with the greatness of being loved by God, it appears light, in the knowledge that the quantity of glory will be boundless. Therefore, to the extent that our union with the Lord increases and that our prayers become intense, we also go to the essential and understand that it is not the power of our own means, our virtues, our skills that brings about the Kingdom of God but that it is God who works miracles precisely through our weakness, our inadequacy for the task. We must therefore have the humility not to trust merely in ourselves, but to work, with the Lord's help, in the Lord's vineyard, entrusting ourselves to him as fragile "earthen vessels".

Saint Paul refers to two particular revelations that radically changed his life. The first—as we know—is the overwhelming question on the road to Damascus: "Saul, Saul, why do you persecute me?" (Acts 9:4), a question that led him to discover and encounter Christ, alive and present, and to hear his call to be an apostle of the Gospel. The second revelation consists of the words the Lord addressed to him in the experience of contemplative prayer on which we are reflecting: "My grace is sufficient for you, for my power is made perfect in weakness." Faith alone, trust in the action of God, in the goodness of God, who does not abandon us, is the guarantee that we are not working in vain. Thus the Lord's grace was the power that accompanied Saint Paul in his immense efforts to spread the Gospel, and his heart entered the Heart of Christ, becoming able to lead others toward the One who died and rose for us.

In prayer, therefore, let us open our soul to the Lord so that he may come and inhabit our weakness, transforming it into power for the Gospel. Moreover the Greek verb with which Paul describes this dwelling of the Lord in his frail humanity is also rich in meaning; he uses *episkenoo*, which we may convey with "pitching his tent". The Lord continues to pitch his tent in us, among us: he is the Mystery of the Incarnation. The divine Word himself, who came to dwell in our humanity, who wishes to dwell in us, to put up his tent in us to illuminate and transform our life and the world.

The intense contemplation of God experienced by Saint Paul recalls that of the disciples on Mount Tabor when, seeing Jesus transfigured and shining with light, Peter said to him, "Master, it is well that we are here; let us make three booths, one for you and one for Moses and one for Elijah" (Mk 9:5). "He did not know what to say, for they were exceedingly afraid", Saint Mark adds (v. 6). Contemplating the Lord is at the same time both fascinating and awe-inspiring: fascinating because he draws us to him and enraptures our hearts by uplifting them, carrying them to his heights where we experience the peace and beauty of his love; awe-inspiring because he lays bare our human weakness, our inadequacy, the effort to triumph over the Evil One, who endangers our life, that thorn embedded also in our flesh. In prayer, in the daily contemplation of the Lord, we receive the strength of God's love and feel that Saint Paul's words to the Christians of Rome are true, when he wrote: "For I am sure that neither death, nor life, nor angels, nor principalities, nor things present, nor things to come, nor powers, nor height, nor depth, nor anything else in all creation, will be able to separate us from the love of God in Christ Jesus our Lord" (Rom 8:38–39).

In a world in which we risk relying solely on the efficiency and power of human means, we are called to rediscover and to witness to the power of God which is communicated in prayer, with which every day we grow in conforming our life to that of Christ, who—as Paul says—"was crucified in weakness, but lives by the power of God. For we are weak in him, but in dealing with you we shall live with him by the power of God" (2 Cor 13:4).

Dear friends, in the past century Albert Schweitzer, a Protestant theologian who won the Nobel Peace Prize, said: "Paul is a mystic and nothing but a mystic", that is, a man truly in love with Christ and so united to him that he could say: Christ lives in me. The mysticism of Saint Paul is founded not only on the exceptional events he lived through, but also on his daily and intense relationship with the Lord, who always sustained him with his grace. Mysticism did not distance him from reality; on the contrary, it gave him the strength to live each day for Christ and to build the Church to the ends of the world of that time. Union with God does not distance us from the world but gives us the strength to remain really in the world, to do what must be done in the world.

Thus in our life of prayer as well we can perhaps have moments of special intensity in which we feel the Lord's presence is more vivid, especially in situations of aridity, of difficulty, of suffering, of an apparent absence of God. Only if we are grasped by Christ's love will we be equal to facing every adversity, convinced, like Paul, that we can do all things in the One who gives us strength (cf. Phil 4:13). Therefore, the more room we make for prayer, the more we will see our life transformed and enlivened by the tangible power of God's love. This is what happened, for example, to Bl. Mother Teresa of Calcutta, who found in contemplation of Jesus and even also in long periods of aridity the ultimate reason and incredible strength to recognize him in the poor and abandoned, in spite of her fragility. Contemplation of Christ in our life does not alienate us—as I have already said—from reality. Rather, it enables us to share even more in human events, because the Lord, in attracting us to him through prayer, enables us to make ourselves present and close to every brother and sister in his love.

38

The Divine Blessing through the Plan of God the Father (Eph 1:3–14)

WEDNESDAY, 20 JUNE 2012

Paul VI Audience Hall

Dear Brothers and Sisters,

Our prayers are very often requests for help in a time of need. Moreover, this is normal for man, because we need help, we need others, we need God. Thus it is normal for us to ask God something, to seek help from him; and we must bear in mind that the prayer the Lord taught us, the "Our Father", is a prayer of petition. With this prayer, the Lord teaches us the priorities of our prayer and cleanses and purifies our desires, and in this way he cleanses and purifies our hearts. Therefore, even though it is in itself normal that we should ask for something in prayer, it should not be exclusively so. There is also cause for thanksgiving, and, if we pay a little attention, we see that we receive very many good things from God. He is so good to us that it is right and necessary to say "thank you". And our prayer should also be a prayer of praise: if our hearts are open in spite of all the problems, we also see the beauty of his creation, the goodness that is revealed in his creation. Therefore we must not only ask but also praise and give thanks;

only in this way is our prayer complete. In his Letters, Saint Paul does not only speak of prayer; he also refers to prayers and, of course, prayers of petition as well, but prayers of praise and blessing for all that God has worked and continues to work in mankind's history.

And today I would like to reflect on the First Chapter of the Letter to the Ephesians that begins, precisely, with a prayer which is a hymn of blessing, an expression of gratitude, of joy. Saint Paul blesses God, the Father of our Lord Jesus Christ, because in him he has made us "know the mystery of his will" (Eph 1:9). There truly is a reason to express gratitude if God enables us to know all that is hidden: his will with us, for us; "the mystery of his will". "*Mysterion*" or "Mystery": a term that recurs frequently in Sacred Scripture and in the Liturgy. I do not want to enter into philology here, but in the common language it indicates what it is impossible to know, a reality we are unable to grasp with our own intellect. The hymn that opens the Letter to the Ephesians takes us by the hand and leads us toward a more profound meaning of this term and of the reality that it points out to us. "Mystery", for believers, is not so much the unknown as rather the merciful will of God, his plan of love which was fully revealed in Jesus Christ and offers us the possibility "to comprehend with all the saints what is the breadth and the length and height and depth, and to know the love of Christ" (Eph 3:18–19). The "unknown mystery" of God is revealed: it is that God loves us and has loved us from the beginning, from eternity.

Let us therefore reflect a little on this solemn and profound prayer. "Blessed be the God and Father of our Lord Jesus Christ" (Eph 1:3). Saint Paul uses the verb "*euloghein*", which more often translates the Hebrew term "*barak*"; it is praising, glorifying, and thanking God the Father as the source of the goods of salvation, like the One who "has blessed us in Christ with every spiritual blessing in the heavenly places".

The Apostle thanks and praises, but he also reflects on the reasons that spur man to offer this praise, this thanksgiving, presenting the fundamental elements of the divine plan and its stages. First of all, we must bless God the Father because, Saint Paul writes, "he chose us in him before the foundation of the world, that we should be holy and blameless before him" (v. 4). What makes us holy and blameless is love. God called us to existence, to holiness. And this choice even precedes the foundation of the world. We have always been in his plan and in his mind. With the Prophet Jeremiah, we too can say that he knew us before he formed us in our mother's womb (cf. Jer 1:5); and in knowing us, he loved us. The vocation to holiness, that is, to communion with God belongs to an eternal design of this God, a design that extends through history and includes all the men and women of the world, because it is a universal appeal. God excludes no one; his plan is solely of love. Saint John Chrysostom says: God himself "rendered us holy but then we must continue to be holy. A holy man is he who is a partaker of faith" (*Homilies on the Letter to the Ephesians* 1, 1, 4).

Paul continues, "he destined us in love to be his sons through Jesus Christ", to be incorporated in his Only-Begotten Son. The Apostle underlines the gratuitousness of this marvelous plan of God for mankind. God did not choose us because we are good but because he is good. And antiquity had a phrase to say on goodness: *bonum est diffusivum sui*; goodness is communicated, it spreads. And thus, since God is goodness, he is the communication of goodness, he wishes to communicate; he creates because he wants to communicate his goodness to us and to make us good and holy.

At the heart of the prayer of blessing, the Apostle illustrates the way in which the Father's plan of salvation is brought about in Christ, in his beloved Son. He writes: "In him we have redemption through his blood, the forgiveness of our trespasses, according to the riches of his grace" (Eph 1:7). The sacrifice of the Cross of Christ is the unique and unrepeatable event with which the Father showed his love for us in a luminous way, not only in words but in practice. God is so real and his love is so real that he enters into history; he becomes a man to feel what it is, how it is to live in this created world, and he accepts the path of suffering of the Passion and even suffers death. God's love is so real that he participates not only in our being but also in our suffering and our dying. The sacrifice of the Cross ensures that we become "God's property" because the Blood of Christ has redeemed us from sin, cleanses us from evil, removes us from the slavery of sin and death. Saint Paul invites us to consider the depths of God's love that transforms history, that transformed his very life from being a persecutor of Christians to being an unflagging apostle of the Gospel. Here once again the reassuring words of the Letter to the Romans resound: "If God is for us, who is against us? He who did not spare his own Son but gave him up for us all, will he not also give us all things with him? . . . For I am sure that neither death, nor life, nor angels, nor principalities, nor things present, nor things to come, nor powers, nor height, nor depth, nor anything else in all creation, will be able to separate us from the love of God in Christ Jesus our Lord" (Rom 8:31–32; 38–39). We must integrate this certainty—God is for us and no creature can separate us from him because his love is stronger—in our being, in our awareness as Christians.

Lastly, the divine blessing ends with the mention of the Holy Spirit, who has been poured out into our hearts; the Paraclete whom we have received as a promised seal: "who is the guarantee of our inheritance until we acquire possession of it, to the praise of his glory" (Eph 1:14). Redemption is not yet finished—as we know—but will reach its fulfillment when those whom God has ransomed are totally saved. We are still on the path of redemption, whose essential reality has been given with the death and Resurrection of Jesus. We are on our way toward definitive redemption, toward the full liberation of God's children. And the Holy Spirit is the certainty that God will bring his plan of salvation to completion, when he will bring back to Christ, the only head, all "things in heaven and things on earth" (Eph 1:10). Saint John Chrysostom comments on this point: "God has chosen us for faith and has impressed in us the seal of the inheritance of future glory" (*Homilies on the Letter to the Ephesians* 2, 11–14). We must accept that the journey of redemption is also our journey, because God wants free creatures who freely say "yes"; but it is above all and first of all his journey. We are in his hands and to walk on the way disclosed by him is now our freedom. Let us walk on this path of redemption together with Christ and understand that redemption is brought about.

The vision which Saint Paul presents to us in this great prayer of blessing has led us to contemplate the action of the three Persons of the Blessed Trinity: the Father who chose us before the creation of the world, who thought of us and created us; the Son who redeemed us through his Blood; and the Holy Spirit, the pledge of our redemption and of our future glory. In constant prayer, in our daily relationship with God, let us learn, as Saint Paul did, to perceive ever more clearly the signs of his plan and his action: in the beauty of the Creator that emerges from his creatures (cf. Eph 3:9), as Saint Francis of Assisi sings: "*Laudato sie mi' Signore, cum tutte le Tue creature*" (FF 263). It is important to be attentive at this very moment, also in the holiday period, to the beauty of creation and to see God's face shining out in this beauty. The saints showed clearly in their lives what God's power can do in human weakness. And he can also do it in us. In the whole of the history of salvation, in which God has made himself close to us and patiently awaits our times, he understands our infidelities, he encourages our commitment and guides us.

We learn in prayer to see the signs of this merciful plan in the Church's journey. Thus we may grow in the love of God, opening the door so that the Blessed Trinity may come and dwell within us, may illuminate, warm, and guide our lives. "If a man loves me, he will keep my word, and my Father will love him, and we will come to him and make our home with him" (Jn 14:23), Jesus said, promising the disciples the gift of the Holy Spirit who was to teach them all things. Saint Irenaeus once said that in the Incarnation the Holy Spirit became accustomed to being in man. In prayer we must become accustomed to being with God. It is very important that we learn to be with God and thereby see how beautiful it is to be with him, who is the redemption.

Dear friends, when prayer nourishes our spiritual lives, we become capable of preserving what Saint Paul calls "the mystery of faith" with a pure conscience (cf. 1 Tim 3:9). Prayer as a way of "accustoming" oneself to being with God brings into being men and women who are motivated, not by selfishness, by the desire to possess, or by the thirst for power, but by gratuitousness, by the desire to love, by the thirst to serve, in other words, who are motivated by God; and only in this way is it possible to bring light to the darkness of the world.

I would like to end this Catechesis with the epilogue of the Letter to the Romans. With Saint Paul, let us too glorify God, for he has expressed himself entirely to us in Jesus Christ and has given us the Consoler, the Spirit of truth. Saint Paul writes at the end of his Letter to the Romans: "to him who is able to strengthen you according to my Gospel and the preaching of Jesus Christ, according to the revelation of the mystery which was kept secret for long ages but is now disclosed and through the prophetic writings is made known to all nations, according to the command of the eternal God, to bring about the obedience of faith—to the only wise God be glory for ever more through Jesus Christ! Amen" (16:25–27).

39

The Christological Hymn

WEDNESDAY, 27 JUNE 2012
Paul VI Audience Hall

Dear Brothers and Sisters,

Just as we saw over the past Wednesdays, our prayer is composed of silence and words, of singing and of gestures that involve the whole person: from the mouth to the mind, from the heart to the entire body. We find this characteristic in Jewish prayer, especially in the Psalms. Today I would like to speak of one of the most ancient songs or hymns of the Christian tradition, which Saint Paul presents to us in the Letter to the Philippians. In a certain sense, this is his spiritual testament. Indeed, it is a Letter that the Apostle dictated while he was in prison, perhaps in Rome. He must have felt that his death was close at hand, for he says that his life will be offered as a libation (cf. Phil 2:17).

In spite of this situation of grave danger to his physical safety, throughout this text Saint Paul expresses his joy in being a disciple of Christ, of being able to go to meet him even to the point of seeing death not as a loss but rather as a gain. In the last chapter of the Letter, there is a pressing invitation to joy, a fundamental characteristic of being Christian and of our prayer. Saint Paul writes: "Rejoice in the Lord always; again I will say, Rejoice" (Phil 4:4). But how is it possible to rejoice in the face of a death sentence whose execution is now imminent? From where, or better, from whom did Saint Paul draw the serenity, strength, and courage to go forward to meet martyrdom and the outpouring of his blood?

We find the answer in the middle of the Letter to the Philippians, in what the Christian tradition calls the *carmen Christo*, the hymn to Christ, or, more commonly, the "Christological hymn"; it is a hymn in which all the attention is focused on the "mind" of Christ, that is, on his way of thinking and on his practical approach to life. This prayer begins with an exhortation: "Have this mind among yourselves, which was in Christ Jesus" (Phil 2:5). These sentiments are presented in the following verses: love, generosity, humility, obedience to God, the gift of self. It is not only or not merely a matter of following Jesus' example, as something moral, but of involving one's whole life in his way of thinking and acting. Prayer must lead Christians to knowledge and union in ever deeper love with the Lord, if they are to be able to think, act, and love like him, in him, and for him. Putting this into practice, learning the sentiments of Jesus, is the way of Christian life.

I would now like to reflect briefly on several elements of this concentrated hymn which sums up the entire divine and human itinerary of the Son of God and englobes the whole of human history: from being in the form of God to the Incarnation, to death on the Cross, and to exaltation in the Father's glory, the behavior of Adam, of man, is also implicit from the start. This hymn to Christ begins with his being "*en morphe tou Theou*", the Greek text says, that is, with being "in the form of God" or, rather, in the condition of God. Jesus, true God and true man, does not live his "being as God" in order to triumph or to impose his supremacy; he does not see it as a possession, a privilege, or a treasure, to be jealously guarded. On the contrary, he "stripped" himself, he emptied himself, the Greek text says, taking the "*morphe doulos*", the "form of a slave", human reality marked by suffering, poverty, and death; he assumed the likeness of men in all things save sin, so as to behave as a servant totally dedicated to serving others. In this regard, Eusebius of Caesarea said:—in the fourth century—"he took upon himself the labors of the suffering members and made our sicknesses his and suffered on our account all our woes and labors by the laws of love, in conformity with his great love for mankind" (*Demonstratio Evangelica* [*Proof of the Gospel*] 10, 1, 22). Saint Paul continues, delineating the "historical" background in which Jesus' humbling of himself took place: "he humbled himself and became obedient unto death" (Phil 2:8). The Son of God truly became man and completed a journey of total obedience and fidelity to the Father's will, even to the point of making the supreme sacrifice of his life. Furthermore, the Apostle specifies: "unto death, even death on a cross". On the Cross Jesus Christ attained the greatest degree of humiliation, because crucifixion was the penalty kept for slaves and not for free men: "*mors turpissima crucis*", Cicero wrote (cf. *In Verrem* V, 64, 165).

Through the Cross of Christ, man is redeemed and Adam's experience is reversed. Adam, created in the image and likeness of God, claimed to be like God through his own effort, to put himself in God's place, and in this way lost the original dignity that had been given to him. Jesus, instead, was "in the form of God" but humbled himself, immersed himself in the human condition, in total faithfulness to the Father, in order to redeem the Adam who is in us and restore to man the dignity he had lost. The Fathers emphasize that he made himself obedient, restoring to human nature, through his own humanity and obedience, what had been lost through Adam's disobedience.

In prayer, in the relationship with God, we open our mind, our heart, and our will to the action of the Holy Spirit to enter into this dynamic of life, as Saint Cyril of Alexandria—whose feast we are celebrating today—tells us: "the work of the Spirit seeks to transform us by grace into a perfect copy of his humbling" (*Festal Letter* 10, 4). Human logic, instead, often seeks self-fulfillment in power, in domination, in forceful means. Man still wants to build the Tower of Babel with his own efforts, to reach God's heights by himself, to be like God. The Incarnation and the Cross remind us that complete fulfillment lies in conforming our human will to the will of the Father, in emptying ourselves of our selfishness in order to fill ourselves with God's love, with his charity, and thereby become capable of truly loving others. Man does not find himself by remaining closed in on himself, by affirming himself. Man finds himself only by coming out of himself; only if we come out of ourselves do we find ourselves. And if Adam wanted to imitate God, this was not a bad thing in itself, but he had the wrong idea of God. God is not someone who only wants greatness. God is love, which was already given in the Trinity and was then given in the Creation. And imitating God means coming out of oneself, giving oneself in love.

In the second part of this "Christological hymn" of the Letter to the Philippians, the subject changes; it is no longer Christ but God the Father. Saint Paul stresses that it is precisely out of obedience to the Father's will that "God has highly exalted him and bestowed on him the name which is above every name" (Phil 2:9). The one who humbled himself profoundly, taking the condition of a slave, is exalted, lifted up above all things by the Father, who gives him the name "*Kyrios*", "Lord", the supreme dignity and lordship. Indeed, it is before this new name, which is the very name of God in the Old Testament, "every knee should bow, in heaven and on earth and under the earth, and every tongue confess that Jesus Christ is Lord, to the glory of God the Father" (vv. 10–11). The Jesus who is exalted is the Jesus of the Last Supper who lays aside his garments and girds himself with a towel, who bends down to wash the Apostles' feet and asks them: "Do you know what I have done to you? You call me Teacher and Lord; and you are right, for so I am. If I then, your Lord and Teacher, have washed your feet, you also ought to wash one another's feet" (Jn 13:12–14). It is important to remember this always, in our prayers and in our life. "The ascent to God occurs precisely in the descent of humble service, in the descent of love, for love is God's essence, and is thus the power that truly purifies man and enables him to perceive God and to see him" (*Jesus of Nazareth* [New York: Doubleday, 2007], p. 95).

The hymn in the Letter to the Philippians offers us important instructions for our prayers. The first is the invocation "Lord", addressed to Jesus Christ, seated at the right hand of the Father: he is the one Lord of our life, among so many "dominant" people who desire to direct and guide it. For this reason, it is necessary to have a scale of values in which the primacy is God's, in order to affirm, with Saint Paul: "I count everything as loss because of the surpassing worth of knowing Christ Jesus my Lord" (Phil 3:8). The encounter with the Risen One made the Apostle realize that he is the one treasure for which it is worth expending one's life.

The second instruction is prostration, that "every knee shall bow", on earth and in heaven. This is reminiscent of words of the Prophet Isaiah, where he points to the worship that all creatures owe to God (cf. 45:23). Genuflection before the Blessed Sacrament or kneeling in prayer exactly expresses with the body as well the attitude of adoration in God's presence. Hence the importance of not doing this action out of habit or hastily but rather with profound awareness. When we kneel before the Lord, we profess our faith in him, we recognize that he is the one Lord of our life.

Dear brothers and sisters, in our prayers let us fix our gaze on the Crucified One, let us pause more often in adoration before the Eucharist to let our life enter the love of God who humbly lowered himself in order to lift us up to him. At the beginning of the Catechesis, we asked ourselves how Saint Paul could rejoice when he was facing the imminent risk of martyrdom and outpouring his blood. This was only possible because the Apostle never lifted his gaze from Christ, to the point that he became like him in death, in the hope that "I may attain the resurrection from the dead" (Phil 3:11). As Saint Francis said before the Crucifix, let us too say: "Most High, glorious God, enlighten the darkness of my heart and give me true faith, certain hope, and perfect charity, sense and knowledge, Lord, that I may carry out Your holy and true command." Amen (cf. *Prayer before the Crucifix at San Damiano:* FF [276]).

40

Saint Alphonsus Mary Liguori

WEDNESDAY, 1 AUGUST 2012
Piazza della Libertà, Castel Gandolfo

Dear Brothers and Sisters,

Today is the Liturgical Memorial of Saint Alphonsus Mary Liguori, Bishop and Doctor of the Church, Founder of the Congregation of the Most Holy Redeemer—the Redemptorists—and patron saint of moral theology scholars and confessors. Saint Alphonsus is one of the most popular saints of the eighteenth century because of his simple, immediate style and his teaching on the sacrament of Penance. In a period of great rigorism, a product of the Jansenist influence, he recommended that confessors administer this sacrament expressing the joyful embrace of God the Father, who in his infinite mercy never tires of welcoming the repentant son.

Today's Memorial offers us the opportunity to reflect on Saint Alphonsus' teaching on prayer, which is particularly valuable and full of spiritual inspiration. His Treatise on *The Great Means of Prayer*, which he considered the most useful of all his writings, dates back to the year 1759. Indeed, he describes prayer as "a necessary and certain means of obtaining salvation and all the graces that we require for that object"

(*Introduction*). This sentence sums up the way Saint Alphonsus understood prayer.

First of all, by saying that it is a means, he reminds us of the goal to be reached. God created us out of love in order to be able to give us life in its fullness; but this goal, this life in fullness, has, as it were, become distant because of sin—we all know it—and only God's grace can make it accessible. To explain this basic truth and to make people understand with immediacy how real the risk of "being lost" is for man, Saint Alphonsus coined a famous, very elementary maxim, which says: "Those who pray will be saved, and those who do not will be damned!" Commenting on this lapidary sentence, he added, "In conclusion, to save one's soul without prayer is most difficult, and even (as we have seen) impossible. . . . But by praying, our salvation is made secure and very easy" (II, Conclusion). And he says further: "If we do not pray, we have no excuse, because the grace of prayer is given to everyone . . . if we are not saved, the whole fault will be ours; and we shall have our own failure to answer for, because we did not pray" (ibid.). By saying, then, that prayer is a necessary means, Saint Alphonsus wanted us to understand that in no situation of life can we do without prayer, especially in times of trial and difficulty. We must always knock at the door of the Lord confidently, knowing that he cares for all his children, for us. For this reason, we are asked not to be afraid to turn to him and to present our requests to him with trust, in the certainty of receiving what we need.

Dear friends, this is the main question: what is really necessary in my life? I answer with Saint Alphonsus: "Health and all the graces that we need" (ibid.). He means of course not only the health of the body, but first of all that of the soul, which Jesus gives us. More than anything else, we need his liberating presence which makes us truly fully human and hence fills our existence with joy. And it is only through prayer that we can receive him and his grace, which, by enlightening us in every situation, helps us to discern true good and by strengthening us also makes our will effective, that is, renders it capable of doing what we know is good. We often recognize what is good but are unable to do it. With prayer we succeed in doing it. The disciple of the Lord knows he is always exposed to temptation and does not fail to ask God's help in prayer in order to resist it.

Saint Alphonsus very interestingly cites the example of Saint Philip Neri, who "the very moment when he awoke in the morning, said to God: 'Lord, keep Thy hands over Philip this day; for if not, Philip will betray Thee'" (III, 3). What a great realist! He asks God to keep his hands upon him. We too, aware of our weakness, must humbly seek God's help, relying on his boundless mercy. Saint Alphonsus says in another passage: "We are so poor that we have nothing; but if we pray we are no longer poor. If we are poor, God is rich" (II, 4). And, following in Saint Augustine's wake, he invites all Christians not to be afraid to obtain from God, through prayer, the power they do not possess that is necessary in order to do good, in the certainty that the Lord will not refuse his help to whoever prays to him with humility (cf. III, 3). Dear friends, Saint Alphonsus reminds us that the relationship with God is essential in our life. Without the relationship with God, the fundamental relationship is absent. The relationship with God is brought into being in conversation with God, in daily personal prayer, and with participation in the sacraments. This relationship is thus able to grow within us, as can the divine presence that directs us on our way, illuminates it, and makes it safe and peaceful even amidst difficulties and perils.

41

Memorial of Saint Dominic Guzmán

WEDNESDAY, 8 AUGUST 2012
Piazza della Libertà, Castel Gandolfo

Dear Brothers and Sisters,

Today the Church celebrates the Memorial of Saint Dominic Guzmán, Priest and Founder of the Order of Preachers, known as the Dominicans. In a previous Catechesis I have already illustrated this distinguished figure and his fundamental contribution to the renewal of the Church in his time. Today, I would like to shed light on one of the essential aspects of his spirituality: his life of prayer. Saint Dominic was a man of prayer. In love with God, he had no other aspiration than the salvation of souls, especially those who had fallen into the net of the heresies of his time; a follower of Christ, he radically embodied the three evangelical counsels by combining the witness of a life of poverty with the proclamation of the word. Under the Holy Spirit's guidance he made headway on the path of Christian perfection. At every moment, prayer was the power that renewed his apostolic work and made it ever more fruitful.

Blessed Jordan of Saxony († 1237), his successor as head of the Order, wrote: "During the day, no one was friendlier than he; ... conversely, at night no one watched in prayer more diligently than he. He dedicated the day to his neighbor, but gave the night to God" (P. Filippini, *San Domenico visto dai suoi contemporanei* [Bologna, 1982], p. 133). In Saint Dominic we can see an example of harmonious integration between contemplation of the divine mysteries and apostolic work. According to the testimonies of people close to him, "he always spoke with God and of God." This observation points to his profound communion with the Lord and, at the same time, to his constant commitment to lead others to this communion with God. He left no writings on prayer, but the Dominican tradition has collected and handed down his living experience in a work called: *The Nine Ways of Prayer of Saint Dominic.* This book was compiled by a Dominican friar between 1260 and 1288; it helps us to understand something of the Saint's interior life and also helps us, with all the differences, to learn something of how to pray.

There are, then, nine ways to pray, according to Saint Dominic, and each one—always before Jesus Crucified—expresses a deeply penetrating physical and spiritual approach that fosters recollection and zeal. The first seven ways follow an ascending order, like the steps on a path, toward intimate communion with God, with the Trinity: Saint Dominic prayed standing, bowed to express humility, lying prostrate on the ground to ask forgiveness for his sins, kneeling in penance to share in the Lord's suffering, his arms wide open, gazing at the Crucifix to contemplate Supreme Love, looking heavenward feeling drawn to God's world. Thus there are three positions: standing, kneeling, lying prostrate on the ground; but with the gaze ever directed to our Crucified Lord. However, the last two positions, on which I would like to reflect briefly, correspond to two of the Saint's customary devotional practices. First, personal meditation, in which prayer acquires an even more intimate, fervent, and soothing dimension. After reciting the Liturgy of the Hours and after celebrating Mass, Saint Dominic prolonged his conversation with God without setting any time limit. Sitting quietly, he would pause in recollection in an inner attitude of listening, while reading a book or gazing at the Crucifix. He experienced these moments of closeness to God so intensely that his reactions of joy or of tears were outwardly visible. In this way, through meditation, he absorbed the reality of the faith. Witnesses recounted that at times he entered a kind of ecstasy, with his face transfigured, but that immediately afterward he would humbly resume his daily work, recharged by the power that comes from on High. Then come his prayers while travelling from one convent to another. He would recite Lauds, Midday Prayer, and Vespers with his companions, and, passing through the valleys and across the hills, he would contemplate the beauty of creation. A hymn of praise and thanksgiving to God would well up from his heart for his many gifts and, above all, for the greatest wonder: the redemptive work of Christ.

Dear friends, Saint Dominic reminds us that prayer, personal contact with God, is at the root of the witness to faith which every Christian must bear at home, at work, in social commitments, and even in moments of relaxation; only this real relationship with God gives us the strength to live through every event with intensity, especially the moments of greatest anguish. This Saint also reminds us of the importance of physical positions in our prayer. Kneeling, standing before the Lord, fixing our gaze on the Crucifix, silent recollection—these are not of secondary importance but help us to put our whole selves inwardly in touch with God. I would like to recall once again the need, for our spiritual life, to find time every day for quiet prayer;

we must make this time for ourselves, especially during the holidays, to have a little time to talk with God. It will also be a way to help those who are close to us enter into the radiant light of God's presence, which brings the peace and love we all need.

42

Liturgical Memorial of the Blessed Virgin Mary

WEDNESDAY, 22 AUGUST 2012
Castel Gandolfo

Dear Brothers and Sisters,

Today is the liturgical Memorial of the Blessed Virgin Mary, invoked by the title: "Queen". It is a recently instituted feast, although its origins and the devotion to her are ancient. It was in fact established in 1954, at the end of the Marian Year, by Venerable Pius XII, who fixed the date as 31 May (cf. Encyclical Letter *Ad Caeli Reginam*, 11 October 1954: AAS 46 [1954], 625–40). On this occasion, the Pope said that Mary was Queen more than any other creature because of the sublime dignity of her soul and the excellence of the gifts she received. She never ceases to bestow upon mankind all the treasures of her love and tender care (cf. *Discourse in Honour of Mary Queen*, 1 November 1954). Now, after the post-conciliar reform of the liturgical calendar, this feast is set eight days after the Solemnity of the Assumption to emphasize the close link between Mary's royal nature and her glorification in body and soul beside her Son. In the Second Vatican Council's Constitution on the Church, we read: Mary "was taken up body and soul into heavenly glory... and exalted by the Lord as Queen over all things, that she might be the more fully conformed to her Son" (*Lumen Gentium*, no. 59).

This is the origin of today's feast: Mary is Queen because she is uniquely conformed to her Son, both on the earthly journey and in heavenly glory. Ephrem the Syrian, Syria's great saint, said of Mary's queenship that it derives from her motherhood: she is Mother of the Lord, of the King of kings (cf. Is 9:1–6), and she points Jesus out to us as our life, our salvation, and our hope. In his Apostolic Exhortation *Marialis Cultus*, the Servant of God Paul VI recalled: "In the Virgin Mary everything is relative to Christ and dependent upon him. It was with a view to Christ that God the Father, from all eternity, chose her to be the all-holy Mother and adorned her with gifts of the Spirit granted to no one else" (no. 25).

Now, however, let us ask ourselves: what does "Mary Queen" mean? Is it solely a title, together with others, a crown, an ornament like others? What does it mean? What is this queenship? As mentioned above, it is a consequence of her being united to the Son, of her being in heaven, that is, in communion with God; she shares in God's responsibility for the world and in God's love for the world. There is a worldly or common idea of a king or queen: a person with great power and wealth. But this is not the kind of royalty of Jesus and Mary. Let us think of the Lord; the royalty and kingship of Christ is interwoven with humility, service, and love. It is above all serving, helping, and loving. Let us remember that Jesus on the Cross was proclaimed king with this inscription written by Pilate: "The King of the Jews" (cf. Mk 15:26). On the Cross, at that moment, he is shown to be King; and how is he King? By suffering with us and for us, by loving to the end and, in this way, governing and creating truth, love, and justice. Let us also think of another moment: at the Last Supper he bows down to wash the feet of his followers. Consequently, Jesus' kingship has nothing to do with that of the powerful of this earth. He is a King who serves his servants; he demonstrated this throughout his life; and the same is true of Mary. She is Queen in her service to God for mankind, she is a Queen of love who lives the gift of herself to God so as to enter into the plan of man's salvation. She answered the angel: "Behold, I am the handmaid of the Lord" (cf. Lk 1:38), and in the *Magnificat* she sings: God has regarded the low estate of his handmaiden (cf. Lk 1:48). She helps us. She is Queen precisely by loving us, by helping us in our every need; she is our sister, a humble handmaid.

And so we have already reached this point: how does Mary exercise this queenship of service and love? By watching over us, her children: the children who turn to her in prayer, to thank her or to ask her for her motherly protection and her heavenly help, perhaps after having lost our way, or when we are oppressed by suffering or anguish because of the sorrowful and harrowing vicissitudes of life. In serenity or in life's darkness, let us address Mary, entrusting ourselves to her continuous intercession so that she may obtain for us from the Son every grace and mercy we need for our pilgrimage on the highways of the world. Through the Virgin Mary, let us turn with trust to the One who rules the world and holds in his hand the future of the universe. For centuries she has been invoked as the celestial Queen of Heaven; in the Litany of Loreto, after the prayer of the holy Rosary, she is implored eight times: as Queen of Angels, of Patriarchs, of Prophets, of Apostles, of Martyrs, of Confessors, of Virgins, of all the Saints, and of Families. The rhythm of these ancient invocations and daily prayers, such as the *Salve Regina*, help us to understand that the Blessed Virgin, as our Mother, beside her Son Jesus in the glory of heaven, is always with us in the daily events of our life.

The title "Queen" is thus a title of trust, joy, and love. And we know that the One who holds a part of the world's destinies in her hand is good, that she loves us and helps us in our difficulties.

Dear friends, the devotion to Our Lady is an important element of spiritual life. In our prayers, let us not fail to address her with trust. Mary will not fail to intercede for us with her Son. Looking at her, let us imitate her faith, her full availability to God's plan of love, her generous acceptance of Jesus. Let us learn how to live from Mary. Mary is the Queen of Heaven who is close to God, but she is also the Mother who is close to each one of us, who loves us and listens to our voice.

43

Martyrdom of Saint John the Baptist

WEDNESDAY, 29 AUGUST 2012
Castel Gandolfo

Dear Brothers and Sisters,

This last Wednesday of the month of August is the liturgical Memorial of the martyrdom of Saint John the Baptist, the Precursor of Jesus. In the Roman Calendar, he is the only saint whose birth and death, through martyrdom, are celebrated on the same day (in his case, 24 June). Today's Memorial commemoration dates back to the dedication of a crypt in Sebaste, Samaria, where his head had already been venerated since the middle of the fourth century. The devotion later extended to Jerusalem, both in the Churches of the East and in Rome, with the title of the Beheading of Saint John the Baptist. In the Roman Martyrology, reference is made to a second discovery of the precious relic, translated for the occasion to the Church of San Silvestro in Campo Marzio, Rome.

These small historical references help us to understand how ancient and deeply rooted is the veneration of John the Baptist. His role in relation to Jesus stands out clearly in the Gospels. Saint Luke in particular recounts his birth, his life in the wilderness, and his preaching, while in today's Gospel Saint Mark tells us of his dramatic death. John the

Baptist began his preaching under the Emperor Tiberius in about 27–28 A.D., and the unambiguous invitation he addressed to the people, who flocked to listen to him, was to prepare the way to welcome the Lord, to straighten the crooked paths of their lives through a radical conversion of heart (cf. Lk 3:4). However, John the Baptist did not limit himself to teaching repentance or conversion. Instead, in recognizing Jesus as the "Lamb of God" who came to take away the sin of the world (Jn 1:29), he had the profound humility to hold up Jesus as the One sent by God, drawing back so that he might take the lead and be heard and followed. As his last act, the Baptist witnessed with his blood to faithfulness to God's commandments, without giving in or withdrawing, carrying out his mission to the very end. In the ninth century, the Venerable Bede says in one of his Homilies: "Saint John gave his life for [Christ]. He was not ordered to deny Jesus Christ, but was ordered to keep silent about the truth" (cf. *Homily* 23: CCL 122, 354). And he did not keep silent about the truth and thus died for Christ, who is the Truth. Precisely for love of the truth he did not stoop to compromises and did not fear to address strong words to anyone who had strayed from God's path.

We see this great figure, this force in the Passion, in resistance to the powerful. We wonder: what gave birth to this life, to this interiority so strong, so upright, so consistent, spent so totally for God in preparing the way for Jesus? The answer is simple: it was born from the relationship with God, from prayer, which was the thread that guided him throughout his existence. John was the divine gift for which his parents Zechariah and Elizabeth had been praying for so many years (cf. Lk 1:13); a great gift, humanly impossible to hope for, because they were both advanced in years and Elizabeth was barren (cf. Lk 1:7); yet nothing is impossible to God (cf. Lk 1:36). The announcement of this birth happened precisely in the place of prayer, in the temple of Jerusalem; indeed, it happened when Zechariah had the great privilege of entering the holiest place in the temple to offer incense to the Lord (cf. Lk 1:8–20). John the Baptist's birth was also marked by prayer: the *Benedictus*, the hymn of joy, praise, and thanksgiving which Zechariah raises to the Lord and which we recite every morning in Lauds, exalts God's action in history and prophetically indicates the mission of their son, John: to go before the Son of God made flesh to prepare his ways (cf. Lk 1:67–79). The entire existence of the Forerunner of Jesus was nourished by his relationship with God, particularly the period he spent in desert regions (cf. Lk 1:80). The desert regions are places of temptation but also where man acquires a sense of his own poverty because, once deprived of material support and security, he understands that the only steadfast reference point is God himself. John the Baptist, however, is not only a man of prayer, in permanent contact with God, but also a guide in this relationship. The Evangelist Luke, recalling the prayer that Jesus taught his disciples, the *Our Father*, notes that the request was formulated by the disciples in these words: "Lord, teach us to pray, just as John taught his own disciples" (cf. Lk 11:1).

Dear brothers and sisters, celebrating the martyrdom of Saint John the Baptist reminds us too, Christians of this time, that with love for Christ, for his words, and for the truth, we cannot stoop to compromises. The truth is truth; there are no compromises. Christian life demands, so to speak, the "martyrdom" of daily fidelity to the Gospel, the courage, that is, to let Christ grow within us and let him be the One who guides our thought and our actions. However, this can happen in our life only if we have a solid relationship with God. Prayer is not time wasted; it does not take away time from our activities, even apostolic activities, but exactly the opposite is true: only if we are able to have a faithful, constant, and trusting life of prayer will God himself give us the ability and strength to live happily and serenely, to surmount difficulties, and to witness courageously to him. Saint John the Baptist, intercede for us, that we may be ever able to preserve the primacy of God in our life.

44

Prayer in the First Part of the Book of Revelation (Rev 1:4—3:22)

WEDNESDAY, 5 SEPTEMBER 2012
Paul VI Audience Hall

Dear Brothers and Sisters,

Today, after the holiday break, we resume the Audiences at the Vatican, continuing with the "school of prayer", which I am sharing with you in these Wednesday Catecheses.

Today I would like to talk to you about a prayer in the Book of Revelation, which, as you know, is the last one in the New Testament. It is a complex book, but one containing great richness. It puts us in touch with the vital, vibrant prayer of the Christian assembly, gathered "on the Lord's day" (Rev 1:10): indeed, the text unfolds into this basic premise.

A speaker presents to the assembly a message which the Lord has entrusted to the Evangelist John. The reader and the assembly are, so to speak, the two protagonists of the book's development; right from the start, a festive greeting is addressed to them: "Blessed is he who reads aloud the words of the prophecy, and blessed are those who hear" (1:3). A symphony of prayer wells up from the ongoing dialogue between them and develops with a great variety of forms until it reaches its conclusion. When we hear the speaker deliver the message, hear and observe the assembly's reaction, their prayer tends to become our own.

The first part of Revelation (1:4–3:22) presents three successive stages in the attitude of the assembly which is praying. The first stage (1:4–8) consists of a dialogue which—the only one in the New Testament—takes place between the assembly that has just gathered and the reader, who greets it with a blessing: "Grace to you and peace" (1:4). The speaker continues, emphasizing the provenance of this greeting. It comes from the Trinity: from the Father, from the Holy Spirit, from Jesus Christ, involved together in carrying ahead the creative and saving plan for mankind. The assembly listens, and when it hears Jesus Christ named it jumps for joy, as it were, and responds enthusiastically, raising the following prayer of praise: "To him who loves us and has freed us from our sins by his blood and made us a kingdom, priests to his God and Father, to him be glory and dominion for ever and ever. Amen" (1:5b–6). The assembly, steeped in Christ's love, feels set free from the bonds of sin and proclaims itself the "kingdom" of Jesus Christ, which belongs totally to him. It recognizes the great mission which has been entrusted to it through Baptism: to bring God's presence to the world. And, looking once again directly at Jesus and with mounting enthusiasm, its ends this celebration of praise, recognizing his "glory and dominion" that will save mankind. The final "amen" concludes the hymn of praise to Christ. These first four verses are already full of instructions for us; they tell us that our prayer must first and foremost consist in listening to God who speaks to us. Submerged by torrents of words, we are not very used to listening or, especially, being receptive by creating silence, either within or outside ourselves, so as to be able to pay attention to what God wants to tell us. These verses also teach us that our prayers, especially if they are only prayers of petition, must first of all praise God for his love, for the gift of Jesus Christ, who brought us strength, hope, and salvation.

A further intervention of the speaker then refers to the assembly, moved by Christ's love, the commitment to accept his presence in its own life. He says: "Behold, he is coming with the clouds, and every eye will see him, every one who pierced him; and all tribes of the earth will wail on account of him" (1:7a). After being lifted up to heaven on "a cloud", the symbol of transcendence (cf. Acts 1:9), Jesus Christ will return, just as he was taken up into heaven (cf. Acts 1:11b). Then all the peoples will recognize him, and, as Saint John predicts in the fourth Gospel, "they shall look on him whom they have pierced" (19:37). They will remember their sins, the cause of his crucifixion, and, like those who witnessed it directly on Calvary, will beat their breasts (cf. Lk 23:48), asking him to forgive them so as to follow him in life and thus to prepare full communion with him after his final Coming. The assembly reflects on this message and says: "Even so. Amen" (Rev 1:7b). The assembly's "even so" expresses its full acquiescence with all that has been said to them, and they ask that it may truly become reality. It is the prayer of the assembly which meditates on the love of God in its supreme manifestation on the Cross and asks to live consistently as disciples of Christ. And there is God's answer: "I am the Alpha and the Omega, the One who is, who was and who is to come, the Almighty" (1:8). God, who reveals himself as the beginning and the end of history, accepts the assembly's request and takes it to heart. He was, is, and will be present and active in his love in the future, as he was in the past, until the final destination is reached. This is God's promise. And here we find another important element: constant prayer reawakens within us the sense of the Lord's presence in our life and in history. His is a presence that sustains us, guides us, and gives us great hope, even amidst the darkness of certain human events; furthermore, every prayer, even prayer in the most radical solitude, is never isolation of oneself and is never sterile: rather, it is the life blood of an ever more committed and consistent Christian life.

The second stage in the assembly's prayer (1:9–22) examines in greater depth the relationship with Jesus Christ: the Lord makes himself seen; he speaks, acts, and the community, ever closer to him, listens, reacts, and understands. In the message presented by the speaker, Saint John recounts his personal experience of an encounter with Christ: he was on the Island of Patmos, on account of the "word of God and of the testimony of Jesus" (1:9), and it was the "Lord's day" (1:10a), Sunday, on which the Resurrection is celebrated. And Saint John was "in the Spirit" (1:10a). The Holy Spirit permeated him and renewed him, expanding his ability to receive Jesus, who asks him to write. The prayer of the assembly which is listening gradually takes on a contemplative attitude, punctuated by the verb "to see", "to look", that is, it contemplates what the speaker suggests, interiorizing it and making it its own. John hears "a loud voice like a trumpet" (1:10b). The voice orders him to send a message "to the seven churches" (1:11), which are located in Asia Minor, and, through them, to all the Churches of all times, together with their Pastors. The words "voice . . . like a trumpet", taken from the Book of Exodus (cf. 20:18), recall God's self-manifestation to Moses on Mount Sinai and indicate the voice of God who speaks from his heaven, from his transcendence. Here the voice is attributed to the Risen

Jesus Christ, who speaks to the assembly in prayer from the glory of the Father, with the voice of God. Turning "to see the voice" (1:12), John sees "seven golden lampstands and in the midst of the lampstands one like a son of man" (1:12–13), a term particularly dear to John which means Jesus himself. The golden lampstands, with their candles lit, mean the Church of every time, in an attitude of prayer in the Liturgy: the Risen Jesus, the "Son of man", is among them and, clad in the vestments of the high priest of the Old Testament, carries out the priestly role of mediator with the Father. A dazzling manifestation of the Risen Christ, with characteristics proper to God—which recur in the Old Testament—follows in John's symbolic message. He describes "hair white as white wool, white as snow" (1:14), a symbol of God's eternity (cf. Dan 7:14) and of the Resurrection. Fire is a second symbol, which, in the Old Testament, often refers to God, to indicate two of his properties. The first of these is the jealous intensity of his love, which motivates his Covenant with man (cf. Deut 4:24). And it is this same burning intensity of love that is perceived in the gaze of the Risen Jesus: "his eyes were like a flame of fire" (Rev 1:14b). The second property is the uncontainable capacity for overcoming evil, like a "devouring fire" (Deut 9:3). Likewise Jesus' "feet", as he walked on to face and destroy evil, are compared to "burnished bronze" (Rev 1:15). Then Jesus Christ's voice, "like the sound of many waters" (1:15c), has the impressive roar of "the glory of the God of Israel" moving toward Jerusalem, of whom the Prophet Ezekiel speaks (cf. 43:2). Three other symbolic elements follow. They show all that the Risen Jesus is doing for his Church: he holds her firmly in his right hand—an extremely important image: Jesus holds the Church in his hand—he speaks to her with the penetrating force of a sharp sword and shows her the splendor of his divinity: "His face was like the sun shining in full strength" (Rev 1:16). John is so struck by this wondrous experience of the Risen One that he faints and falls as though dead.

After this experience of revelation, the Apostle has before him the Lord Jesus, who speaks to him, reassures him, lays his hand on his head, reveals his identity as the Risen Crucified One, and entrusts to him the task of passing on his message to the Churches (cf. Rev 1:17–18). This God was just so beautiful that John fainted before him, falling as though dead. He is the friend of life and places his hand on the Apostle's head. And this is how it will be for us: we are friends of Jesus. Then the revelation of the Risen God, of the Risen Christ, will not be terrible but will be an encounter with the friend. The assembly, too, experiences with John the wonderful moment of light before the Lord, but this is combined with the experience of the daily encounter with Jesus, perceiving the riches of the contact with the Lord, who fills every space in existence.

In the third and last stage of the first part of the Apocalypse (Rev 2–3), the speaker proposes to the assembly a sevenfold message in which Jesus speaks in the first person. Addressed to the seven churches located in Asia Minor around Ephesus, Jesus' discourse starts with the specific situation of each Church and then extends to the churches of every era. Jesus immediately enters into the situation in which each Church lives, highlighting its lights and shadows and addressing to the Church a pressing invitation: "Repent" (2:5, 16; 3:19c); "hold fast what you have" (3:11); "do the works you did at first" (2:5); "be zealous and repent" (3:19b). . . . If these words of Jesus are listened to with faith, they immediately begin to take effect. The Church in prayer, on receiving the word of the Lord, is transformed. All the

Churches must listen attentively to the Lord, opening themselves to the Spirit as Jesus asks insistently, repeating this order seven times: "He who has an ear, let him hear what the Spirit says to the Churches" (2:7, 11, 17, 29; 3:6, 13, 22). The assembly listens to the message, receiving an incentive for repentance, conversion, perseverance, growth in love, and guidance on the journey.

Dear friends, the Book of Revelation presents to us a community gathered in prayer because it is precisely in prayer that we become ever more aware of Jesus' presence with us and in us. The more and the better we pray, with constancy, with intensity, the more like him we shall be, and he will truly enter into our life and guide it, bestowing upon us joy and peace. And the more we know, love, and follow Jesus, the more we will feel the need to pause in prayer with him, receiving serenity, hope, and strength in our life.

45

Prayer in the Second Part of the Book of Revelation (Rev 4:1—22:21)

WEDNESDAY, 12 SEPTEMBER 2012
Paul VI Audience Hall

Dear Brothers and Sisters,

Last Wednesday I talked about prayer in the first part of the Book of Revelation. Today let us move on to the second part of the Book. While in the first part, prayer is oriented to the Church's inner life, in the second part attention is focused on the whole world; in fact, the Church, on her pilgrimage through history, is part of it in accordance with God's plan. The assembly, which by listening to John's message as it is presented by the speaker has rediscovered its task of cooperating in the development of the Kingdom of God as "priests of God and of Christ" (Rev 20:6; cf. 1:5; 5:10), opens itself to the world of man. And here emerge two ways of living, in a shared dialectic relationship. We might define the first as the "system of Christ", to which the assembly is happy to belong, and the second as "worldly systems opposed to the kingdom and the covenant and activated by the power of evil", which, by deceiving men, wishes to create a world that is the opposite of the one willed by Christ and by God (cf. Pontifical Biblical Commission, *The*

Bible and Morality: Biblical Roots of Christian Conduct, no. 70). Consequently the assembly must be able to read in depth the history it is living, learning to discern events with faith in order to cooperate, with its action, in spreading the Kingdom of God. And this work of interpretation and discernment in addition to action is linked to prayer.

First of all, after the insistent appeal of Christ, who says seven times in the first part of the Book of Revelation: "He who has an ear, let him hear what the Spirit says to the Churches" (Rev 2:7, 11, 17, 29; 3:6, 13, 22), the assembly is invited to come up to heaven to see reality with God's eyes; and here we rediscover three symbols, key reference points for interpreting history: the throne of God, the Lamb, and the scroll (cf. Rev 4:1–5:14).

The first symbol is the throne, on which a figure is seated whom John does not describe because it is beyond the scope of any human representation. John can only hint at the sense of beauty and joy he feels in its presence. This mysterious figure is God, almighty God, who did not stay closed in his heaven but made himself close to man, entering into a Covenant with him; in a mysterious but real way, God makes his voice, symbolized by thunder and lightning, heard in history. There are various elements that appear around God's throne, such as the twenty-four elders and four living creatures who ceaselessly praise the one Lord of history. Thus the first symbol is the throne.

The second symbol is the scroll, which contains God's plan for events and for people; it is hermetically sealed by seven seals, and no one can read it. In the face of this human inability to scrutinize God's design, John feels a deep sadness that causes him to weep. Yet there is a remedy to man's bewilderment before the mystery of history; someone is able to open the scroll and to enlighten him.

And here the third symbol appears: Christ, the Lamb immolated in the sacrifice of the Cross but who is standing, which is a sign of his Resurrection. And it is the Lamb himself, Christ who died and is risen, who breaks open the seals one by one and reveals God's plan, the profound meaning of history.

What do these symbols mean? They remind us of the way to take to be able to interpret the events of history and of our own life. By raising our gaze to God's Heaven, in a constant relationship with Christ, opening our hearts and minds to him in personal and community prayer, we learn to see things in a new light and to perceive their truest meaning. Prayer is, as it were, an open window that enables us to keep our gaze turned to God, not only to remember the destination toward which we are bound, but also to let God's will illuminate our earthly pilgrimage and help us live it with intensity and commitment.

How does the Lord guide the Christian community to a deeper interpretation of history? First of all, by asking it to consider realistically the present in which we are living. The Lamb then opens the first four seals of the scroll, and the Church sees the world in which it is inserted, a world in which there are various negative elements. There are the wicked deeds of men, such as acts of violence that stem from the desire to possess, to dominate each other, even to the point of self-destruction (the second seal); or injustice, because men fail to respect the laws that they have given themselves (the third seal). To these are added the evils that men must suffer, such as death, hunger, and pestilence (the fourth seal). In the face of these all too often dramatic situations, the ecclesial community is asked never to lose hope, to believe firmly that the apparent omnipotence of the Evil One comes up against the real omnipotence which is God's.

And the first seal which the Lamb breaks open contains this very message. John recounts: "And I saw, and behold, a white horse, and its rider had a bow; and a crown was given to him, and he went out conquering and to conquer" (Rev 6:2). God's power, which can not only offset evil but can actually overcome it, entered human history. The color white refers to the Resurrection: God made himself so close that he came down into the darkness of death to illuminate it with the splendor of his divine life; he took the evil of the world upon his own shoulders to purify it with the fire of his love.

How can we grow in this Christian interpretation of reality? The Book of Revelation tells us that prayer nourishes this vision of light and of deep hope in each one of us and in our communities: it invites us not to let ourselves be overcome by evil, but to overcome evil with good, to look at the Crucified and Risen Christ, who associates us with his victory. The Church lives in history; she does not withdraw into herself but courageously continues on her journey through difficulty and suffering, forcefully asserting that in the end evil does not overcome good, that darkness does not conceal God's splendor. This is an important point for us; as Christians we can never be pessimistic; we know well that on our journey through life we often encounter violence, falsehood, hatred, and persecution, but this does not discourage us. Prayer teaches us above all to see God's signs, his presence, and his action, indeed, to be lights of goodness ourselves, spreading hope and showing that the victory is God's. This prospect leads to raising thanksgiving and praise to God and to the Lamb: the twenty-four elders and four living beings sing together the "new song" which celebrates the work of Christ the Lamb, who will "make all things new" (Rev 21:5). However, this renewal is first of all a gift to be requested. And here we find another element that must characterize prayer: to pray to the Lord insistently that his Kingdom come, that the human heart be docile to the lordship of God, and that it be his will that guides both our life and the life of the world. In the vision of the Book of Revelation, this prayer of petition is portrayed by an important detail: "the twenty-four elders" and "the four living beings" hold in their hands, together with the harp that accompanies their singing, "golden bowls full of incense" (5:8a) which, as is explained, "are the prayers of the saints" (5:8b), namely, of those who have already reached God but also of all of us who are journeying on. And we see that in front of God's throne an angel is holding a golden censer in his hand into which he continues to put grains of incense, which is our prayer, whose sweet fragrance is offered together with the prayers that rise to God (cf. Rev 8:1–4). It is a symbolism that tells us how all our prayers—with every possible limitation, effort, poverty, dryness, and imperfection they may have—are, so to speak, purified and reach God's heart. In other words, we can be sure that there is no such thing as superfluous or useless prayers; no prayer is wasted. And prayers are answered, even if the answer is sometimes mysterious, for God is Love and infinite Mercy. "The angel", John writes, "took the censer and filled it with fire from the altar and threw it on the earth; and there were peals of thunder, loud noises, flashes of lightening and an earthquake" (Rev 8:5). This image means that God is not indifferent to our entreaties; he intervenes and makes his power felt and his voice heard on the earth; he causes the system of the Evil One to tremble and collapse. Often when confronting evil, we have the feeling that we are powerless, but our prayers themselves are the first and most effective response we can give, and they strengthen our daily commitment to spread goodness. God's might makes our weakness fruitful (cf. Rom 8:26–27).

I would like to conclude by referring to the closing dialogue (cf. Rev 22:6–21). Jesus repeats several times: "Behold, I am coming soon" (Rev 22:7, 12). This affirmation indicates not only the future prospect at the end of time but also that of the present: Jesus comes, he makes his dwelling place in those who believe in him and receive him. Thus, guided by the Holy Spirit, the assembly repeats to Jesus a pressing invitation to make himself ever closer: "Come" (Rev 22:17a). It is like the "Bride" (22:17) who ardently longs for the fullness of the nuptials. The invocation recurs for the third time: "Amen. Come, Lord Jesus" (22:20b); and the speaker concludes with words which demonstrate the meaning of this presence: "The grace of the Lord Jesus be with all" (22:21).

The Book of Revelation, despite the complexity of its symbols, involves us in an extremely rich prayer, which is why we too listen, praise, give thanks, contemplate the Lord, and ask him for forgiveness. Its structure as a great liturgical prayer of the community is also a strong appeal to recognize the extraordinary, transforming power of the Eucharist. I would particularly like to extend a pressing invitation to be faithful to Holy Mass on the Lord's Day, Sunday, the true center of the week! The wealth of prayer in the Book of Revelation is reminiscent of a diamond which has a fascinating series of facets but whose value depends on the purity of its one, central core. Likewise the evocative forms of prayer we encounter in the Book of Revelation make the unique, inexpressible preciousness of Jesus Christ shine out.

46

The Liturgy, School of Prayer: The Lord Himself Teaches Us to Pray

WEDNESDAY, 26 SEPTEMBER 2012
Saint Peter's Square

Dear Brothers and Sisters,

In these months we have journeyed in the light of the word of God so as to learn to pray ever more authentically, looking at several important Old Testament figures, at the Psalms, at the Letters of Saint Paul, and at the Book of Revelation, but, especially, at the unique and fundamental experience of Jesus in his relationship with the heavenly Father. In fact, only in Christ can a person be united to God with the depth and intimacy of a child in his relationship with a father who loves him, only in Christ can we address God in all truth, calling him affectionately, "Abba! Father!" Like the Apostles, we too have repeated in these past few weeks and repeat to Jesus today: "Lord, teach us to pray" (Lk 11:1).

Furthermore, to learn to live more intensely our personal relationship with God, we have learned to invoke the Holy Spirit, the first gift of the Risen One to believers, because it is he who "helps us in our weakness; for we do not know how to pray as we ought" (Rom 8:26), Saint Paul says, and we know how right he is.

At this point, after a long series of Catecheses on prayer in Scripture, we can ask ourselves: how can I let myself be formed by the Holy Spirit and thereby become able to enter into the atmosphere of God, of prayer with God? What is this school in which he teaches me to pray, comes to help me in my attempts to speak to God correctly? The first school of prayer—as we have seen in these weeks—is the word of God, Sacred Scripture. Sacred Scripture is an ongoing dialogue between God and man, a progressive dialogue in which God shows himself ever closer, in which we can become ever better acquainted with his face, his voice, his being; and man learns to accept God, to know God, and to talk to God. Therefore, in these weeks, in reading Sacred Scripture, we have sought to learn from Scripture, from this ongoing dialogue, how we may enter into contact with God.

However there is yet another precious "place", another precious "source" for developing in prayer, a source of living water that is very closely related to the previous one. I am referring to the Liturgy, which is a privileged context in which God speaks to each one of us, here and now, and awaits our answer.

What is the Liturgy? If we open the *Catechism of the Catholic Church*—ever an invaluable and, I would say, indispensable aid—we can read that the word "liturgy" originally meant: a "service in the name of/on behalf of the people" (no. 1069). If Christian theology made use of this word of the Greek world, it obviously did so thinking of the new People of God born from Christ, who opened his arms on the Cross to unite men in the peace of the one God. A "service on behalf of the people", a people which did not exist on its own but was formed through the Paschal Mystery of Jesus Christ. Indeed, the People of God does not exist through ties of kinship, place, or country. Rather it is always born from the action of the Son of God and from the communion with the Father that he obtains for us.

The *Catechism* also indicates that "in Christian tradition [the word 'liturgy'] means the participation of the People of God in 'the work of God'" (no. 1069), because the People of God as such exists only through God's action.

The actual development of the Second Vatican Council reminds us of this. It began its work fifty years ago with the discussion of the draft on the Sacred Liturgy, which was then solemnly promulgated on 4 December 1963, the first text that the Council approved. That the Document on the Liturgy was the first document to be promulgated by the conciliar assembly was considered by some to have happened by chance. Among the many projects, the text on the Sacred Liturgy seems to have been the least controversial. For this very reason it could serve as a sort of exercise in learning conciliar methodology. However, there is no doubt that what at first sight might seem a coincidence also turned out to be the best decision, on the basis of the hierarchy of the subjects and of the most important duties of the Church. In fact, by starting with the theme of the "liturgy", the Council shed very clear light on the primacy of God and his indisputable priority. God in the very first place: this itself explains to us the Council's decision to start with the Liturgy. Wherever the gaze on God is not conclusive, everything else loses its orientation. The fundamental criterion for the Liturgy is its orientation to God, enabling us to take part in his action itself.

However, we might ask ourselves: what is this work of God in which we are called to take part? The answer that the Council's Constitution on the Sacred Liturgy gives us is apparently twofold. In no. 5 it points out, in fact, that the works of God are his actions in history which bring us salvation and which culminated in the death and Resurrection of Jesus Christ; but in no. 7, the same Constitution defines the celebration of the Liturgy as an "action of Christ". In fact, these two meanings are inseparably linked. If we ask ourselves who saves the world and man, the only answer is: Jesus of Nazareth, Lord and Christ, the Crucified and Risen One. And where does the Mystery of the death and Resurrection of Christ that brings salvation become real for us, for me, today? The answer is: in Christ's action through the Church, in the Liturgy, and, especially, in the sacrament of the Eucharist, which makes present the sacrificial offering of the Son of God, who has redeemed us; in the sacrament of Reconciliation, in which one moves from the death of sin to new life; and in the other sacramental acts that sanctify us (cf. *Presbyterorum Ordinis*, no. 5). Thus the Paschal Mystery of the death and Resurrection of Christ is the center of the liturgical theology of the Council.

Let us take another step forward and ask ourselves: how does the enactment of Christ's Paschal Mystery become possible? Twenty-five years after the Constitution *Sacrosanctum Concilium*, Blessed Pope John Paul II, wrote: "In order to reenact his Paschal Mystery, Christ is ever present in his Church, especially in liturgical celebrations. Hence the Liturgy is the privileged place for the encounter of Christians with God and the One whom he has sent, Jesus Christ (cf. Jn 17:3)" (*Vicesimus quintus annus*, no. 7). Along the same lines we read in the *Catechism of the Catholic Church*: "A sacramental celebration is a meeting of God's children with their Father, in Christ and the Holy Spirit; this meeting takes the form of a dialogue, through actions and words" (no. 1153). Therefore, the first requirement for a good liturgical celebration is that there should be prayer and a conversation with God, first of all listening and consequently a response. Saint Benedict, speaking in his *Rule* of prayer in the Psalms, pointed out to his monks: *mens concordet voci*, "the mind must be in accord with the voice." The Saint teaches that in the prayers of the Psalms, words must precede our thought. It does not usually happen like this because we have to think and, then, what we have thought is converted into words. Here, instead, in the Liturgy, the opposite is true: words come first. God has given us the word, and the sacred Liturgy offers us words; we must enter into the words, into their meaning, and receive them within us; we must attune ourselves to these words; in this way we become children of God, we become like God. As *Sacrosanctum Concilium* recalls, "in order that the liturgy may be able to produce its full effects it is necessary that the faithful come to it with proper dispositions, that their minds be attuned to their voices, and that they cooperate with heavenly grace lest they receive it in vain" (no. 11). A fundamental, primary element of the dialogue with God in the liturgy is the agreement between what we say with our lips and what we carry in our hearts. By entering into the words of the great history of prayer, we ourselves are conformed to the spirit of these words and are enabled to speak to God.

In line with this, I would just like to mention one of the moments during the Liturgy itself; it calls us and helps us to find this harmonization, this conformation of ourselves to what we hear, say, and do in the celebration of the Liturgy. I am referring to the invitation that the celebrant expresses before the Eucharistic Prayer: "*Sursum corda*", let us lift up our hearts above the confusion of our apprehensions, our desires, our narrowness, our distraction. Our hearts, our innermost selves, must open in docility to the word of God and must be recollected in the Church's prayer, to receive her guidance to God from the very words that we hear and say. The eyes of the heart must be turned to the Lord, who is in our midst: this is a fundamental disposition.

Whenever we live out the Liturgy with this basic approach, our hearts are, as it were, removed from the force of gravity which has pulled them downward and are inwardly uplifted, toward the truth, toward love, toward God. As the *Catechism of the Catholic Church* says: "In the sacramental liturgy of the Church, the mission of Christ and of the Holy Spirit proclaims, makes present, and communicates the mystery of salvation, which is continued in the heart that prays. The spiritual writers sometimes compare the heart to an altar" (no. 2655): *altare Dei est cor nostrum.*

Dear friends, we celebrate and live the Liturgy well only if we remain in a prayerful attitude, not if we want "to do something", to make ourselves seen, or to act, but if we direct our hearts to God and remain in a prayerful attitude, uniting ourselves with the Mystery of Christ and with his conversation as Son with the Father. God himself teaches us to pray, Saint Paul says (cf. Rom 8:26). He himself gave us the appropriate words with which to address him, words that we find in the Psalter, in the great orations of the sacred Liturgy, and in the Eucharistic celebration itself. Let us pray the Lord that we might be every day more aware of the fact that the Liturgy is an action of God and of man; prayer that wells up from the Holy Spirit and from us, wholly directed to the Father, in union with the Son of God made man (cf. *Catechism of the Catholic Church*, no. 2564).

47

The Ecclesial Nature of Liturgical Prayer

WEDNESDAY, 3 OCTOBER 2012
Saint Peter's Square

Dear Brothers and Sisters,

In last week's Catechesis, I began talking about one of the special sources of Christian prayer: the sacred Liturgy, which, as the *Catechism of the Catholic Church* states, is "a participation in Christ's own prayer addressed to the Father in the Holy Spirit. In the liturgy, all Christian prayer finds its source and goal" (no. 1073). Today I would like us to ask ourselves: in my life, do I leave enough room for prayer, and, above all, what place in my relationship with God does liturgical prayer, especially Holy Mass, occupy, as participation in the common prayer of the Body of Christ which is the Church?

In answering this question, we must remember first of all that prayer is the living relationship of the children of God with their Father, who is good beyond measure, with his Son Jesus Christ, and with the Holy Spirit (cf. ibid., no. 2565). Therefore the life of prayer consists in being habitually in God's presence and being aware of it, in living in a relationship with God as we live our customary relationships in life, with our dearest relatives, with true friends; indeed, the relationship with the Lord is the relationship that gives light to all our other relationships. This communion of life with the Triune God is possible because through Baptism we have been incorporated into Christ, we have begun to be one with him (cf. Rom 6:5).

In fact, only through Christ can we converse with God the Father as children; otherwise, it is not possible. In communion with the Son, however, we can also say, as he did, "Abba". In communion with Christ we can know God as our true Father (cf. Mt 11:27). For this reason, Christian prayer consists in looking constantly at Christ, and in an ever new way, speaking to him, being with him in silence, listening to him, acting and suffering with him. The Christian rediscovers his true identity in Christ, "the first-born of all creation" in whom "all things hold together" (cf. Col 1:15ff.). In identifying with him, in being one with him, I rediscover my personal identity as a true son who looks to God as to a Father full of love.

But let us not forget: it is in the Church that we discover Christ, that we know him as a living Person. She is "his Body". This corporeity can be understood on the basis of the biblical words about man and about woman: the two will be one flesh (cf. Gen 2:24; Eph 5:30ff.; 1 Cor 6:16f.). The indissoluble bond between Christ and the Church, through the unifying power of love, does not cancel the "you" and the "I" but, on the contrary, raises them to their highest unity. Finding one's identity in Christ means reaching communion with him, which does not cancel me out but raises me to the loftiest dignity, that of a child of God in Christ: "The love-story between God and man consists in the very fact that this communion of will increases in a communion of thought and sentiment, and thus our will and God's will increasingly coincide" (Encyclical *Deus Caritas Est*, no. 17). Praying means raising oneself to God's heights, through a necessary, gradual transformation of our being.

Thus, by participating in the Liturgy we make our own the language of Mother Church; we learn to speak in her and for her. Of course, as I have already said, this happens gradually, little by little. I must immerse myself ever more deeply in the words of the Church with my prayer, with my life, with my suffering, with my joy, and with my thought. It is a process that transforms us.

I therefore think that these reflections enable us to answer the question we asked ourselves at the outset: how do I learn to pray, how do I develop in my prayer? Looking at the example which Jesus taught us, the *Pater Noster* [*Our Father*], we see that the first word [in Latin] is "Father" and the second is "our". Thus the answer is clear: I learn to pray, I nourish my prayer by addressing God as Father and by praying with others, praying with the Church, accepting the gift of his words which gradually become familiar to me and full of meaning. The dialogue that God establishes with each one of us, and we with him in prayer, always includes a "with"; it is impossible to pray to God in an individualistic manner. In liturgical prayer, especially the Eucharist and—formed by the Liturgy—in every prayer, we do not only speak as individuals but, on the contrary, enter into the "we" of the Church that prays. And we must transform our "I", entering into this "we".

I would like to recall another important aspect. In the *Catechism of the Catholic Church* we read: "In the *liturgy of the New Covenant* every liturgical action, especially the celebration of the Eucharist and the sacraments, is an encounter between Christ and the Church" (no. 1097). Therefore it is the "total Christ", the whole Community, the Body of Christ united with her Head, that is celebrating. Thus the Liturgy is not a sort of "self-manifestation" of a community; it means, instead, coming out of merely "being ourselves", being closed in on ourselves, and having access to the great banquet, entering into the great living community in which God himself nourishes us. The Liturgy implies universality, and this universal character must enter ever anew into the awareness of all. The Christian liturgy is the worship of the universal temple which is the Risen Christ, whose arms are outstretched on the Cross to draw everyone into the embrace of God's eternal love. It is the worship of a wide-open heaven. It is never solely the event of a single community with its place in time and space. It is important that every Christian feel and be truly integrated into this universal "we" which provides the basis and refuge of the "I", in the Body of Christ which is the Church.

In this we must bear in mind and accept the logic of God's Incarnation: he made himself close, present, entering into history and into human nature, making himself one of us. And this presence continues in the Church, his Body. So, the Liturgy is not the memory of past events but is the living presence of the Paschal Mystery of Christ, who transcends and unites times and places. If in the celebration the centrality of Christ did not emerge, we would not have Christian Liturgy, totally dependent on the Lord and sustained by his creative presence. God acts through Christ, and we can act only through and in him. The conviction must grow within us every day that the Liturgy is not our or my "doing" but, rather, is an action of God in us and with us.

The Liturgy is not, therefore, the individual—priest or member of the faithful—or the group celebrating it; rather, it is primarily God's action through the Church, which has her own history, her rich tradition, and her creativity. This universality and fundamental openness, which are proper to the whole of the Liturgy, are one of the reasons why it cannot be conceived of or modified by the individual community or by experts but must be faithful to the forms of the universal Church.

The entire Church is always present even in the Liturgy of the smallest community. For this reason, there are no "strangers" in the liturgical community. In every liturgical celebration, the whole Church takes part, heaven and earth, God and men. The Christian Liturgy, even if it is celebrated in a place and in a concrete space and expresses the "yes" of a specific community, is by its nature catholic; it comes from all and leads to all, in unity with the Pope, with the Bishops, and with believers of all epochs and all places. The more a celebration is enlivened by awareness of this, the more fruitfully will the authentic meaning of the Liturgy be made present.

Dear friends, the Church becomes visible in many ways: in charitable action, in mission projects, in the personal apostolate that every Christian must carry out in his own walk of life. However, the place in which she is fully experienced as Church is in the Liturgy; it is the act in which we believe that God enters our reality and we can encounter him, we can touch him. It is the act in which we come into contact with God: he comes to us, and we are illuminated by him. For this reason, when in reflections on the Liturgy we focus our attention exclusively on how to make it attractive, interesting, and beautiful, we risk forgetting the essential: the Liturgy is celebrated for God and not for ourselves; it is his work; he is the subject; and we must open ourselves to him and let ourselves be guided by him and by his Body which is the Church.

Let us ask the Lord that we might learn every day to live the sacred Liturgy, especially the Eucharistic celebration, praying in the "we" of the Church, which directs her gaze, not upon herself, but to God, and feeling part of the living Church of all places and of all epochs.